WHERE ANGELS FEAR TO TREAD

LINDA BOOTHERSTONE

Copyright © 2009 Linda Bootherstone

First edition: 2009

Second edition: 2015

This reprint: 2022

All rights reserved.

ISBN-13: 978-0-6455080-2-4

Contents

Dedication
Acknowledgements
Map

PART ONE	FORMING FRIENDSHIPS	
Chapter 1	The Meeting	1
Chapter 2	The Rally	6
Chapter 3	Castellar de la Frontera	12
Chapter 4	Local Connections	18
Chapter 5	Win Some, Lose Some	25
Chapter 6	Northern Morocco	29
Chapter 7	Arrangements in Casablanca	37
Chapter 8	The Mountains and the Sea	44
Chapter 9	The Concert (Song – Morocco)	55
Chapter 10	The South and Goodbye (Song – 'Til We Met Again)	61
Chapter 11	Homeward alone	70
PART TWO	DIVERSE DESTINATIONS	
Chapter 12	Back at Base – First letters (Song – Crusader)	77
Chapter 13	Debby	83
Chapter 14	Bad brakes and Berber Banjos	90
Chapter 15	Into the desert	95
Chapter 16	Marrakesh	100
Chapter 17	Buy Them All Dahling	108
Chapter 18	The Family (Poems – For Mum, The Price)	117
Chapter 19	Hekel, The Flying Fiat (Poem – It's A Dog's Life)	128
Chapter 20	Heading East	137
Chapter 21	To Odessa (Poem – Odessas Odyssey	144

Chapter 22	The Black Sea Pearl	
	(Song – Black Sea Pearl)	156
Chapter 23	Slovakia and the Tooth Fairy	165
Chapter 24	Ja – We Have Ways of Fixing Your Bike.	173

PART THREE CLOSING THE GAP

Chapter 25	Castellar Again	182
Chapter 26	A Judas in the Camp	193
Chapter 27	Way Down Yonder	202
Chapter 28	The Wild West	
	(Poem – Two Trails to Destiny)	210
Chapter 29	Going North	219
Chapter 30	The Reunion	225

POSTSCRIPT	Song – Faraway Friends	233

Dedication

For my Family and all my Faraway Friends

Thank you.

Acknowledgments

This book was written during a wet winter in Andalucia. The metamorphosis from pencilled scribbling on scrap paper by candlelight and gas lamp into this finished copy was made possible with the aid of kind friends and family and with the wonders of modern technology.

I would like to thank the following:

Janet Bootherstone, Erica Robb, Sandra Moss, Viola Weidman, Hilary Walker (née Simkins), Christina Sobey, Choo Choy Lee, Peter Hendricks and Jenny Kelso.

Of course the inspiration for its subject came from Georgia March and our time together. She kindly allowed me to use extracts from her letters and articles and added her comments and suggestions when reading the final manuscript. And thanks to Mary Gudzenovs for publishing assistance.

Finally my thanks must go to all the people I met along the way who, knowingly or unknowingly, have provided the material for this tale, so many of whom have given their hospitality and friendship.

I am still travelling: meeting and parting from so many acquaintances and forming friendships around the world.

* * *

This book was written in 1996 and since then many changes have happened to the places and people mentioned, including myself. It is a true account of my actions and feelings at the time. I did not and do not wish to cause any offence in relating the occurrences herein.

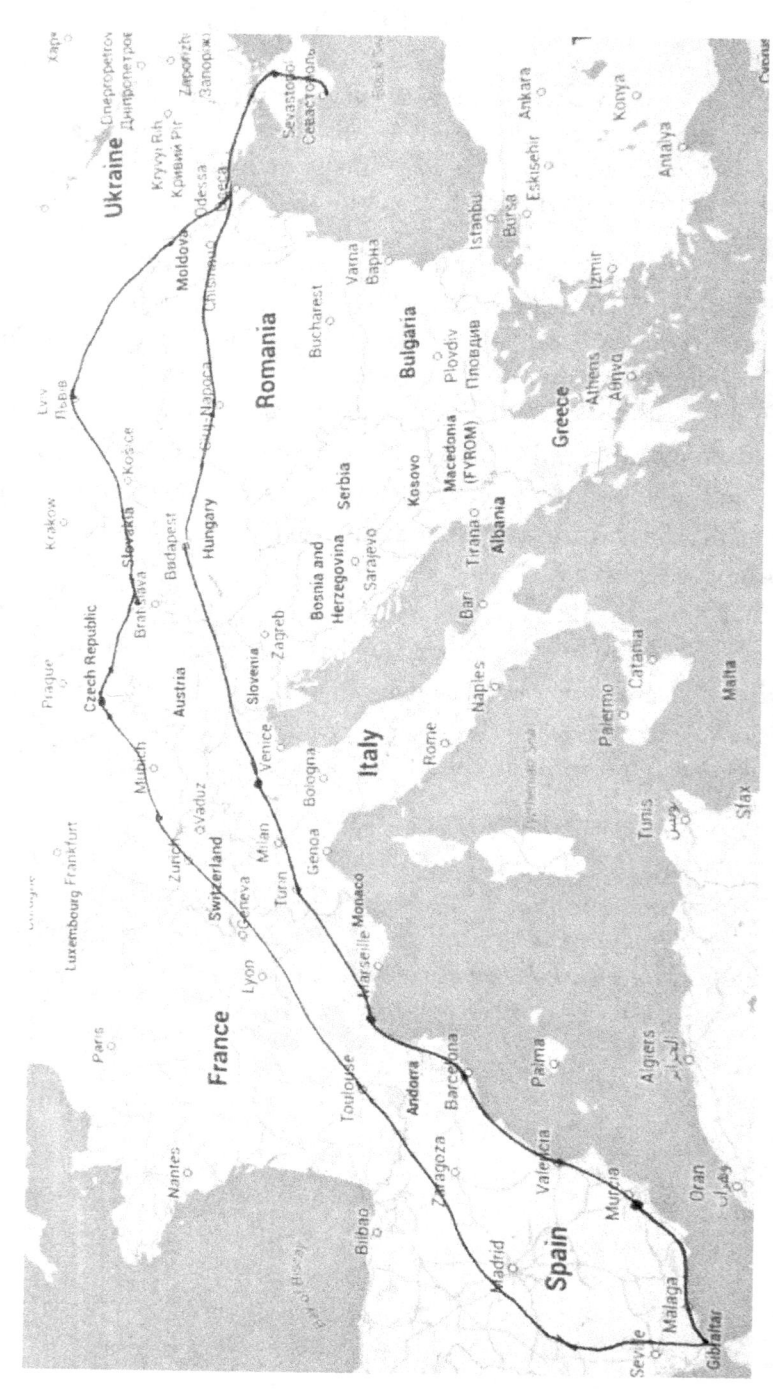

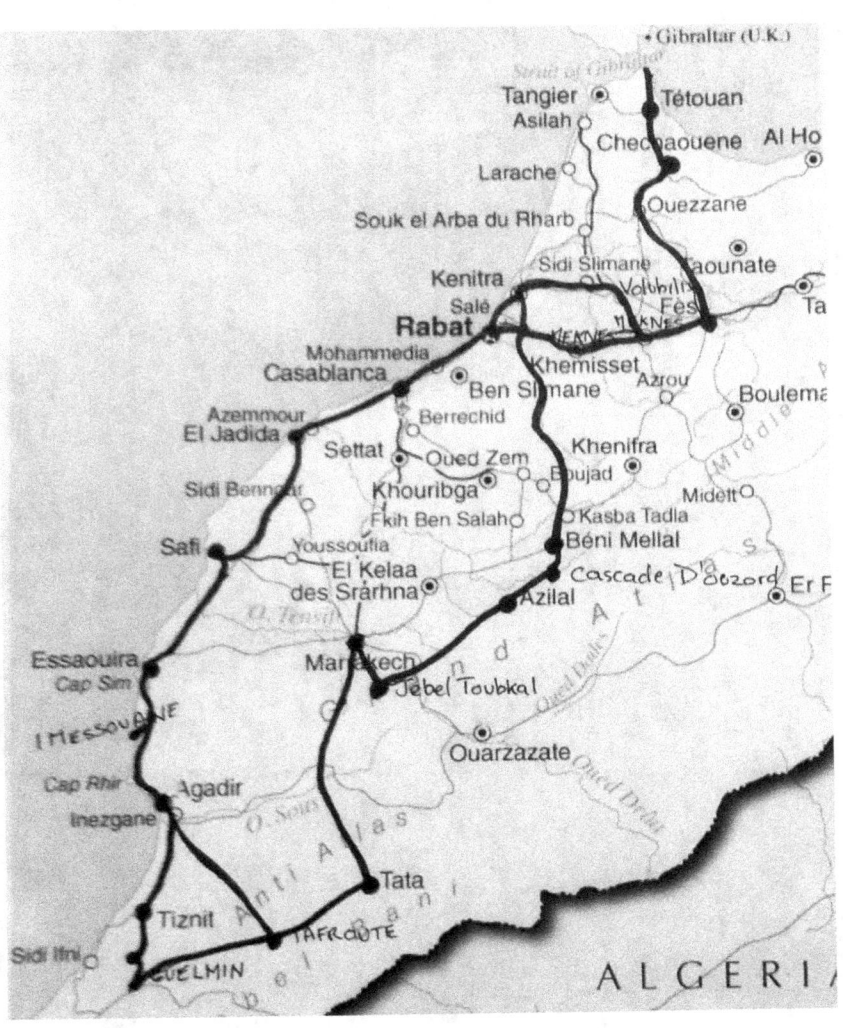

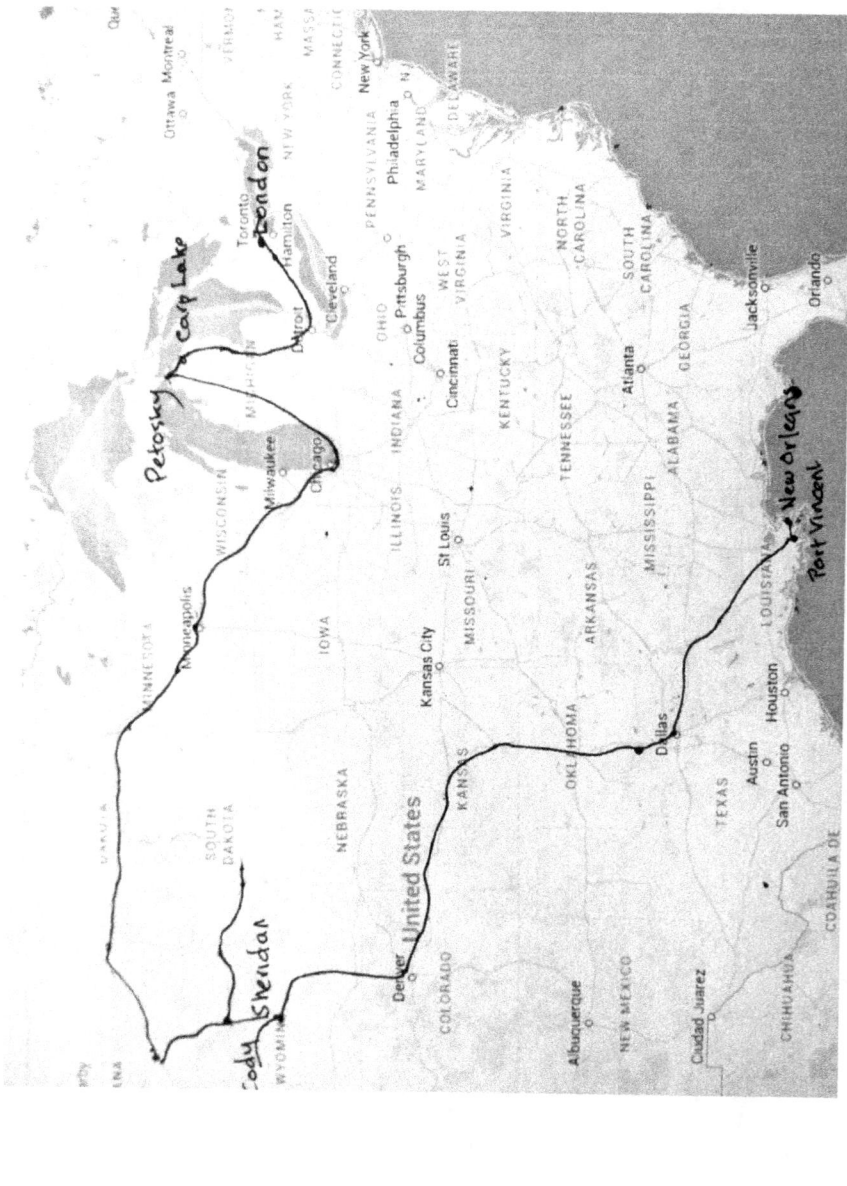

Part One
Forming Friendships

Chapter One

The Meeting

Damn cameras! The BMW stood poised by the old lighthouse at Cape Sagres – the South-West tip of Portugal. Early morning mist swirled around. The ocean pounded on the cliffs nearby and the sun was trying to break through. A perfect picture, but the solid, reliable East German Practika jammed tight. So much for photographic evidence! It was nearly the end of the trip though and many illustrative photos of the ride down through Portugal were already safely on film. I had been visiting my artist friend, Roger Hallett, in the Bearnaise region of France and now I was making my way back to Andalucia.

The weather in Spain was torturously hot with several bush fires reported, including in my own village of Castellar, and I had decided that a route through Portugal would provide a cooler alternative, which in fact it did. However, the ride from Cape Sagres to the popular tourist town of Lagos became warmer as the sun broke through the mist and, on stopping to draw money from a bank, I decided to take a drink and lunch break. I had plenty of time to continue the day's journey to Faro where a popular motorcycle rally I wished to attend was being held.

Parking the bike next to the fishing docks, I walked across the road and into a pleasant park. A square of four benches stood facing each other. I sat on a vacant one and took out my tucker bag with the remains of yesterday's loaf and my ration of 'La Vache qui Rit' cheese. I often thought I should hold shares in the company as it's my constant travelling diet. It was about midday and a few people were wandering through the shade of the well watered parklands. As I chewed my somewhat stale sandwich, a woman in a long flowing skirt walked by.

She was definitely not a local; her long blonde hair, slim figure and fine features were very different from those of the solid, dark Portuguese. She walked past me and I immediately noticed the odd-shaped backpack she was carrying. Familiarity jogged my memory; I had played with a Celtic harpist in Australia who had carried a similarly shaped pack. The woman unswung her load, placed it on the bench opposite and, undoing it, took out that very instrument. I watched her with interest as she sat down, tuned the harp and then began playing warm-up scales. No longer able to keep silent, I walked over.

'Where did you get your Celtic harp?' I asked.

'I had it made for me in Canada,' she replied with the tell-tale accent. I introduced myself and asked her about her involvement with the instrument and what type of music she played. She replied that her name was Georgia and she had only acquired the harp earlier that year. She was from London, Ontario and for many years owned and toured with a theatre company in Canada and the US with her husband. Unexpectedly, last year the marriage had ended and during the trauma she had somehow felt the need to learn to play the harp. She was a trained vocalist and felt she could accompany herself on the instrument. She approached a harp maker in London and was disappointed to hear that it would take many months to have one personally built. However, the very next day an offer of the loan of a harp was made, to practice on while hers was in the making. Her love affair with the instrument began. Three months later, in June, and two days before her departure from Canada, the instrument was ready and Georgia set off to see the world, confident that her harp playing would enable her to survive.

She had planned on staying in France for a year but this country had proved to be too expensive and an American traveller met on a bus suggested she try her luck in Portugal. En route to Lagos in the Algarve, Georgia decided she would start writing a book about her life and travelling adventures and, to this end, she stayed with a Portuguese family, writing in the mornings and spending the afternoons practicing the harp, exploring her new found locality and learning Portuguese. After a month she felt confident enough to play in public and compose her own music. She had developed a unique style and took her music and voice to the streets of Lagos to play for the people. Public reaction, she told me, was immediately rewarding. Toddlers stood in awe before her, crying when busy mothers tried to drag them away. A French woman wept tears of compassion and Georgia had to stop playing to put her arms around her. A dog put his head in her lap at the debut of one her songs, and people of all nationalities showered her with gifts and invitations. She was indeed able to cover her meagre needs with the money she was earning from busking. However, she had her Canadian savings with her to continue the trip. I told her about my involvement with other harpists and singers in Australia and then asked if she knew any traditional tunes. We found that she'd heard of the Canadian harpist Loreena McKennit and was familiar with her version of Greensleeves. So, I dug into my bag for my selection of tin whistles and found one that was in tune with her harp. As the strains of Greensleeves (Commonwealth harp and whistle version) wafted over the parklands, an interested audience gathered. Even the young men with 'Guns & Roses' t-shirts applauded!

For the next hour we chatted and played each other tunes, then I needed to get to the bank and be on my way.

'When you've finished your book or want a break from it, come and visit me in Spain,' I said. 'Here's my address. My cottage is very basic but there's room for you to stay and we can make some more music together.'

'Thanks,' she replied swiftly, 'I'm sure I will.'

I walked away smiling. Even if we didn't reconnect, I had enjoyed the hour with this sunny-faced woman. It had been a great musical interlude and I was happy with that. These chance meetings always brighten up the day; sometimes they developed into real friendships, sometimes not. It didn't matter, I had learnt to enjoy and appreciate whatever came along.

At an early age I became interested in meeting people and had never been shy. My first job, at age 15, during school holidays was demonstrating toys in a department store in South London. By 17 I was selling to housewives, door to door. Looking back it amazes me that, even though I was the youngest, I was the most successful rep in the area, especially as my appearance was not conducive to the norm of that mainly upper middle class district. My peroxided mop of blonde hair was often tinted varying shades of purple—quite outrageous in the early 1960s! In winter it was covered with a woolly hat as I trudged through the snow, my diminutive 5' 2' figure swathed in jumpers and waterproofs. Completing my strange attire were my father's size 7 flying boots, filled with numerous pairs of socks to keep them on my size 4 feet! It must have been my cheeky smile and chat that attracted the housewives, who invited me in for so many cups of warming tea that I often had to ask for the loo. Their conversations and varying lifestyles opened my eyes to the diversities of human nature, and perhaps that's where I developed my quick judge of character. With the experience gained in this job, I was accepted early for training as a market research interviewer with Lever Brothers' then elite team. Here I learnt how to obtain information politely, and it has helped to satisfy my natural curiosity about people and places ever since.

At junior school my favourite subject was social geography. One of my early school photos has a map of the world behind me and a travel book, showing a camel and sand dunes, in front. How apt. Little did I know that I would see many of the places that I read about, making connections by my twin loves of music and motorcycling.

And why motorcycling? While still a child I was fascinated by the skill of driving and, on our Sunday outings in the family jalopy, I was forever watching my father at the wheel and asking him about the controls. I saved my pocket money by collecting Post Office Savings Stamps and, at last, the day came when I had enough to buy the wreck of a three wheeler Bond mini car. My father helped me rebuild it and also risked life and limb teaching me to drive. Obtaining a licence for it also qualified me for riding a motorcycle.

My elder sister, Anne, had a boyfriend with a beautiful BSA Gold Star which fascinated me (and so did he, but to no avail), and by the time I was 18 I'd joined the local motorcycle club (Saltbox MCC, Biggin Hill, Kent) but was too independent to spend long on the many pillion seats I was offered. Buying a bike of my own, I toured England and the Continent; firstly with my fellow club members but latterly on my own. I had no fear of travelling alone or breaking down for I soon found that in the world of motorcycling there is always someone who comes to your aid in times of need.

As for the music, my parents both had good voices, which I luckily inherited, and I loved singing. I became interested in folk music when one of my interviewer colleagues invited me to her wedding in Scotland (to which I rode on my 350cc Triumph). At the reception everyone took a turn at singing a traditional song and I was entranced. This sort of live music involved people, for it gave so much pleasure when everyone could join in the chorus. I was hooked, bought every Clancy Brothers record I could find and learnt many traditional English and Celtic songs. When I emigrated to Australia in 1969 at age 23, complete with a newly acquired 600cc BMW, I met some Irish musicians and was soon singing in folk bands around the country.

From then on I made contacts in motorcycling and music, both in Australia and the other countries I'd visited during my 48 years of life. This present meeting with Georgia was no exception. It added to the colour of my life. I would try and keep in contact with my new-found harp playing friend. I continued through the busy town, past the red and white striped English tourists, their skin tone indicating exposure time in the bright Portuguese sun. After locating the bank, I repacked the bike and headed off in the rising heat to Faro and the bike rally.

Chapter Two

The Rally

A 'rally' in the motorcycle world is the name given to a social gathering of motorcyclists, usually for a weekend camp, in a given place chosen by the organisers. Most rallies are run by motorcycle clubs to bring motorcyclists together from different countries or areas. They can be a fund-raising event for the club or just a way of having fun.

The idea originated in Germany in the early 1950s when a group of Zündapp owners decided to hold a camping weekend in mid-winter. The nickname for Zündapps with sidecars at the time was 'Green Elephant' as they were issued in that colour. The place this group chose to hold their 'Green Elephant Rally' was originally in the north near Stuttgart.

In true Teutonic fashion, the participants found that camping in the snow, thermometer well into minus, was great fun. No only did it necessitate having a huge bonfire but also downing a large quantity of Schnapps—to keep out the cold, you understand. With the warmth and alcohol in these adverse conditions a great feeling of camaraderie, mates against the elements, ensued and the event was turned into an annual pilgrimage. Then a few other motorcycle groups began to attend, mainly with sidecars to battle the road conditions but not necessarily painted green, and the event became simply known as 'The Elephant Rally'. Over the years its popularity grew, attracting overseas riders as well, and the location was moved to the Nürburgring. The British bikers braved the elements crossing the channel and skidding along miles of frozen autobahn in January to clink glasses and sing 'Eins, Zwei, Suffa!' with their European brethren.

To keep up with the 'Fritzes', the Brits held a rally of their own, 'The Dragon Rally' in Llangollen, North Wales, in February. If they couldn't promise snow, at least there was a 90% chance of torrential rain to challenge those 'enthusiasts' from home and abroad.

Towards the end of the 60's both these rallies were attracting motorcyclists in plague proportions. The 'Dragon' organisers had to advertise the event as 'invitation only' in order to reduce the numbers to a manageable level. The 'Elephant Rally' turned into a motorcycle trade exposition, local hotels and hostels filled to overflowing while the tough campers lit their own fires.

By the early 1970's the original cosy ambience of these gatherings was lost but, as the popularity of motorcycling grew, more clubs sprang up and other rallies were organised in many countries on almost every weekend of the year. Some were purely camp-outs and many ran gymkhanas and presented long distance and other awards. Later, rather than just campfire sing-songs, live groups and rock bands were engaged to play, and other attractions such as the wet T-shirt competition (for the girls to take part in and the boys to judge) began to appear.

I had attended many rallies in different countries and at such meetings made many friends with motorcyclists from all over the world. It is a great networking system and also the location of rallies often draws riders to areas and countries they have not seen before, thus widening knowledge of different regions and cultures and cementing international bonds.

The attraction of a rally for me is that it provides an enjoyable focus for a journey. I enjoy a good campfire sing-song at the end of a trip but the ride there is equally, if not more, important than the event itself. I prefer to take my time and investigate places of interest along the way. Included in the registration fee for the rally is a metal lapel badge to commemorate the event. Many bikers go to as many rallies as they can in a short time to collect badges. Also, now organisers advertise their rallies with attractions such as laser shows, discos and raffling a motor bike to make more money for their club. To me the collection of new friends and memories is more important, and once the rallies became large and commercial my enthusiasm for them waned.

I knew this Faro Rally in Portugal was now one of the largest in Southern Europe and possibly not my style but I hadn't been to such a meeting for years and was interested to see what was on offer. Also it was on my way home. A further incentive was that I knew that some of the Gibraltar MCC would be attending and it would be a chance to do a write-up for a Gibraltar magazine for which I was freelancing. Somehow I'd have to borrow a camera for accompanying pictures but I'd cross that bridge when I came to it. I was hoping that the music wouldn't be too loud and the lads letting their hair down not too raucous. Late afternoon saw me and my old BMW in amongst the crowds of men and women with much more up-to-date machines, heading towards the rally site. It was like gradually being drawn from a small tributary to a stream and then into the great flow of a river. I was caught up in the excitement. After my lone trip, where I had been a novelty, suddenly I was just one of thousands of bikers, many of whom had travelled many hundreds of kilometres to be there.

The camping area was huge—in a eucalyptus grove. Bikes were parked in small groups with accompanying tents. Here and there a club banner waved. Of course the majority were Spanish and Portuguese and I felt rather an outsider, especially with my woeful lack of language. However, amongst all these new, super racing, up-to-date machines, I at last spotted a BMW of similar vintage to mine, with a German licence plate. There seemed to be a space amongst the group and most travelling Germans can speak English, so I was able to make myself understood and was immediately accepted into the circle.

Despite my doubts about attending such a large commercial meeting, I had a very interesting and entertaining weekend. We had our own campfire which was visited at various times by Portuguese, Spanish, English and Austrians, who joined in our multi-national sing-songs. There were approximately 9,000 bikers registered from many countries—quite an organizational headache for the relatively small Moto Clube Faro but I was amazed at their professional approach. For £15 a head they managed to keep everyone fed and watered for the weekend and even provided showers and toilets, kept clean by an ever changing team of workers.

A sardine bake sizzled during the day and, on Friday and Saturday nights, bands provided the music at a main stage. There was also a girlie strip show, which gave me my usual moral and ethical headache about such things. Though I believe in freedom of choice in career and how one wants to display one's own sexuality, I'm still embarrassed by male or female strip shows. Public nudity is not entertaining to me, but then I didn't have to watch and went off to have a beer.

Commercial stalls sold their wares, which included leather clothing, badges, spare parts and bike magazines. A tattoo artist stood at the ready for those wishing to indelibly mark the occasion. There was a concours d'elegance and rat bike (worst bike) competition, and people milled around in the hot summer sun, admiring or laughing at each others machines. The Gibraltar bike club was there in force—downing a large quantity of beer—and I luckily found some friends who kindly lent me their camera.

Gibraltar MCC at Faro

I stayed on for Sunday night when the numbers had dwindled to the last stalwart 200, mainly bikers from other countries who, on their annual holidays, were in no rush to get home. The Faro MCC provided a free chicken BBQ and let us finish off the remaining kegs of beer, so we were all singing and dancing until 4am. On request, I brought out my whistle and was highly amused to see many tough looking, leather clad lads clapping in time to and applauding my favourite tune 'King of the Fairies'. Perhaps they wouldn't have cheered so loud had they known the title. My solo was followed by two Belgian boys from the Gremlin MCC performing a double act of comedy song and dance on the tables.

A more sober Monday morning saw me helping clean up the rubbish from the various camping spots in the eucalyptus grove. The last few stragglers were leaving and the time came for me too to hit the road for my last day's ride back to Castellar. I had not been along this stretch of road before and was interested in finding the Doñana National Park. However, I gave up the hunt for the heat was intense and I was dehydrating and had to stop often to drink cold fluids and pour water over my head. In all my years travelling in Oz and Africa I could not remember feeling this bad. Perhaps it was the humidity as well as the 40+ degrees of heat. Or perhaps I was getting soft. The road from Seville to the coast is flat, straight and boring and I was glad to see the sea on reaching the little port of Barbate where the fishing boats bobbed colourfully in the harbour. After an ice-cream stop I rode along the winding and more interesting coast road, past the great modern windmills at Tarifa. I had friends to visit in a community nearby, so chatted with them for a while before looking at the map to see if I could take a short cut home.

A road was marked which looked interesting and I turned on to it just as the sun was beginning to set. Big mistake. Darkness fell quickly and I found myself on a very rough track which had lost its road markings and most of its tarmac. There were several worrying forks and huge potholes that were hard to see in the gathering gloom. When I hit them it shook the bike so badly I nearly lost the tent bag off the back and the gas plate that I'd brought all the way from Roger's house in France for my kitchen. Fatigued and anxious I wondered if I should just stop and camp by the side of the road and negotiate the rest of this unfamiliar road in daylight. However, I really wanted to be home. It was only a matter of 30kms away! After proceeding at a snail's pace for several more nerve-wracking kilometres, I eventually found the sealed main road and quickly covered the last stretch home.

The house key, usually kept in the kennel, was nowhere to be found, so instead, I wrenched open the door of my small caravan parked in the garden and fell into an exhausted sleep with my little dog, Shilpit, happily snoring under the bed. She had waited five weeks for my return and couldn't quite believe that it was really me home again. She wasn't going to let me out of her sight till morning in case she was dreaming. My own dreams were of an endless road with bike-swallowing potholes. They would probably have turned into a full scale nightmare had I known that the area I had passed through was a National Park full of wild boars!

Chapter Three

<u>Castellar de la Frontera</u>

Castellar de la Frontera is 22 kms from Gibraltar or Algeciras on the southern tip of Spain. How come I am living here? How can one describe it? I often asked myself the same questions. To answer the former is very complex but I'll try and put it briefly.

Like Georgia, I had run away from home when my long-term relationship with my writer/musician boyfriend broke up. 'Home' had been South Australia where I had lived happily for the best part of 20 years after emigrating from the UK in the '60s. On my return to the UK in 1989 I spent a short time lodging with my brother in the Midlands town of Burton-on-Trent. There I met Julia Bartlett, a go-ahead granny who wanted to attempt a single-handed Atlantic crossing. She had a Morgan Giles 30ft sloop in Malta, was looking for sponsorship for the project (Mermaid Initiative) and was hoping to raise money for the Children's Society while completing the trip.

Another girl, Mel Bradfield, and I joined the project in UK, working on publicity there and in Malta where we were to refit the boat and later crew it to the Canaries via Gibraltar. From Las Palmas to USA Julia would go it alone. While Julia flew ahead, Mel and I rode down to Malta on my BMW and worked on the boat, 'Forlanda', in Manual Island boatyard. However, the project took a different turn for me when the boat came off the land and into the water. I discovered that, despite all the latest medical and psychological aids, I became so motion sick that I had to escape the boat when we had been less than two weeks at sea. I left it on the Aeolian Islands and took a ferry back to Malta. Here I rethought my 'crew' status when I was safely on dry land and sitting firmly on my BMW, which had been stored there by members of a Maltese MCC. I could continue to perform my duties as publicity writer and photographer as long as Julia, the boat and I were still in the Mediterranean region. By taking a cargo ship from Malta to Marseilles it was possible to ride down to Gibraltar and promote the project there before the arrival of Mel and Julia. This I did and, as Mel also had to leave the project in Gibraltar due to a knee injury, I found another female crew member, Sally Read, to take her place.

When 'Forlanda', Sally and Julia finally sailed out of my sight in October 1992, my involvement was more or less over. Julia was now only contactable by radio. I could hope to receive intermittent news of her through 'ham' operators in Gibraltar but it was not important. Apart from writing up my part of the story for the book we eventually hoped to put together, Julia's success or failure was now in her own hands and could only be related by herself. Whether I stayed in Spain or went back to UK was irrelevant to the project but a decision by which I was now confronted.

Winter was approaching and I couldn't face spending it in England, so I stayed in Andalucia instead, buying a small caravan to keep off the torrential rain. I began my Spanish occupation by living at a campsite run by a local rogue, Pepe, and whilst there I observed the strange mix of people who had accumulated in the area of Costa del Sol (often referred to as Costa del Crime) and the Campo de Gibraltar.

La Linea, the border town between Gibraltar and Spain, has a high crime rate as junkies beg on the streets and steal to survive. I could understand why certain folk had chosen this part of the world to live. Its close proximity to Morocco has led to a very ancient tradition of smuggling all sorts of commodities (mainly drugs) from the 'dark continent', but also the British goods shipped into Gibraltar had their attractions for the previously less fortunate Spanish. Big money was (and is) to be made by many unscrupulous people there to make it. On the fringe of this scene were many no-hopers or, to use the less polite Australian expression *'deadshits'*, those who had failed in some way in other parts of Europe and had come south to live in a less organised and much sunnier clime. Here they could, literally in some cases, get away with murder.

Up until 1992 it was still possible for the British to work legally in Gibraltar without regulation and there was much building work in progress. So a large British labouring force made the place carry on the tradition, started by British occupation in 1704, of being a 'Little England'. The numerous English style pubs give the place a certain 'East Enders' appeal. The Isthmus is over-crowded and relatively expensive compared to Spain but here the language-lazy Brits can speak their native tongue and drink British beer.

Andalucia, of which Gibraltar is geographically a part, is one of the poorest areas of Spain. Donkeys and mules are still used as beasts of burden, especially for the cork cutting in the surrounding cork oak forests. There is little permanent work available, however, and the people easily succumb to the temptation of hashish and tobacco smuggling rather than be amongst the thousands of unemployed.

I found the whole area fascinating. The characters were forever changing as people came and went. Living on a campsite I met tourists en route to Africa and took a trip to Morocco myself in 1993, accompanied by an Australian and an English guy, both on BMW bikes. Our three week sojourn there together gave me a much better insight into Moroccan life than I had acquired 20 years before on my previous trip through Africa. During the next two years I went back as often as I could to make more Moroccan friends and to explore the beautiful country and its many traditions. My collection of artifacts increased and, especially when I started oil painting, the frustrations of living in a 12ft caravan overcame me and by my second Christmas I was actively searching for a larger space in which to live. A chance conversation with a German smuggler in a bar in Gibraltar led me to rent his somewhat derelict property in Castellar de la Frontera. No toilet, no electricity, water from a well by way of a deposit and a house which needed a thorough cleaning, repairing and repainting. It did, however, have a lovely setting and was only £6 per week rent. I had my caravan towed over and put it in the garden and used it as living quarters while I worked on the house. At last I could spread out!

Little by little I began to explore and understand the history and character of Castellar, the area around my new home. On my first visit as a naive tourist I had been impressed by its beauty and air of mysticism. It lies about 20kms inland off the main 340 route. A small road leading from the flat valley floor winds up for 8kms to reach an old Moorish castle. The first few kilometres pass the farmlands of Almoraima, previously a convent. Their cattle and horses graze amongst cork forests which are selectively harvested every year. The road dips to where the venta (bar & restaurant) La Jarandilla nestles next to a river bridge and then winds upwards past the spectacular Guardarranque dam, through rocky outcrops until it reaches a huddle of houses. These lie outside the looming castle walls and, passing them, on the brow of the hill a vehicle can be left in a small car park while the castle is explored on foot. A walk upwards on a cobbled street takes you through the entrance arch of the castle wall and along a circular route of alleys. Moorish style houses face directly out on to the street, shaded in some cases by bougainvillea and other creeping plants. Deceptively small facades hide interior courtyards and terraces that open out on to splendid views across the dam or to where the Andalucian white villages nestle in the surrounding hills. Vultures fly above and, in springtime, flowers carpet the area. A sense of history pervades. During the occupation of Andalucia by the Moors in the 11th century, Castillo de Castellar was built as a part of a line of garrison defences which spread inland from the Mediterranean coast. A minor outpost, the fortress was built atop a rocky outcrop and was big enough to house a small garrison. The Moors sank two water cisterns within the walls and defended themselves against invading Spanish Christians. However, during the next few hundred years the 'castillo' was constantly besieged and changed hands many times between Spanish and Moorish victors. In 1504 the Spanish finally took control and the Moors were either expelled or integrated.

Castellar, Andalucia

Built as a garrison, the castle was not equipped for peace-time settlement. As the population grew, small peasant houses sprang up on the rocky slopes outside the walls and women had to walk 3kms to the Guadarranque river to draw water. The surrounding terrain made access difficult and donkeys were the main transport. While the rest of Andalucia, the most backward area in Spain, began to catch up with the 20th century, Castellar's isolation left it still without electricity or water services.

In 1969 the government decided to dam the Guadaranque river to make a reservoir in the adjacent valley. While the earth-moving machinery was around they also built a new town on the other side of the valley and allowed the people the chance to sell their hovels and buy cheaply in this new, modern area which had all facilities including schools, shops and health clinics, and a much better road to Gibraltar and Algeciras. The people jumped at the opportunity and the old village and castle were left almost deserted. By chance, this change in Castellar coincided with the hippy movement in Europe in the early 1970s, where many young people left their industrial towns in search of peace and love. The trail to Marrakech in Morocco began and en route many of the flower power, combi driving pilgrims found Castellar. Its appeal was obvious; there was not only a beautiful setting but close proximity to the hashish producing areas of North Morocco. Many of these wanderers had dropped out of middle-class backgrounds in Germany and were able to raise the small amount of capital needed to buy a deserted house or cottage in or around the castle. They stayed to find that their lifestyle could only be supported by a continuation of the centuries old custom of smuggling and dealing. No other type of work was available in the depressed Andalucian economy. And so the village of Castellar developed, and unfortunately became known as a drug town, a reputation that it has only lately wanted to throw off. Police and Guardia mostly looked the other way unless there was any real trouble.

So what was I doing in Castellar, I who don't even smoke cigarettes? Well, the rent was cheap and I did know some English inhabitants who lived in the castle and had respectable jobs in Gibraltar. Also there were other inhabitants who were developing tourist bars, souvenir shops and an art gallery. Some houses were bought and renovated by incoming people not part of the hippy scene, so it seemed that the place could become popular with the genuine tourists who were interested in the history and beauty of the place and not just the availability of drugs. I felt that I might be able to cope with the situation, if I trod carefully, and perhaps became involved with the 'arty' scene. As a runaway myself, I felt that maybe here I had the chance to find a home.

On my return from the rally in Portugal I continued the process of making the rented house habitable. At some stage I remembered the blonde woman Georgia whom I'd met in Lagos and I sent some copies of music to her. I received a short, cheerful note in reply and went about my normal daily life.

Chapter Four

Local Connections

My normal daily life involved a number of things to try and make a living. Having finished work on Julia's boating project in October '92, I wrote a musical show for Gibraltar schools with an American singer/songwriter, Michael 'Beans' Gardner, who was temporarily in the area. Freelance writing for a Gib magazine and local newspaper expanded my contacts and I became involved with the making of an educational film about energy conservation. I spent a great deal of time riding around the area interviewing people, researching and writing but not, however, acquiring much money.

After my return from Portugal in July '94 I took on casual English teaching for the Algeciras franchise of the Kids Club, but this folded so I turned my creative talents to other things. The receding waters of the Guardarranque dam at Castellar during a dry summer left tree roots on its banks. Their weird shapes inspired me to varnish them, add dried flowers and name them 'Riddle Roots'. Artfully designed promo labels said 'Each unique root holds the hidden secret of the drowned valley of Castellar'. I sold them in a souvenir shop in the castle. However, it seemed the bottom had already fallen out of the Riddle Root market for, after I sold about five over two months, I realised it wasn't a really reliable source of income.

During 1993/94 I had been promoting motorcycle trips to Morocco especially catering for women travellers. So far three women friends had come as pillion passengers on my trips to that country. They enjoyed it so much that I thought it might be worth trying to turn it into a business. I was busy writing publicity for this and researching the logistics of the enterprise.

As for my social life, it waxed and waned with the flow of interesting people who came into the area. However, many of these were just travelling through and I could but briefly enjoy their company over a drink or a meal in my caravan while I passed on information about Spain or Morocco. A few more permanent contacts lived up the coast around Estepona and some in the Castle of Castellar. I had no close friends but had been helped out once or twice when I'd had bike trouble by a big, Father Christmas figured Scotsman, PC. He had a beard, smoked a pipe and had a deep, gentle voice with a lovely west coast accent. A few years previously in the UK I had had what can only be described as a 'mad passionate love affair' with a singing Scotsman with a similar timbred voice, so the vibration of PC's accented tones hit a familiar note within me.

I met PC soon after my arrival in Gibraltar in '92 when, as a good friend of Sally, the girl who volunteered to crew the Canaries with Julia on the Mermaid Initiative, he brought her luggage aboard the night before they sailed out of Gibraltar. That was our first 'hello'. His home was a Winnebago campervan that he'd driven down from UK a couple of years previously, and he invited me to drop by whenever I was passing. As his Winnebago was parked in La Linea en route from Gibraltar to my campsite, I did in fact call a few times for a beer, wine or a cup of coffee. He had worked in Canada and Russia in the catering trade and, over the course of a few visits, I discovered that he too had changed his lifestyle considerably after the break-up of his marriage and was now hoping to start life again in a new country. I appreciated his taste in good wines and classical music and, as he was well educated and informed, we had some stimulating conversations.

Lacking my normal points of contact with like-minded people (folk clubs or touring motor cycling clubs), I was experiencing difficulty in finding a new circle of real friends. Though I met many people who were pleasant and helpful, I still had the feeling of being an oddity, unable to discuss things in depth or reveal my true opinions. With PC, though our lifestyles had little in common, his intelligent attitude led me to relax my guard a little and use him as a sounding board for some of my ideas.

I like someone else to read through my articles before I submit them for publication in case there are spelling or grammatical errors I have overlooked and PC did this for me. I sounded him out on my touring business ideas as he seemed to have a logical mind and experience in the management area. He appeared to be a fairly reliable type, often helping other travellers with information about the area and lending them tools or videos, for the Winnebago was well equipped and had a TV and VHS set. After my trips to Morocco or France I would find wherever he was parked and regale him with stories of my adventures. I realised that there was a deep, dark side to this man but, thinking that this often happens when people have been disillusioned in life, I did not pry into his past but tried to keep our relationship light and bright and on casual terms. This seemed OK for him too. He had a labouring job and a pub circle in Gibraltar, and I was busy with my home in Spain.

My best friend by far was my little dog, Shilpit. A scruffy little white goat-haired mutt with a red nose and yellow eyes, she had been abandoned but adopted me just before I moved to Castellar. Despite my protests, my neighbours on the campsite put her into the caravan as I was being towed away, saying

'You'll be lonely there in Castellar by yourself, you'll need a friend.'
'But I can't have a dog. I've only got a motorbike and I go away too much.'

However, Shilpit (it's an old Scottish expression meaning pathetic/useless) stuck by me. Despite my erratic lifestyle, I tried my best to be caring and responsible, leaving extra food if I was away overnight and arranging for other people to look after her if my absence was longer. She was a camp dog, used to rough treatment and being alone. She found food by begging around venta kitchen doors. She often went off walking by herself, although she preferred me along too, and where I lived was ideal. I enjoyed taking her for walks and the extra exercise did me good.

The Shilpit Wants a Walk

Morning mist lies in the valley
As the sun lights up the sky
Cuckoo calls his gentle greeting
And the Shilpit wants a walk

Busy bees at midday buzzing
In and out among the flowers
Lazy breeze plays o'er the hillside
And the Shilpit wants a walk

Goat bells jangle on the rock ledge
Lake lies calm in evening's still
Twittering birds fly home to settle
BUT the Shilpit wants a walk

The Shilpit

She did have a nasty habit of chasing the odd goat, just for fun, and I told her to be careful about this as the goat herders don't like it. She just wagged her tail. I hadn't had a dog since leaving school and it was a great ego booster to have her adoring eyes on me as she lay at my feet in the bar, but she wasn't an over possessive, clinging dog. I thought that she and I had a good understanding of each other and were of a similar temperament. We were both loyal and faithful in our friendships but needed our own space to go off and explore different worlds. Then a strange event occurred which made me realise just how mentally attached we must be.

When I went away to Roger Hallet's art exhibition in France (and came home via Portugal) it was on the motorcycle, so Shilpit had to stay behind. I originally planned to be away for only two weeks and left dog food with a friend in the castle, Pam, who would kindly drop in to feed Shilpit on her way home from work. However, through my involvement with the exhibition (I showed some poems), it became obvious that I would be away longer. I sent Pam a letter with some more money for food and an explanation of my delay. In this communication I also mentioned a nightmare that I'd had about Shilpit. In this I'd seen her running down the road from the castle towards me with a gaping wound in her side. That was all, no explanation, but it was very upsetting.

As I was not sure how long the letter would take to arrive and my original ETA was overdue, I rang Pam at her office in Gib. No, she hadn't received the letter but all was well and Shilpit was OK now. As I put down the phone I realised that if she hadn't received the letter she wouldn't know about the dream, and what did she mean by 'Shilpit is OK *now*'? Pam said later that when my letter arrived it gave her the shivers. Shilpit *had* received a wound in her side. Pam and her partner thought that maybe it was a gunshot wound, perhaps fired by one of the goat herders. Not too serious, they treated it and it soon healed. But I was amazed how this trouble had been related to me by the dream. Had Shilpit transmitted this information to me psychically?

However, there was something she hadn't told me but which became obvious by her increased girth. While I had been in France, dodging Roger's advances, she had been very actively courting the local Boxer. As no-one knew the date of conception, it was a matter of guesswork as to when the puppies were due – bets were laid.

About three weeks after my return from Portugal I stayed away overnight in Gibraltar and in the morning brought the pretty 8 year old daughter of some friends back to my house for a ride on the bike and a visit. It was a hot day and Kirsty was going to help me clean out the well. I had bought doggy shampoo to wash Shilpit and keep away the tics that were plaguing her. As we drew up, the scruffy white animal came running to the gate as usual but I happened to notice that she had come out of the caravan. This was out of bounds, but it was my fault for not shutting the door properly. She jumped up and down, pleased to see me.

'Come on Shilpit, you lucky dog, bath time!'

I filled a bucket with cool well water, poured in the shampoo mix and grabbed my very unwilling pet, dunking her in the bucket. With Kirsty's help, I sluiced her down thoroughly with the cold, antiseptic water and she looked at me with a dazed expression. This beneficial treatment was obviously not appreciated and she seemed almost to be in shock. After a good wash I pulled her out and briskly towelled her dry. With a shake, she bounded back towards the caravan.

'Shilpit, you're not allowed in there!' But she dived inside, so I followed. Then it dawned! My bed (although I now slept in the house) was covered in blood and there, underneath it, hidden away in the corner were four brand new puppies. Shilpit eyed them and me sheepishly. 'Thought I'd surprise you, Mum.' She had! 'Oh, you poor dog! You've just had babies and I've thrown you in a bucket of cold water! I didn't even notice you were thinner.' I shuddered to think what sort of reaction I would have had at such treatment.

Luckily, Kirsty was so thrilled with the new puppies that she didn't mind helping me with the job of washing the duvet and other bedding. At least the heat of the day saved Shilpit from pneumonia or shock, and it dried the sheets.

Right from the start Shilpit was torn between affection for me and her maternal duties. It was a sweltering August afternoon and I'd promised Kirsty that we would go for a swim in the lake. Shilpit usually accompanied me on such a trip and she looked longingly at us as we gathered our swimming togs to go. Not being conversant with the do's and don'ts of new born pups, I decided to pop them in a basket and take them with us. That way Shilpit could come without feeling bad about it. It wasn't a good idea for she kept jumping up at the basket in a worried fashion as I carried it. On arrival at the beach I positioned the pups under a large rock to provide shade. Shilpit joined us for a swim in the cool water several times and after each dip rushed back to her offspring.

After a couple of hours I went to gather the clan to take them home in the basket but found the tiny, squirming bodies buried in sand and wedged firmly under the lip of the rock. It took quite some digging to retrieve them. I looked Shilpit deep in her yellow eyes. From that moment I felt that she may have realised that romance with the Boxer had left her with more than she'd bargained for and that perhaps an 'accident' or two might be a relief. This made me feel better about my intentions because there was no way I was going to keep all these puppies and I had to dispose of them as kindly as possible. Obviously I had to wait for Kirsty to go home but the sooner I did it the better. Still, I couldn't brace myself to do the dirty deed. I had been told that I should keep one for the mother's sake as she needed to use up her milk and, some said, that is psychologically wrong to leave her with none. Having seen Shilpit's reactions I felt that she was quite strong-minded over these matters but I decided that one should live and picked the most attractive to facilitate later adoption.

I woke up every morning that week to the sound of mewing pups and promised myself that 'today was the day' I would take the bull by the horns – the pups by the throat – and that would be that! But I couldn't do it. At night Shilpit would leave her pups and follow me to the bar, then reluctantly go home early to feed them. Everyone remarked how unusual it was for a mother to leave her pups when they were so young. But, let's face it, not all females want to be mothers; I could empathise with her.

After days of procrastination it *had* to be done and in this instance one of the junkies, who lived directly behind me, obliged. During one of his more down to earth moments I enquired if he had experience in puppy killing and, when he replied in the affirmative, asked if he would oblige.

'Sure,' he said, 'you'll have to divert the mother for about half an hour.'

'That's no problem, she'll follow my bike if I ride up to the castle.'

Sure enough, as I pulled away she ran behind and I kept her occupied for the required time. More over, when we returned she made no attempt to find her offspring. Still wagging her tail and communing with me, she froze when there was a whimper from the nest. Her head went up, she shot me a questioning look and then walked slowly, tail down, to the kennel. When I peered in she was settled with a little gold puppy suckling at her teat. With her front paws crossed in an attitude of complete exasperation, her glaring yellow eyes said 'You've left me one. Why didn't you get rid of them all?' So much for motherly love.

Chapter Five

<u>Win Some, Lose Some</u>

Midway through September when the weather, thankfully, starts to cool, Georgia with the harp from Lagos suddenly appeared on my doorstep. 'Linda, I'm here,' she laughed as we embraced, 'I've come to make
some music with you.'

I soon had her established in the caravan and she told me of the bus journey from Lagos, her rather stressful overnight stop in a hostel in La Linea, and the final stretch up to Castellar to where she and her harp had been given a lift. I was very pleased to see her for her presence was like a ray of sunshine in this, what I was beginning to find, somewhat negative place. For me, living among people I didn't really understand or identify with was becoming hard work. Georgia had a positive attitude which rekindled my own and we found many songs and tunes in common and could appreciate each other's anecdotes about the music and theatre world. She had finished the first draft of her book and her harp playing had improved with the extra practice on the streets in Portugal where she had made quite a name for herself, 'The Angel of Lagos'!

Although appearing small and dainty, she had a surprising amount of strength and displayed no trouble climbing upon the pillion seat of my BMW with her harp for our forays into Gibraltar and along the coast to perform. We were lucky enough to score a few weekends playing at the Sotogrande Market, for which the estate office gladly paid. Georgia's harp was a hit, as was the gracious style with which she played it and her rich, flowing voice. My lively whistle was a complementary contrast and, with practice, our vocal harmonies improved and rang out with confidence among the craft stalls. We received as much applause from the stall holders as the punters.

As the weeks went on we were interviewed and sang on Gibraltar radio and the Costa del Sol. We enjoyed performing together and I felt I would miss her when she continued her journey. Though she loved the countryside in my area, Georgia was not too impressed with some of the people around me. In an effort to lift PC's more frequent depressed moods, I introduced Georgia to him and left them alone together for a long chat. She had healing qualities, read Tarot cards and had a way with people that gave them inspiration. I hoped that maybe she could touch some vital chord in PC's consciousness and show him a way to combat his depressions; something, it seemed, I was unable to do. She left him her 'Purpose Plan', which I shall explain later. She was, however, doubtful about his attitude. He did not seem to want to break out of his negative mode and, as Georgia said, 'You can't help someone who doesn't want to help themselves.' She felt my energy was being sapped by people such as him and that it was good that we were able to regenerate positive energy by our singing together. I agreed.

Although our music was attracting interest and offers of work along the coast, Georgia's aim was not to stay in Spain but to continue her journey, both physical and mental, by travelling through Africa and experiencing the life and music there. Not wanting to lose her lively company so soon, I suggested that we go to Morocco together on my bike. I could at least take her to Agadir in the South to start the next part of her trip. Georgia was enthusiastic about this suggestion. As I'd been there before I could give her an introduction to Africa without the trials of facing it alone and maybe we could find some work en route. So it was decided and a departure date provisionally fixed for the beginning of October. Meanwhile we would make money towards the trip and enjoy the pleasant weather in Castellar. All seemed well in the world.

Shilpit was busy being a dutiful mum to her remaining puppy, Gremlin, who was now a month old. Although still preferring to follow me around than suckle her child, she had resigned herself to the responsibility of parenthood.

One evening Georgia and I had an invitation to dinner with Sam, another English girl who lived in a cottage close by. We arrived about 8pm, armed with the guitar and harp, bottles of wine and Shilpit in tow. A most enjoyable evening ensued, laughter and singing after the well prepared dinner and we all became a little tipsy. As usual Shilpit disappeared during the latter part of the evening to feed the pup, Gremlin, back at the house. About midnight Georgia and I staggered home; she to the caravan and me into my house. I noticed that Shilpit was not in the kennel but thought she must have gone walkabout. I fell immediately into a drunken sleep but was awakened about 3am by the sound of Gremlin crying. Why wasn't Shilpit around? I brought the pup into the bedroom to comfort her and began to worry. There must be something wrong – she wouldn't stay away this long, especially as I was home. Although she slept outside in the kennel, Shilpit's habit was to come in and check on me at night to make sure I was there and have a quick cuddle before going outside again. Tonight she hadn't done so. Now I began to be afraid for her and slept fitfully.

In the morning light I started the search around the house, up and down the trail we had walked the night before, tracing the route over the fence and up the garden path. Halfway across the garden I found her – eyes glazed, tongue lolling and her poor little white body stiff as a board. I stood frozen, staring at her, a huge lump in my throat and a numb feeling of disbelief. But it was true. The goat herders in the area often put poison bait down for dogs. Shilpit was naughty. She did chase goats, not viciously but for a moment's fun. I'd often warned her but of course she didn't understand. Now, on the way home to feed her baby she had stopped to try a tasty snack lying on the track. My little friend was gone.

I remained dry-eyed as Georgia, Sam and I took turns in digging the spade into the rock-hard, dry earth for a pit deep enough to bury Shilpit. We lowered her in, replaced the earth and scattered wild flowers on her grave. Georgia spoke the 'goodbyes' – my throat was too tight – and we all shed a farewell tear. Gremlin, her offspring, bounced around the garden, wondering what the fuss was about. She was a distraction for us and now we had to wean her. A lovely little puppy but not my soul mate – I tried not to think about it – and I was surprised how bereft I felt.

After this distressing event, however, our lives were brightened by a visit from Craig, a very nice young man whom Georgia had befriended in Lagos. They made a good couple. He, too, was full of life and enthusiasm and between them they cooked me some wonderful meals and Craig hung a door in this house that I was trying to make both weatherproof and attractive. Craig was imminently flying back to South Africa and Georgia hoped to catch up with him there eventually after her journey through Africa. She, Craig and I spent several days checking the bike over, effecting minor repairs and having new tyres fitted for the long journey. It was a productive and fun time.

Craig flew out, the weather cooled, and storms began heralding the start of the normal rainy season in October. I felt we were leaving Spain just in time and would enjoy dry and pleasant weather in Southern Morocco. We found a home for Gremlin and both excitedly looked forward to our departure.

Chapter Six

Morocco—The North

In mid-October Georgia and I took the midday ferry from Algeciras. The hour and a half crossing gives gull's eye views of the pillars of Hercules; one being the great limestone Rock of Gibraltar jutting impertinently from the European coast, and the other Jebel Musa, beckoning grandly from the most northerly tip of Africa.

We had no trouble checking through the Moroccan border, 5 miles from the port of Ceuta, and then the start of our journey really began with the 100 km ride to Chefchaouen, a beautiful town in the Rif mountains. The magic of Chaouen, as it is affectionately called, begins on the approach road. From the floor of the valley it can be seen nestling in the arms of the surrounding hills, an overgrown village moulded into the mountain and spilling out from its original walled centre. Remnants of these walls are on the upper side, just below the new Asmaa Hotel, the campsite and the Youth Hostel. The walking track in from these locations is through a gate in this wall and down the narrow, cobbled streets, which on first acquaintance seem an impenetrable maze. The outsides of the street-front houses, shops and workshops are whitewashed, but in many cases not just white but with varying shades of blue. I was told that this colour discourages the mosquitoes but, whether this is true or not, the effect is more soothing to the eye than the stark white of many Spanish towns. The shadows and hollows of the roughly-shaped archways and alleys give an impression of Bilbo's Hobbit land. This is especially so in the cooler months when jelaba-clad figures, their pointed hoods covering their heads, shuffle on slippered feet through the alleys.

The cloistered dwellings are full of life. Tiny shops bursting with carpets and crafts from all over Morocco are like Aladdin's caves. In tiny workshops huge looms take up nearly all the floor space, while men and women, dwarfed by their apparatus, weave carpets and cloth.

The maze of streets finally burst out on to the main square to another welcoming world. Cafes selling all kinds of Moroccan food and fresh squeezed orange juice or the famous 'whisky Moroccain' (mint tea), tourist style with each glass jammed full of mint leaves. Up the street, open displays of fossils from desert areas make a troglodyte seem almost commonplace. The trendiest clothes in Morocco can be bought at a price way below any in Europe.

Chaouen is proud of its cultural community. There are up-market art and craft galleries with almost European prices which cater for the more selective buyer. The kasbah sports a museum with antique pieces, space for art exhibitions and a sweet smelling, green and tranquil garden. On Mondays the souk (market) in the lower part of town is alive with travelling street vendors selling spices from colourful piles, pots and pans and other household commodities, vegetables and live animals, second-hand clothes and shoes. All is hustle and bustle, with fast food stalls cooking tasty snacks and selling the ever present 'hobs', Moroccan flat bread.

As an introduction to Morocco I find Chaouen colourful and exciting but also hassle-free and peaceful. I get an immediate rush of satisfaction and happiness every time I arrive.

Leaving the bike at the Youth Hostel set in a woody area above the town, we dashed through the narrow streets and climbed the opposite hill to an old tower in order to view the sunset; always a spectacular sight as the orange glow fades behind the mountains and the lights of the town gradually appear and twinkle amongst the deepening shadows of the buildings. The evening call to prayer rang out and there was a feeling of peace accentuated by the silhouette of a lone shepherd on the hillside. He was also taking in the view, puffing contentedly on his kif pipe.

We descended the track, just before complete darkness overtook us, and made our weary way back to the town. Too tired to cook a meal, we bought a cake to have at the Youth Hostel with our cup of tea. Taieb, the Youth Hostel 'official' met us in town and accompanied us up the rocky hill and back down to his domain and our dormitories.

An early start was necessary the next morning to walk up the hill behind us to visit Hadja, a Berber woman who, although only in her late 30s, had 11 children ranging from a babe in arms to teenagers. I played my whistle and we sang for them while Hadja and her older daughters provided us with mint tea in their interesting home. A small, low house, the main room served as a kitchen, lounge, bedroom, storeroom and chicken hutch. Goats wandered in and out as we drank. The children were red-cheeked and snotty-nosed and very inquisitive. All laughing faces and waiting hands, hoping I would let them try the whistles and maybe keep them; I left one behind as one of the boys showed some talent.

As we walked back down to the village, Hadja came with us as it was market day and she needed provisions. She sang a Berber song to us which we tried to imitate, bringing forth gales of laughter from our guide. She skipped across the rocks, showing us short cuts that took twice as long for our fumbling feet. On reaching town we explored the shops and galleries. One of the local artists, Mohcin, invited us to have a meal at his house and gave Georgia one of his watercolours, which I was to pick up on my return.

Back at the campsite next to the Youth Hostel we met three South African boys travelling in a utility. They were some of the first of their nationality to cross Africa from south to north overland. Previously, during apartheid, it was impossible but now they were welcomed at most black nations' borders as being men from 'Mandela's Country'. They were euphoric at having completed the arduous journey despite many obstacles; one was illegally crossing the Mauritanian border (where internal fighting still persisted) at night. Now they were looking forward to relaxing in Europe and I told them where my house key was located so that they could have a 'European' rest in at Castellar. (I heard later that they made the most of their time there toasting their success with local beer. They did leave me an appreciative note).

We left Chefchaouen for the ride through the hills to the industrial town of Kenitra. It is about a four-hour ride, a good road and pretty scenery. The town of Kenitra itself is not very attractive but the camp is in a walled park with plenty of trees and a friendly proprietor who provides guard dogs (which invariably run off with any boots or shoes not kept safely inside the tent). I had stayed there many times before so we were greeted with a friendly wave.

Kenitra is the home of a wonderful Moroccan family who took me under their wing a few years before on an enforced stay when one of my party ended up in hospital. The head of the family was very definitely Fatima, the then 55 year old matriarch. With her headscarf tied in the Moroccan fashion, tight across her forehead and down under her chin, her full jelaba covering her ample body from head to foot and with a purposeful frown on her face when bargaining with a street vendor, she was formidable. But at home, scarf and jelaba free, loose top with rolled up sleeves over her baggy pantaloons, round smiling face with twinkling eyes, she laughed and joked and combated her hard life with an abundant sense of humour. She was up at 5.30 every morning, catching the bus to the fish factory at Medhia where she worked six days a week, arriving back home at 7.30 in the evening.

The 'monsieur', her husband, was 20 years her senior and, at that time, though in good health was obviously senile. Shuffling around in his brown jelaba, a serene smile on his face, he talked about when he was a soldier in France during the war. He endlessly repeated questions and either slept or made pots of tea. Fatima fondly called him an old fool but considered herself lucky that they had his French army pension. She had 8 children by him over the course of their married life. At this time only two were at home; Zohre, a 30 year old looking for a husband and Mohammed, 21, looking for a job.

Zohre had a lively personality like her mother, a full moon face and a very expressive way of talking, rolling her brown eyes while she almost spat out the Arabic words. To hear her relate the day's incidents was a dramatic experience—even without understanding the language. She was a very hard worker, helping out by doing the house cleaning in the morning and going to her job as seamstress in the afternoon and evening.

Mohammed was a good looking boy with short, dark, curly hair and a gentle open face. He worked at the same factory as his mother or out on the fishing boats when he could and, like any lad of his age, liked to go out with his friends. He smoked and was especially pleased when I produced a gift of American cigarettes from Gibraltar.

The beauty of the family was Hinde, Fatima's grandchild. Her mother, now living with a new husband, worked in Rabat and Hinde stayed with Fatima to attend the local schools. Although only 14, she was already taller than me with a graceful, well formed, woman's body and an oval face with intelligent brown eyes. She learnt French at school and pronounced it well. She had a delightful manner, for her way of speaking and body language were at once playfully innocent and yet seductive.

This little family was housed in a two-storey dwelling in a back street not far from the old medina. The street-fronted door opened on to a main area with a skylight, used as both a room and a hallway and, when they insisted on pulling my bike inside for safety, a garage. A 'squat-upon' toilet lay behind a door to the left and a cubicle kitchen to the immediate right. Off the main entrance square was the formal living room for visitors which had the best cushioned seats and a table for serving the ceremonial tea and couscous. This room doubled as Fatima's and the old man's bedroom and was where visitors stayed overnight as well. Another room off the square, directly facing the front door, served as the normal living and eating room where the television was situated. The sofas were not so grandly covered here. This was Zohre's bedroom at night. On the right lay yet another small area, Hinde's enclosure. She had a wardrobe in which everyone's best jelabas were hung. Like any teenager, posters and photos adorned the walls and knick-knacks cluttered the shelves but, with limited space, she had to be tidy.

We arrived at the house early evening and were sent to the market with Hinde to buy vegetables and then, while Fatima was preparing the meal, Zohre and Hinde took us off to the hammam. This is not just a public bath, it is a social event. For many Moroccan women it is a once-a-week chance to get away from the tedium of their family chores and have several hours for themselves. Not only do they completely clean their own bodies, washing, scrubbing and rewashing it many times, but they also wash each other, family and friends. It's a place to sit and chat, gossip, and even fight if differences have to be settled. The echoing chambers of the bathing rooms are filled with noise; laughter, shouts, children's cries (if the soap is in their eyes) and singing.

The process starts in the changing room, a large square area with a surrounding bench upon which people undress and then leave their clothes in a bag for the attendants. From there they go through to the first chamber, armed with soap, henna, scrubbing cloth and small washing bowls. Inside there are buckets to fill with hot water from an ever-flowing tap. Each chamber is a tiled area where people sit in copious water on the floor. There are usually about three chambers, each one hotter than the next. It's normal to go to the hottest to begin the washing process there. Then, when the heat becomes too overwhelming, move back to the next one, start the process again, then finish in the coolest chamber.

Hinde and Zohre took control. Georgia and I were scrubbed,

rubbed and rinsed for almost three hours. Surprisingly, layer after layer of dirt came away under the insistent scrubbing cloth. Our western ideas of cleanliness through frequent showering is laughable when it is seen just how deeply the dirt is buried and how long it really takes to remove it. Zohre and Hinde were tireless in their efforts with us. Just as I thought I was squeaky clean with no more dirt in my pores, Zohre would start scrubbing me again and lo, yet another layer of scum appeared. Eventually, exhausted, we made our escape back to the changing room where we watched as women, skinny in their nakedness, began adding layer after layer of clothing, vests, knickerbockers, petticoats, and when the final jelaba covered them they appeared solid and buxom.

The feeling of the whole process is of love and friendship. Womankind sharing their mutual lifestyles, linked by the common bond of the female form in all its various shapes and sizes. A great feeling of sisterhood. Afterwards, we were shepherded back to the family house in its narrow alleyway and only just managed to keep our eyes open long enough to eat the delicious couscous.

As the hammam is not just a bath but a sharing experience, so couscous takes in the same feeling of community. When made properly, the process takes about three hours and the whole family is involved. Firstly, choosing the ingredients at a Moroccan market is far removed from our supermarket experience. Food is handled and haggled over—human communication. The preparation of the vegetables can include the whole family, peeling and chopping while swapping gossip.

Couscous is a ground grain. Its tiny particles are hard when dry and need to be steamed with added fats to make it light and fluffy. Traditionally the process requires three steaming periods with the grains separated and fat rubbed in between each one. The vegetables are cooked in a pot below the steamer and the meat in a separate container. The complete meal is served on a large, circular, ceramic dish with the meat (or fish) and vegetables piled high in the centre on top of the couscous. Deft fingers take a little of the vegetables and squeeze them together with the couscous to form balls by tossing and rolling the mixture in the palm of the hand. The ball magically clings together and is then popped into the mouth. The light, fluffy morsel melts into the waiting salivic juices with a mixture of taste and texture. Pieces of meat or fish are taken separately. Each person only takes from the segment of this food plate directly in front of them, but the hostess will select various choice pieces of the meat and put them into the guest's sector.

Caring and sharing accompanies the preparation and eating of couscous. Fatima and her family revelled in this traditional meal and usually served it for Sunday lunch. I found it reminiscent of my early years when my family all helped prepare our weekend roast beef and Yorkshire pudding and we would sit around the dinner table discussing the week and sharing our lives.

It was with great difficulty that Georgia and I tore ourselves away from this friendly family environment to continue our trip south.

The Hammam

Jelabas fall and pantaloons tumble
Vests and slips lie in array
Then tied neatly in a bundle
Bagged with the purse and put away

Check equipment for the bathroom
Scrubbing cloth and pumice stone
Stools and mats and soap and buckets
Ladling bowls and brush and comb

Buckets sploshing, splishing, splashing
Shampoo foams and henna dyes
Bodies glistening, water streaming
Children wailing, soap in eyes

Through hot steam bare bellies shine
Opening pores release the sweat
Rubbing, scrubbing, dirt is scraped
From every crease and inch of flesh

In the change room long hair streaming
Then tightly tied against the head
Figures fill with layer on layer
Bosoms bulge and waists are spread

Chitter chatter of the children
Smiling eyes across the floor
Friends are meeting, passing gossip
Weekly respite from the chores

Chapter Seven

Arrangements In Casa

Before we left Spain I had contacted Gwen, a woman met on a previous trip who invited me to stay at her house when next in Casablanca. An attractive woman in her forties, she was married to a Moroccan, Kamal, and had lived and worked as an English teacher for many years in Morocco. Gwen had faxed me to say that, having other guests at the time of our visit, she had arranged for us to stay with a friend, Jo, and she included a map to guide us to a flat close to the centre of the city.

Georgia and I made an early start from Kenitra in overcast but dry weather. After a short stop in Rabat, incorporating a quick tour of the kasbah, we took the scenic, coastal route for the 100kms to Casablanca rather than the dull motorway, and timed our trip to arrive late afternoon. We found the address, no problem, and were expecting Jo to be a woman as Gwen had written the name without an 'e'.

The apartment door was answered by a young Moroccan man who ushered us in and through a spacious dining-room to a large lounge furnished with black leather sofas. Rising to meet us, wearing a silk dressing gown and holding a long cigarette holder between his fingers, was a man in his early forties.

'How do you do?' he said in a very British accent, 'I've been expecting you all day. Gwen didn't say exactly when you were arriving.'

We shook his proffered hand, hiding our surprise, so Jo was Joe. We weren't sure of an arrival time ourselves, we told him as he waved a hand elegantly at the sofa to indicate making ourselves comfortable. He called to the young Moroccan man to bring some wine.

'This is Hassan,' he told us as the handsome man returned, smiling politely but shyly, 'he helps me around the house. Do you smoke?'

We said thanks but no and settled back to enjoy the ice cold white wine while Joe regaled us with stories of his life in Casa over the last 16 years—chain smoking all the while. Hassan hovered in the background, topping up our wine and providing nibbles while Joe spoke. Joe had originally come to Morocco in the '70s on the hippy trail and stayed as an English teacher. He found life very amenable in this profession and had many comforts that weren't readily available back in the UK, some of which we were to learn about more clearly later. In the evening Hassan cooked us a delicious fish meal which was served in the large dining-room.

Kamal and Gwen arrived after dinner and the latter said that she had made a contact for us on the music scene and would set up an appointment. It was a pleasant evening in convivial company and interesting to learn more about the life of the ex-pat teaching community in the big city. At last Georgia and I retired exhausted to the comfy lounge that had been designated as our bedroom.

During the next few days we met some funny, larger-than-life characters and found ourselves in situations that did seem like something out of a film set. No wonder Casablanca, the movie, was such a success. Even though it wasn't actually filmed there, the town of today seemed to want to live up to its reputation, with its characters if not its buildings.

Casablanca is a large sprawling city but has a motorway bypass with well signposted exits and the connecting streets are wide and reasonably easy to negotiate. In the centre, not far from the port area, lie the large modern hotels and main tourist shopping area. This includes the ancient medina, a bright contrast to the surrounding western influence. There are many English language schools, one in which Gwen and Joe taught, and large expensive shops with European goods.

Not far from the centre are large tree-lined parklands to which city people can escape for their lunch break, and it is a short ride out to the coast where the new mosque, constructed by Hassan II, commands attention and magnificently displays his wealth and power. The green and white marbled structure is an imposing and beautiful sight. However, the slums opposite were a reminder that much public money went to build this great mosque and not all was voluntarily given. Wages were docked for contributions to the building work and we met many Moroccans who were unhappy about this. However, as a tourist attraction it must bring wealth to the city.

One evening Georgia and I looked for the famous 'Rick's Cafe' of the movie 'Casablanca' but were disappointed when all we found was a poor imitation in one of the 5 star hotels. Sure, the waiters all wore high-collared trench coats but it lacked atmosphere so we didn't stay for an overpriced drink. The city itself has little to offer in the way of ancient sites but it is the commercial capital of Morocco and the place to find any commodity you need. It also has a variety of cultural centres and is the nightlife hot spot. It has a reputation for rogues and we played if safe by paying a parking attendant to watch the bike night and day, but we experienced no trouble in any of the areas we frequented.

Hoping to find some outlets for our blossoming musical abilities as a duo, we made enquiries at several embassies and were put in contact with a Mr Smouni, the head of the Sidi Belyout Community Theatre in the centre of town. This gentleman was a large, extremely well dressed, typically theatrical character. He waved us expansively into his spacious office and demonstrated his importance by instructing one of his numerous pecking order of assistants to bring us tea. He was very taken with the blonde Georgia and her harp and offered us a concert on Saturday night, 5th November, two weeks hence. After agreeing a percentage fee for our performance, we were told to speak to his second in command, Mr Ishman, to arrange publicity. Things were going well, we thought.

We also spoke to Rachid, a contact of Gwen's, who ran a children's home and he booked us to perform two shows for children on the same weekend, so it seemed we could make a fair amount of money in a short period of time. Happy with our organisation, we decided to go to the Atlas Mountains for the next two weeks to exercise our lungs, plan and rehearse the shows and come back in time for our grand performances.

It all seemed too good to be true. Before we left Mr Ishman set up an interview with the newspaper 'Le Matin' and the reporter arrived at the centre the next day. He had no note pad and seemed not at all interested in asking us any questions—only in drinking tea. We provided both the write-up and a photograph. Perhaps this was an omen. We offered to do a radio interview but Mr Ishman said it wasn't necessary and that he would arrange posters and put in information on our performance in the November program shortly to be printed.

Our stay at Joe's was proving very interesting. We weren't the only house guests as another English friend of Gwen's, Judith, was also in residence. A middleclass, middle-aged lady, she played the oboe and had been a professional orchestral musician for many years until modern technology with pre-recorded and synthesised music had depleted demand for her talents. Now she was trying out TEFL teaching to diversify her means of making a living. It was her first time in Casa and she was working with some private students that Gwen had arranged. It was obvious that she thought that Georgia's and my music was not in her class and was amazed that we had lined up a concert. However, we befriended her by sharing our supply of Tesco tea bags, which were a great improvement on the weak Lipton's available in the local shops.

In contrast to Judith's 'straight' manner it was becoming increasingly obvious to us that Joe's was decidedly not. On closer observation we noticed that the pictures around his flat were all of young boys, the books included some on sex in Thailand, and the relationship he had with Hassan, the live-in houseboy, seemed rather peculiar. We started to piece a few bits of stories together to make two and two add up and were finally given undeniable evidence of our conclusions at Joe's dinner party.

He had an extensive collection of music, mainly '70's era, and one evening asked my opinion of which to select as suitable music to play for the elderly mother of his Swiss colleague. She was coming with her daughter that night to join Georgia, Judith and myself for a meal. The conversation at the pre-dinner drinks was in French and too fast for me but I followed the theme. Joe was a charming entertainer, the mood was congenial with Hassan intermittently topping up our glasses when there was a knock at the door. Hassan opened it and a tall, slim and very pretty young Moroccan man strode in and immediately began a precocious banter with Joe. He demanded Coca-Cola, which was not in the house but Joe gave him money to buy it. This gave the party a few minutes grace but the young man returned as we were sitting down to dinner and, much to my surprise, he joined us and flirted outrageously with our host throughout the meal. It was hard to hold together a reasonable conversation while this distraction was occurring. I was seated next to the older woman and her daughter at one end of the table while Judith and Georgia were opposite Joe and his playboy at the other. Eventually, unable to stand the strain of the now very uncongenial atmosphere any longer, I finished my meal and went into the bathroom to prepare for bed.

When I came out five minutes later the Swiss ladies were leaving, Judith was disappearing to her room and Joe and his paramour were heading for his. Hassan looked uncomfortable. A giggling Georgia explained that the banter had ended with Joe making such a sexually suggestive comment that the guests could no longer ignore the situation and had decided to bail out—and I had missed it!

Needless to say we were quite relieved when, all concert dates and arrangements set, we left Casablanca, glad to be out of the big city and its strange appetites. We were grateful for Joe's hospitality, however, and one other thread he showed us in the great tapestry of life.

I had a Moroccan teacher friend, Ahmed, in El Jadida, about another 100kms down the coast. It was a sunny, warm day and we enjoyed the coastal scenery—Atlantic waves crashing on to low rocks or sandy beaches. Stopping at the old port city of Azemour for lunch, we ate our bread and 'Vache qui Rit' on the crumbling walls overlooking the river mouth. On arrival at El Jadida, the coastal playground for inhabitants of inland Marrakech, we left the BM, our bike gear and the harp in the safety of the guards of the seaside Sable d'Or cafe where Ahmed was a regular customer. Lightened of our thick jackets as we were in warmer weather, we walked in to explore the old walled city.

El Jadida was in the hands of the Portuguese for about 400 years and they built a water cistern which is now only used as a tourist attraction. It has a beautiful arched ceiling which is stunningly reflected in the shallow residue of water on the floor. The acoustics are brilliant and Georgia and I entertained two groups of people on guided tours by bursting into Amazing Grace and Pie Jesu, and the sound of our harmonies echoed hauntingly around the building. Even the ticket lady came to listen. Outside, we walked around the top of the city walls, looking across at the yards where the colourful fishing boats were built, and chatting to the local children who played among the iron canons, the rusty muzzles of which pointed uselessly out to sea.

We picked up the bike from Sable d'Or and, as there was no sign of Ahmed for his usual after school coffee with the other teachers, we drove around to his house. However, a neighbour said he had moved and showed us his new residence close by. The man next door to this abode informed us that Ahmed wouldn't be back until after 6, so we positioned ourselves on the pavement and Georgia began to play the harp. Within seconds we were surrounded by children, like magic they appeared, running from all directions. By the time we finished the first song the crowd was ten deep. Little fingers reached out to touch us and the harp, eyes opened in wonder and hands clapped in spontaneous appreciation. After half a dozen more songs we were beginning to attract adults too and the situation became a little worrying, as we were now hemmed in on all sides and in danger of being crushed. Fortunately a young man came to our rescue, after we explained what we were doing there.

'I have a sports centre across the road,' he said, 'you can come there and wait inside away from the crowd.'

We gratefully accepted his offer, and were safely behind closed doors yet close enough to see when Ahmed returned. The young man gave us a soft drink and we were entertained by the sight of chubby Moroccan women doing the equivalent of Jane Fonda exercises led by another muscular Moroccan lad, who obviously thought he was the bees knees.

After half an hour or so Ahmed eventually appeared and explained the reason for his move—he was now married. I had only seen him six months previously and had not been aware of a fiancée on the scene, so it was a surprise. However, his pretty, new wife Nezrah, also a teacher, was friendly and hospitable and we soon had our gear inside their new flat and the bike safely guarded at the local garage. Luckily I had brought one of my paintings for him, so presented it to them both as a wedding gift.

Moroccans seldom have pictures on their walls, though. Except for a photo of Hassan II or an occasional family portrait, they keep their walls bare. The decoration lies mainly in the richness of the fabric for their cushions and sofas. These are positioned against the walls and double as beds for visitors or family. Carpets are also decorative. Nezrah was very proud of the beautiful material she had chosen for her lounge and they were saving to decorate another room. It was a big change from Ahmed's previous bachelor pad.

We settled in for a comfortable night's chat and the meal that Ahmed prepared for us. It is unusual for a Moroccan male to cook when he has a wife but Ahmed enjoyed it and, having lived abroad for some time, was less stuck in the traditional ways than many of his contemporaries. We spent a very pleasant evening, glad of the less stressful company of our Moroccan friends.

Chapter Eight

The Mountains And The Sea

Bidding a fond farewell to Ahmed and Nezrah, we left El Jadida early. It was market day at Asni, our destination, and I wanted to be there in time to take advantage of the occasion to buy our supplies for the mountain walk. The ride inland to Marrakech was beautiful. As the day was clear, the snows capped mountains of the high Atlas rose spectacularly on the horizon and were clearly visible from about 50kms before we reached the city. Georgia had bad vibes about Marrakech brought on by the previous night's dream, so we didn't stay long but rode out a further 50kms to the Youth Hostel at Asni.

The Road to Marrakech

The market was in full swing and we soon located my friend Brahim. A tall, handsome man with dark, curly hair and a moustache that accentuated his winning smile, he came to greet us with a slow, regal walk and firm handshake. His business as a jewellery dealer between the local crafts people and foreigners was aided enormously by his grasp of five languages and his immaculate dress, either in well pressed T-shirt and jeans or his 'blue man' traditional robes. He was one of my favourite Moroccan men; great to look at and a real gentleman who took on the financial responsibility of his mother and siblings. His father's wanderings kept him away much of the time and he was not a great earner. In contrast Brahim was well known and respected in the local community and one of the more successful dealers.

Georgia and I had tea with Brahim in one of the market tea houses where we also sang a few songs with 'Bob Marley', the Berber boy with dreadlocks and no front teeth who played his Berber banjo on market days to earn a few dirhams busking. He spoke only Berber dialects so our conversations had always been very limited, but music formed the common bond.

I love the Asni market. Every Saturday the mountain people come into town on their donkeys and mules and leave them in the 'donkey park' while they do their weekly trading. Anything is obtainable at the market. There are doctors, dentists, barbers, cobblers and a host of other services all under the little canvas structures or in tiny shops on the perimeter of the market square. While the stallholders ply their wares, their donkeys can be shod, have saddles made or mended, and the family can have their teeth pulled or buy remedial concoctions from the medicine man. Local fruits and vegetables are piled high on the ground, colourful mounds of spice catch the eye and nose. Jewellery sellers constantly tempt with their trinkets. They often followed us around until we told them we were Brahim's friends and then they dropped back, for he was the big boy around there. Under Brahim's watchful eyes we bought a supply of fruit and vegetables, dates and peanuts and several packets of the all important chocolate bars.

The Youth Hostel, run by a gentle Berber couple, was a good place to leave the bike, our camping gear and Georgia's precious harp, locked safely in their storeroom. We packed our rucksacks with sleeping bags and food and took the early taxi to Imlil, a village a few kilometres away where the walking track to Mount Toubkal begins. A pretty village at the head of a valley, Imlil has souvenir shops, a mountain hostel and a place to hire a guide. However, I had done the walk before and was confident I knew the way without assistance.

The route starts off gently among the more lush vegetation of the lower slopes but then takes a steep rise up to the first pass. Fortunately I remembered the short cuts and we were well on schedule to reach the mountain hut for the first night. Here altitude lowers the temperature and we were glad to snuggle into our sleeping bags after dark. The last time I was here, in the spring season, it snowed heavily overnight and it was necessary to take a guide to the top of the pass as my English female companion, Sam, and I couldn't find the track under the blanket of snow. However, this time the morning dawned clear, with not a sign of the white stuff, so we made an early start on the hard climb uphill.

It took four hours of scrambling over the rocky terrain to reach the cradle of the pass. The scenery is quite stark here with little vegetation on the westerly slope. It was noon when we reached the top and we used our last gasps of breath to sing 'Happy Birthday' to Jason, Georgia's then 24 year old son. We wondered if he could hear us in Banff, Canada, from our high vantage point!

High Atlas

The weather was magnificent, crisp and clear, and the valley on the eastern, downhill slope more fertile and pleasing to the eye. We lunched by a stream and finally, exhausted, reached the Berber village of Idbassen and the welcome abode of Mr Lahcen. He was a small, laughing man who had enterprisingly turned his home into a hostel.

On my previous walk with Sam we had wandered off the beaten track and, tired and hungry at the imminent onset of nightfall, had found ourselves on the edge of a precipitous drop with a dangerous climb to the correct route we could see in the valley below. It was then my first time on this track and we'd left the guide at the top of the pass. Things hadn't looked too good, but then as we started our first tentative steps down—hi ho, hi ho—along came a walking party with picks and shovels over their shoulders like the seven dwarfs of Snow White. They rescued us by gallantly helping us down over the rocky ledge and leading us to the village. 'Smiley' was Mr Lahcen, who took us to the refuge of his home in this lovely mud-brick building.

That was six months before. This time he had spotted us, footsore and weary, as we descended the correct track and sent his son Mohammed to meet us. He cooked a tasty tarjine, wrapped our aching bodies in thick Berber blankets as the cool of the night set in, and made us comfortable with rugs and cushions in his simple accommodation. Reviving a little with the food and hot mint tea, Georgia and I sang Australian action songs to the village children, who giggled merrily at our antics.

From Mr Lahcen's house the route gradually descends along a fertile valley with many small villages. The inhabitants of these rural communities cultivate intensively on terraces near the river. On our continuing journey the following morning, children asked us persistently for bonbons, dirhams and other 'cadeaux' and became tedious at times, but we just laughed and sang to them instead. We had been teaching each other songs en route and Georgia's ability to sing and climb at the same time was amazing. Her lung power in such a small frame was remarkable.

It's a long day's walk to the tourist resort of Seti Fatma, where the road winds in from Marrakech. The village sprawls along a fertile valley and there are seven beautiful waterfalls. Our priority on arrival was to find a hotel and a meal.

During the meal a somewhat inebriated man, Hussein, talked to us about the mountain walks. He said he was a guide and asked who was ours. When we replied that we had come by ourselves from Imlil he refused to believe us.

'If you had no guide, then which book did you use?' he demanded. 'No book, we know the way,' we explained.

'Rubbish,' he kept muttering. Two European women alone on the mountain was a situation too incredible for him to believe.

After a visit to the first cascade the next morning, we started our journey by road transport to Oukaimeden, the winter sports village about 50kms away. We wanted to make this the next point to begin walking on the circular route back to Asni. This necessitated taking the road toward Marrakech, then diverting back into the mountains on a dead-end road. The first part was easy as from Seti Fatma 90% of vehicles return to Marrakech. A lift came immediately in a van with two young Moroccan lads who thought their luck had changed picking up two blonde European women at once! However, as they snuggled up to us in the front seat, Georgia said sternly, 'Ne touche pas! Nous sommes les femmes formidables!' Their hands immediately retracted from our shoulders. We suffered no more advances, just engaging in friendly chat until the turn-off where we paid them the going rate and waved goodbye as we started on the uphill climb to Oukaimeden. Traffic to this destination was much more limited but a Swiss family stopped in their roomy Mercedes, transporting us with speed and comfort to the French mountain hut. Here I knew a hot shower, comfortable room and good meal were available.

As a ski resort, Oukaimeden is at its best under snow. Without it, it is a barren, desolate place, not at all inviting. However, it is a high point of the mountain range and, on a clear day, gives spectacular views across the hill tops and down to Marrakech.

Our departure morning was misty and it was hard to see the route down the mountainside. Had I not walked this way before in better conditions I doubt we would have found the route and, in some places, I was unsure if we had indeed taken the right track. On one such occasion I asked some small children to guide us over the rocks and, when I finally recognised the area, turned to thank them. On their request for bonbons I reached into my pocket, not for sticky sweets but another prize. Some time before I worked on a science exhibition for children in Gibraltar and it was sponsored by local industries, one of which sold computer ware for one of Richard Branson's Virgin companies. For publicity I was given dozens of little red tin badges, the logo on which was a heart and the words 'I am a Virgin Lover'. I was instructed to hand them out to the kids and teachers who came to view the exhibition. Some of the latter were amused but I baulked at handing them to the nuns of the Loreta Convent! Having some spare, I brought them for gifts on such an occasion as this. Waste not, want not. The children certainly seemed proud when I pinned them on to their tatty clothing. So now, if anyone reading this finds a small child in the High Atlas Mountains sporting such a badge you'll know who is responsible.

The walk to Asni is a long one but mainly all downhill. We found many places to have tea, sing to the children and cool our hot, tired feet in the streams. As it happened we were very lucky as, on arriving back at the Youth Hostel at Asni, the clouds that had gathered in the high peaks all day let themselves go and it started to rain. On looking behind us we saw that on the passes we had just overcome snow was falling. The angels had let us through.

For several weeks now I had a very painful elbow joint on my right arm. The feeling ranged between a dull ache to a stabbing pain running up and down from wrist to elbow. Riding the bike with my arm in one position was bearable but when I bent the elbow to take off my helmet the pain increased. Brahim, on hearing about the malady, insisted that I go to the Berber doctor at the market and he said he would take us personally the next day. I didn't dare refuse his generous offer.

Back at the Youth Hostel we met a newcomer, Raya. She was a Russian born girl, now living in America, who was touring Morocco alone. She felt quite threatened, not knowing how to deal with the constant male attention, and was very happy to be able to relate to two other English speaking women. She gladly accompanied us to the market, happy to have the pressure of her sole journey relieved.

Brahim took us immediately to the 'doctor', who held his 'surgery' in a small shed. When my eyes become accustomed to the dark interior contrasting with the bright sun outside, I saw the place was filled with many bottles containing powder and potions. Also a few small animal and frog skins, bird claws and herbs – all the usual paraphernalia of a man of his profession. Dubiously I sat on the floor. Brahim informed the man in Berber what the problem was and he gently took my arm in his hands, daubed it with some kind of oil and began to lightly massage.

'This is OK,' I thought, 'obviously some kind of magic potion to be absorbed into my muscles.'

While I knelt on the floor, bemused by the doctor and his cure, Georgia was sitting outside strumming her harp with Raya. Of course this attracted a few people who stopped by to see what was going on.

The doctor suddenly yanked at my elbow, bending it backwards. I yelped with pain. It wasn't what I expected a doctor to do with an obviously traumatised joint. I protested loudly but Brahim said 'Be quiet Linda, this is good for you.' I had my doubts but held back any more complaints while my arm was very tightly wrapped in the extended position. The bandage was sewn into place and it was now totally impossible for me to bend the joint. Brahim translated the instructions that I must leave the bandage in position for one week and now would I please hand over 30DH. I doubted the cure very much, and was the experience worth £2? After all, it was the onlookers who had the entertainment, not me.

Feeling somewhat sore, I followed the others as we threaded our way through the busy souk and out to where the taxis stood. Brahim issued instructions to the driver of one to take us the next village of Moulay Brahim to have our hands hennaed. This is a decoration that is usually done on special occasions such as weddings or feasts. Moulay Brahim, however, is a tourist village for holiday makers from Marrakech and is famous for its henna artists, so many Moroccan women have their hands and feet decorated as a holiday treat.

Brahim has many friends and relatives in this village and unfortunately they are not always the most skilled. He would invariably choose an artist to oblige us, which probably means keeping the commission in the family. I also think it added to his 'street cred' to be seen with white women, and he certainly gained a few more points in that direction that day with the three of us.

Henna is a plant which is dried and ground down to form a powder. It is green when dry but when mixed with water and applied it leaves a reddish brown stain. It is a softening treatment for both the skin and the hair. To make patterns on the hands and feet it is mixed to a fairly thin consistency and put into a small plastic syringe which is adapted to pipe a fine stream of the mixture on to the skin. The client can select the pattern of her choice from photos and this is copied on to the hands and feet. The piped henna dries but has to do so slowly. In order to do this, when the design is complete cologne is sprinkled on it, then cotton wool placed over the area, where it must be left in place as long as possible, preferably overnight. This applies to the hair also which, when treated with henna, should be kept wrapped in a towel. Then the caked residue can be washed off. The pattern remains as a dark red/brown stain which takes several weeks to fade, depending on the henna and how many times the area is washed. Funnily enough the stain lasts longer on the palm of the hands than the backs. As we were to perform in concert shortly, Georgia and I decided to have just a small, simple design on our palms only so our hands would not look 'dirty' on stage.

In order to give ourselves more rehearsal time in a warmer climate than the mountainous region, we decided to go straight out to the coast at Essaouira. It was necessary to remove the bandage from my arm for two reasons; one was that I couldn't bend my right arm to play the whistle or ride the bike, and the other was that the wrapping was so tight that I felt the circulation was restricted. out came the scissors. What a relief to get the wretched thing off! So much for Berber doctors.

The ride to Essaouira was a lucky one, along a good straight road. We just missed rain all the way and arrived in plenty of time to search out a good camping spot, 'Tangaro', 6 kms south of the main town. The site was owned by a Frenchman and incorporated a hostel with a restaurant. After witnessing a magnificent sunset made spectacular by the flaming skies, we asked if we could go into the dining-room to practice. As there were few clients, it was allowed and we found that the acoustics were very good, so resolved to use this as the rehearsal room while we camped at the site.

For the next few days we explored the beach area where an old seaside fortress eroded by the action of the waves had sunk into the sand. One such spectacular ruin was supposed to have inspired Jimi Hendrix to write 'Castles in the Sand'. The little village, Diabet, perched on the dunes overlooking the long white beach was a hippy village in the 1970's (Castellar's equivalent) and many musicians and artists stayed there. The cemetery, on a hillside, had beautiful grave stones with peaceful country scenes and Arabic script painted on ceramic tiles.

Castle in the Sand

In the campsite were a young German couple with a combi-van. They had been in Morocco for two weeks and were unhappy with the hustlers. Unable to cope with the constant hassling to buy, they were almost too afraid to venture out of the security of the campsite. Georgia and I found this very sad as it differed so much from our own attitude and experience. For example, on one of our walks into the village we were looking for a place to buy bread and, on enquiring by mistake at a private house, were invited in, given tea and a meal and sent off with a loaf of bread and an invite to come back any time. We always welcomed opportunities to meet the local people and found their generosity and friendliness more than compensated for the few times we were hassled.

Essaouira is another old Portuguese port. The fishing fleet is very active and every night the boats return full and the little harbour is alive with people. The fish are unloaded and salted or sold fresh to the waiting women. The gulls fly overhead in their thousands, screeching and squabbling over the pickings. Small open-air fish restaurants offer fresh fish and crustaceans in a very basic setting where one can watch the action while eating. For those on a bigger budget there is a very nice up-market restaurant, 'Sam's' on a jetty right among the colourful fishing boats. The whole port has a festive feel about it and attracts many tourists.

Essaouira town is an old walled city with narrow streets, art and craft shops, galleries and colourful souks. It is a very laid-back place with less hustlers than the larger centres such as Marrakech and Fes. We loved it and spent hours in the day exploring, while rehearsing in our restaurant at night. The Moroccan waiters and the mainly French diners were most appreciative. We by now had enough songs and tunes for an hour-and-a-half performance and were happy with our harmonies and arrangements. As Georgia's French was fluent, it was easier for her to do most of the introductions but I also wanted to say a few words and was busy rehearsing my speech in 'Franglais'.

The programme was varied. Georgia was to perform her original songs, written with her harp, and I had my Celtic whistle tunes and my composition 'Morocco' which I could accompany with guitar if one was available for the occasion. While on our mountain walk we had taught each other folk songs from Australia, Africa, America and Celtic countries that we had collected on our travels. We wanted to make the performance an interesting combination of voice and instruments and a variety of style and tempo. We were ready for Casablanca – was Casablanca ready for us?

Saturday Souk at Asni

Donkeys braying by the river
Roughly tethered for the day
Saddle off and panniers empty
Chewing on a pile of hay

Shouts and laughter as the dawn breaks
Steaming glasses passed around
Poles and planks and canvas awnings
Rise swiftly on the dusty ground

Lorries fill the main street junction
Disgorging goods and bodies dazed
Gas bottles clink, ungracious landing
Diesel fumes lie in a haze

Linda Bootherstone

Distorted speakers start their crackle
Announcing ointments sure to cure
Fruits and veggies colourfully tumble
On well-worn kilims on the floor

Amethysts twinkle, bracelets glitter
Studded boxes, silver chains
Babushkas soft and kaftans pretty
Treasures brought by camel train

A chance to get that aching tooth pulled
Dentures smile a welcome bright
The barber's blade can trim your moustache
The medicine man can ease your plight

'Plastic, plastic' shout the children
Beggars plead among the fray
In the tea room hopeful buskers
With Berber banjos sing and play

Striped jelabas of the men folk
Colourful cloth that women wear
Bargaining, buying, mingling, watching
Hustle, bustle everywhere

As daylight fades the town falls quiet
Departing donkeys, trucks and cars
Back into the hills to travel
Home lights twinkling under the stars

Chapter Nine

<u>The Concert</u>

The day came for us to leave the peace of Tangaro for the long ride back to Casablanca. Leaving later than we planned we took the same coast road to Safi, the famous pottery town. Cliff-top views looked down upon white-tipped waves on miles of sandy beaches, fertile coastal plains were checked with crops and now and again a team of camels loaded with vegetation could be seen lolloping among them, their handler's cries lost to us in the wind. We stayed overnight in the campsite in the new part of Safi—our voices echoing in the shower block as we continued rehearsing.

The next stop was at Ahmed and Nezra's flat in El Jadida. This location put us in striking distance of Casablanca to arrive early Thursday morning. The arrangements, as we had left them two weeks before, were for us to perform a children's show at Rachid's orphanage on Friday, an adult concert in the Sidi Belyout Theatre on Saturday night and another children's show on Sunday. They were all planned and well-rehearsed and we were looking forward to the performances.

Gwen had arranged for us to stay at her home this time. She was away in England but Kamal was to take care of us. On arrival in Casablanca we tried to ring him and also Rachid and Mr. Smouni, the theatre director, but none of those contacts was available at the time. Eventually, in pouring rain we rode to the theatre in the centre of town to find that Mr. Smouni was now in his office. Our glamorous 'artiste' image was somewhat dampened by our arrival in waterproof motorcycle clothing but he was charming as usual and offered us tea.

The mint tea was most welcome. However, we were somewhat perturbed to find that although there had been an article in the paper (the promotion written by ourselves, with photos that we had provided), no posters had been produced and our concert was not included in the recently printed November program. Mr. Smouni loftily dismissed this omission to us by saying that we must talk to Mr. Isham who would arrange photocopy posters for us to distribute ourselves. Before shooing us benignly out of his office, he kindly let us use his phone to contact Kamal who said he would be home shortly. It took until 5.30 that evening for us to help Isham design the posters and we were now caught in Casablanca's rush hour traffic in the rain and diminishing light.

On arrival at Kamal's place he was still not at home and his servants refused to admit us without his permission. We were somewhat baffled by this and persuaded them to phone him at his office. I spoke to him and he replied that he would be there immediately. The servants stood by sullenly while Georgia and I unloaded the bike and carried our many bags up the stairs to the first floor apartment. It was richly decorated with brocade cushion and we felt horribly grubby dripping water onto the spotless floor. No sooner had we brought up the last bag when Kamal arrived in a state of agitation.

'You can't stay here!' he said roughly. 'Put your stuff in my car and follow me. I will take you to a hotel.'

We were gob smacked! He grabbed our bags as we staggered back downstairs with them, threw them into the boot of his Mercedes and took off. Georgia and I jumped on the bike and followed as best we could. He drove fast and I had difficulty keeping up in the dark and slippery conditions. We couldn't lose him as all our luggage was in his car and I didn't know where he was heading. On arrival at a small hotel very near the theatre he unceremoniously dumped our belongings, booked us into a room and paid for one night, saying he would return to pay the other two later. Without further explanation he drove off into the gloomy night.

Georgia and I were in a state of shock! We unpacked, had a shower and went out for a cheap meal, wondering what it was all about. Why, at the last minute, had he changed his mind and not let us stay? Was someone else arriving? Did Gwen know? Why didn't he tell us when we rang earlier? We felt totally unwanted. However, looking on the bright side of things the theatre was in easy reach for rehearsals and there was a bike park across the road.

Our closer acquaintance with the organization of the Sidi Belyout Theatre the next day left us with a distinctly 'Fawlty Towers' impression. Mr. Smouri, as director, was the big boss and had a large office where he could entertain business clients with tea on a sofa at one end or sit officiously at his large desk at the other surrounded by papers and telephones. Apart from setting a date for a performance and giving his approval it appeared he had nothing more to do. The whole mechanics of the theatre management were passed on to the swarm of underlings.

To be able to see him in the first place it was necessary to approach one of the three receptionists in an office in the large reception hall. When he was ready to receive the visitor, he alerted his doorman who sat motionless outside his door all day waiting for the bell to ring summoning his services. This individual kept his head set down and to one side and his hands dangling straight, palms facing inwards in front of his legs. When the awaited signal was given he went to the door, cautiously opened it and, if instructed, would shuffle over to the visitor, give a waggle of his head and show them in before returning po-faced to his seat.

Mr. Isham, the second in command had a tiny office and no bell boy. He was short and with a large bottom and one leg longer than the other, possible the evidence of earlier polio. When we met him two weeks earlier we were impressed with his lively personality and enthusiasm but, as it transpired, he was sadly lacking in efficiency. He still hadn't made the posters and it was nearly 24 hours later and the day before our Saturday morning performance. A room further along the corridor from Isham's office contained a bank of secretaries male and female who sat at typewriters looking very busy, but we weren't sure at what.

We managed to procure an empty room in which to rehearse and requested that we had a sound check the following afternoon on stage in the concert hall. This was set for 2p.m. Rachid arrived while we were rehearsing to say he was terribly sorry but he had the dates muddled for his children's shows and could we do them in December instead! We were beginning to be mighty suspicious of any 'arrangements'. Georgia had the presence of mind to demand a cancellation fee which, much to our surprise, he paid.

Joe kindly agreed to lend us his guitar to play with my recent composition 'Morocco'. We picked up the instrument from his flat the next morning and also rushed around the language schools distributing the posters that Mr. Isham had eventually photocopied for us. At 2 p.m. prompt we presented ourselves at the theatre for the sound check. However, only then were we informed that the technician did not finish lunch break until 3. Now resigned to the status quo we tuned up, found a comfortable chair and stool for Georgia and her harp and practiced our songs yet again until the engineer, Mustapha, arrived.

As he was finally arranging microphones Isham came in to ask what we had done about the tickets! We were non-plussed. 'What do you mean, Isham, what have we done about the tickets? It's your theatre!'

He then informed us that we were responsible for having our own tickets printed and doing all the publicity. He said as it was a community theatre we were supposed to run our own show—completely! So, what all these hordes of people did, goodness knows!

This information had not been forthcoming two weeks ago when we discussed contracts with the director. By this time our tempers were short. We were there to sing, we replied tartly, not to the theatre managers. *He* could buy the bloody tickets. (It transpired they were only raffle books anyway). At that he said 'Ok' and, smiling as usual, scuttled off.

Finishing the sound check at 5.30p.m., we returned, exhausted to the hotel for a rest. Things were not looking too hopeful for the evening performance. Georgia and I mixed and matched our clothes for our image as the duo 'Enchante', put on our make-up and arrived at the theatre 7.45pm, 15 minutes before the show was due to start. Composing ourselves in the dressing room, which was complete with make-up lights, all shining brightly, we waited for our curtain calls, and waited . . . and waited . . .

Eventually at 8.30pm, the silence weighed too heavily and our nerves were at breaking points. I went out to the reception. The auditorium was full—of empty seats, but Rachid, and his wife Leila, were standing in the reception area in full evening dress, ready for our performance. They were our only audience. I called Georgia and we agreed that it did not matter, we would do the show for two people. After all our rehearsal and tensions, we were ready to sing! Isham said we couldn't because of some legality involving taxes!? Rachid took him aside and eventually persuaded him, probably with dirhams, and all the stage crew, security men and any other staff that could be found, were shepherded into the auditorium. Needless to say they had the best seats. Georgia and I agreed to do half the show for nine people. What troopers we were! We had to imagine a full house (seating was for about a thousand). This isn't too difficult, however, with blazing stage lights in your eyes.

We wowed them! The harp tinkled angelically, the whistle gaily piped its jigs, the guitar strummed and our voices rose and fell in perfect harmony. Thunderous applause from 18 hands after each song. The sound man was so impressed that he completely forgot to press the button to record our historic performance on the tape that we had bought especially for the purpose.

Rachid and Leila came to shower us with compliments after the show and we actually received 270 dirhams! At least it paid for our hotel (as expected Kamal had not returned to cover the other two nights) and a tank full of petrol. It wasn't enough to cover a drink at the Sheraton Hotel opposite. So, we made do with coffee and cake in a nearby café to unwind from our Casablanca debut. Fame at last? It was certainly a show that *we* would never forget.

Duo Enchante

Morroco

You stole my heart away from me
For you I'd always cross the sea
Your mountains high and your valleys low
Again you call me, Morocco

As birds fly south, then so will I
Their beating wings across the sky
For they all know the place to go
I'll meet them there in Morocco

From Jebel Toubkal to the sea
Or in desert south that's where I'll be
Your gorges deep and your plains so wide
Provide a place for me to hide

Cascading waters thundering down
Or mud brick houses red and brown
Palms silhouette in sunset's glow
Your timeless beauty, Morocco

Brown sparkling eyes, *ça va bien?*
Small outstretched hands for *un dirham*
Cous-cous and tarjine and nana tea
A welcome's always there for me

You stole my heart away it's true
And now I'm never far from you
Your mountains high and your valleys low
Again you call me, Morocco,
Again you call me, Morocco.

Chapter Ten

The South And Goodbye

Such were our feelings the next day that number one priority was to pack up and leave as soon as possible. But it was necessary to return Joe's guitar and we knew the household would not appreciate an early visit on Sunday morning, so filled in time dropping off a note to the Youth Hostel for Raya, the Russian girl met in Asni who had told us she'd soon be in town.

When we were fully loaded it was difficult to carry the extra instrument and Georgia had it precariously perched across the seat between us. As I steered the bike into a busy roundabout in the centre of the city a policeman blew his whistle and stopped us right in the middle of the junction to check our passports. We rather fancied that the guitar had looked like a gun case. So it was with great relief that we dropped off the offending item (much as we had appreciated its use the night before) and headed for the road south, riding nonstop to Essaouira. My arm had become very painful and I popped a few aspirins before collapsing, exhausted, in the tent.

For the next two days we relaxed, even indulging in a bottle of wine one night, and Georgia taught me how to make a 'Purpose Plan', an aid to focusing ideas and direction. It was an exercise she had given PC to help him. The plan goes as follows:-

- Firstly write your vision of how a perfect world will be.
- Next write down 10 positive things about yourself, things you are or can do.
- Choose 2 of these positive things; call them a and b.
- Describe two ways in which you have shown these qualities; call these descriptions c and d.
- Then make a sentence that shows how, by being a and b and doing c and d, you can create your perfect world.

This forms your purpose if you repeat this exercise every day for seven days and then once a week for three weeks and once a month for a year. By the end of that time you will have evolved and decided your purpose.

Tentatively, I started, and my first attempt at the exercise went like this:-

1) My vision of a perfect world is—a world without deadshits.
2) Ten positive things about me are:-

1. I can eat anything
2. *I can sing* (b)
3. I talk to people easily
4. *Willing to learn new things* (a)
5. Observant
6. Tolerant (fairly)
7. Non-aggressive
8. I feel comfortable in most situations
9. I'm mostly healthy
10. I'm tenacious

I picked No. 4 as my a) and No. 2 as my b) How do I demonstrate these?
   c) I have done a great number of different things in my life
   d) I have just performed in Casablanca with Georgia

My purpose is – to experiment and perform in order to rid my world of deadshits.

This was my first Purpose Plan. Georgia nagged me for days and I spasmodically did more. It was interesting and by the end of a couple of weeks I had evolved different ideas and purposes. I could see that it was an affirmation exercise that kept one thinking about the positive things one could do and how ideas and actions *do* come out of positive thinking and we *can* change our world by our own efforts. Well, after Casablanca we needed to think positively.

We revisited the Moroccan family in Diabet who had previously been so kind to us. Their old granny had leg pains, so Georgia rubbed them with

Tiger Balm and we sang. The girls even joined in with some French songs. On our way back to the campsite one of the sisters ran after us to give us a bar of strawberry chocolate. It tasted awful but the thought was there.

The weather was cool and bright and we packed unhurriedly one morning to begin the ride south to Agadir. The scenery changed to rolling hills and villages of white stone. There were small, shrubby trees which we later learnt were Argan trees. As we stopped for fuel I studied the map and saw a small road detouring out to the coast. We felt like exploring and the bike was going well so we took the turn off to Imessouane and followed a narrow, windy, though paved road out to the edge of the towering cliffs. Then the road, now running parallel to the coast, dipped down into a river valley and, at the mouth, ended right in the midst of a perfectly picturesque fishing harbour. We rolled to a halt next to the small boats pulled up on the beach and were almost immediately surrounded by jeleba-clad men who were fascinated by the bike. They smiled at us but were not intrusive, just inquisitive.

As we stood surveying the scene I looked across the bay and noticed a sign for a Galerie. I asked one of the men if it was a Galerie d'Art and he said yes, it was the studio of a local artist, Abdullah Aoerik, who would be pleased to meet us.

'Will it be OK if we leave the bike here?' I asked.

'Yes, no problem, we will watch it for you,' came the reply.

I felt quite safe in this village. No-one was rushing up to demand dirhams, cadeaux or bonbons. One of the fisherman, Brahim, even said he'd like us to call in on his wife for tea and gave us directions to his house.

We walked across the pebbly beach to the Galerie, set on a prominent point at the centre of the bay. We were greeted by a very hairy artist. Abdullah had long grey hair and beard, he spoke good English and proudly showed us a book full of press cuttings about his many art exhibitions, especially in America. A true Berber, he was very interested in the origins of his race and culture and not only painted scenes of traditional Berber life but was well known in the area for his anthropological and philosophical writings. Though he liked to be taken seriously, he was enchanted by Georgia's harp and as we played our tunes and songs for him he rushed to find his tape player and record our music. He was very excited by our visit, offering us tea and coffee and insisted that we should stay in Imessouane for at least one night. He would arrange a place for us and make a meal.

We talked and sang all afternoon and then Abdullah showed us a tiny room in a house set in the cliff. Next door, in a similar space, were three French surfers and their Moroccan cooks. By pooling our resources we arranged to have a meal with them, but not before following up one of Abdullah's suggestions.

Imessouane is famous among surfers as there are good Atlantic waves along two beaches and also a sheltered swimming spot, but there is also another more artistic attraction. A little further way from the main village area, ten minutes walk along the cliff, lies a row of rocks, just offshore, and the restless sea crashes into them, sending spray so high that it resembles a blow hole or geyser. The setting sun on this spray creates rainbows and glittering streaks of foam stream up the beach and form whirls of bubbles. The higher the seas, the more spectacular the effect. We arose early next morning to reach the rocks by 7.30 and watch the sun creep up over the hills behind us and cast a pearly pink glow on the tips of the waves out to sea. Gradually, as the shadows shortened, the sun's rays came into the shore and finally burst on the rock-flung spray. More sparkling rainbows. Early fishermen stood silhouetted against the golden foam as they cast their lures from precarious positions on the rock ledges. It was a show that lasted a good hour at either end of the day and sometimes whales could be spotted in this area, enjoying the sea's motion.

During the day we visited the fisherman's wife, Latifa, and sang 'My Johnny' (the song about a seafarer's woman) for her and 'All around my Hat' for her mentally challenged son, who laughed and clapped. Later we explored the rest of the village and found many surfers who were either camped, parked in their vans or renting, like us, the little 'hole in the cliff wall' rooms.

It was a very relaxed spot. The villagers didn't seem to mind the invasion of travellers and surfers; indeed the tourist trade helped their fishing industry. There was no harassment. That evening we ate another meal with the boys, this time teaching them a few bush dances after dinner. Everyone joined in and spirits were very high with lots of laughter. No-one worried about the absence of alcohol. Coca cola, mint tea and good company were our stimulants.

We resumed our southward journey to Agadir the next day, taking with us a letter of introduction to a friend of Abdullah's, a manager in one of the five star hotels in Agadir. We thought that maybe we could obtain work playing music for a while before I had to return to Spain. It would be interesting and help finances.

The countryside soon took on a more tropical feel, especially when we arrived in a little place they call Banana Village. Here the streets were lined with stalls selling a variety of baby bananas. The beaches were now closer to the road, more accessible to both travellers and, so we were warned, locals, who wished to relieve them of their possessions. Tarazoute, a beach which is well known to many campervan owners, held no appeal for me but I had heard it is very popular with Northern Europeans at Christmas and New Year.

Agadir is a tourist town. Almost completely destroyed by an earthquake in 1966, it has been rebuilt in a very modern style and is geared toward the rich tourist who can fly in from Northern Europe and UK. Many hotels lie directly on the beach and the next few blocks inland are filled with tourist shops, usually with fixed prices so the embarrassed newcomer doesn't need to bargain. There are restaurants, supermarkets, theatres and very little evidence of the poorer element who are housed further out of town. These folk can be found shopping in the large old medina, which is far more dirty and interesting than the town centre. We spent one night in the 'insulated' town campsite and then, on finding the address that Abelmounim, one of the Moroccan boys in Imessouane gave us, went to the other part of town to stay with his friendly family.

We looked up Mr Gloughi, Abdullah's contact who, though unable to find us work, invited us to dine with him at his Hotel Amadil. After the meal we were taken to see the in-house entertainment, a Russian group 'Katinka' who put on an excellent cabaret show, including puppetry, juggling, singing and dancing. A real spectacular. After the show we were invited to meet them and were amazed to find there were only seven in the troupe; it had seemed like at least twenty with all the costume changes and different skills involved. We sang 'Amazing Grace' for them and were whisked into their dressing room and, amid much laugher, draped in some of their finery for a photo session.

Russian Theatre

The next few days passed looking unsuccessfully for work in a variety of hotels and clubs, so for a break in our endeavours we rode out to find the waterfall in Paradise Valley. The scenery was enchanting. A narrow road gradually wound up through palm trees and coloured rocks, often following a river bed, mostly dry but running in places or forming pleasant pools.

The waterfall, when we finally reached it, was an anti-climax. On the lower level the track that led to the fall was crowded with souvenir stalls and very pushy guides latched on to us, even though we insisted their services were not necessary. The falls were dry anyway and the unwanted attention of those, now abusive, guides caused us to hurry away back to the parked bike to escape as soon as possible along the same road.

We had noted a pretty village with a rose garden on the way up and stopped to investigate. The garden was for a little tea house, the owner of which, Ahmed, showed us around his mill for grinding almonds for oil, as well as the ever present olives. He also explained how argan oil was made. We had noted plenty of argan trees on the way out to Imessouane as they were full of goats. The animals actually climb the branches to eat the nuts, they digest them and regurgitate the clean kernels. These are then gathered by the women and ground by hand to make a fine oil which is very nutritious and used in cooking, but its texture is so fine that it is also used as a base for cosmetics. The complicated and labour intensive production process makes it a highly prized and expensive commodity.

Ahmed was a great entrepreneur. Not only did he run his tea shop, oil making enterprise and an antique shop but he also offered accommodation. We regretfully declined his offer to stay over and have cous-cous with his family and headed back to Agadir instead.

As we had no luck in obtaining work, Georgia had decided to leave the relative civilisation of Morocco behind and take the giant step toward Mauritania. As I could go no further we needed to arrange her onward travel by bus. At the terminus she bought a ticket to Dakhla in the south of Morocco where she would have to find a way to pick up transport to cross the Moroccan/Mauritanian border. We weren't sure at this stage if the border was open as we had received conflicting reports, but the latest had been from a transport manager who said that his trucks were now getting through. Georgia decided to take the chance and go. In Africa borders open and close all the time and one has to be on the spot to know the true state of affairs. However, I felt confident that if there was a way through she would find it and had no real worry about her managing alone.

As a striking blonde European woman, Georgia did attract attention from men of many races but, although there were always some who would be a nuisance, most men seemed to be in awe of her. The harp helped, it gave her the angelic angle and most people don't want to jeopardise their dealings with the hereafter by insulting an angel. In all our contacts with aggressive and uneasy situations Georgia, like myself, knew when to read the signs and get out.

For example, early one evening in Agadir we went down to the fishermen's quay to watch the boats come in with their daily catch. As we had some time so spare while waiting for an appointment, we went to the fishermen's tea room for a drink. It was obvious we were the only women there. As usual Georgia had her harp and I the whistle, so we played a few tunes. The men were delighted and a crowd began to gather. After a while the cafe owner came over and asked us very quietly and politely to leave. He loved our music but felt that we were attracting too much attention and he didn't want to be responsible for our safety. Two white women amongst many Arabic fishermen could lead to trouble.

We thanked him and left immediately. There was no problem, the men waved us goodbye and it was a great experience for us all. I knew that Georgia would be looked after in ways like this and with her own spiritual powers that she used to help her self-preservation.

We spent the night in Agadir with our Moroccan and French friends, for the surfers from Imessouane were also in town. They were going to take Georgia to the bus station the following night while I had to leave early for the ride back to Marrakech or, hopefully, beyond.

My bike was now lighter of Georgia's body and the harp but the panniers and back seat were full of all the motorcycling clothing and helmet she had borrowed. She was leaving me the same way as we met, just the clothes she wore, one small bag with a change of clothing and her harp. The lady sure travelled light. She even gave me her camera. It was an emotional farewell that morning. I was envious of her journey into the unknown; it would have been nice to be going too. However, I had to be back to meet other obligations, so we gave each other a big hug and kiss and both had a lump in our throat and a tear in our eye. I had sung 'Til We Meet Again' to her the night before and given her the words of 'Crusader' to sing in the desert.

'Goodbye Georgia and good luck. I know you'll have a great adventure. I was glad to have been part of it and I know we'll meet again somewhere—some day.'

'TIL WE MEET AGAIN
(MacLean Limetree Arts)

Chorus

'Til we meet again, I wish you well
I hope your light shines easily
And when we meet again,
It doesn't matter how we've done
On Kurrugh side, I'll see you further on

You may struggle, you may toil
To support the walls around you
Or lonely burn the midnight oil
'Til the pool of light shines on you

Chorus

This day is almost done
And in the space between
We'll be afraid of what's to come
But we will gently dream, dream on

Chorus

Chapter Eleven

Homeward Alone

It's amazing how quickly I can adapt to being on my own again. As long as I'm with the bike I don't really feel alone because we are already a team with which a pillion passenger has to fit. Not only was Georgia a good friend but she was a great pillion passenger. Her weight was not a problem, she learnt to get on and off with the least disruption to my balance and always helped push the bike around when parking. She also gave me encouragement in bad weather or road conditions, complimenting me on my riding skills. However, she had gone and I was now quickly happy to be just alone with the bike. When you travel with another person, no matter how close you are, there is always some kind of discussion or compromise on direction or events. This is a necessary process to ensure that everyone is happy with the decisions that are made. Now it was just up to me, and the bike who also has her say—if, for example, she wants to break down.

Both Georgia and I knew that when travelling alone you are more vulnerable but also more open to other people's advances. People react in a different way to a solo soul and in some ways it can be a bolster to one's self confidence when they say 'What, are you doing this on your own?' 'Yes I am.' A lone person is more readily invited into a group or family situation.

Whilst travelling together we enjoyed the companionship and our singing in which we taught one another and harmonised beautifully but, for the time being, this was over and we were both ready to be thrown back on our own resources. On re-meeting, whenever that may be, we would be able to appreciate each others stories of our separate journeys and, hopefully, in the meantime we could keep in touch by pigeon post.

Leaving warm, sunny Agadir behind me I found a small adventure for myself by taking a road back to Marrakesh that I hadn't previously travelled. It proved to be well surfaced, interesting and fast and I was in Marrakesh early enough to push on through to Cascades d'Ouzoud, hoping to arrive before dark.

Possibly the most photographed waterfall in Morocco, Cascades d'Ouzoud is in the mid Atlas, east of Marrakesh and tends to be a mite chilly in November at night. Dusk was falling as I rode up the approach road to the village. There was a police control on it. The uniformed officer checked my passport as I sat patiently astride the bike.

'Vous êtes seule?' he enquired politely when he realized it was a woman riding this big machine.

'Oui, monsieur.' 'Porquoi?' 'Porquoi pas?'

He threw his head back and laughed. 'Allez.'

Apparently I was the main talking point in town that night.

I knew the three brothers in the family who owned the campsite and was interested to find that one of them, Maroum, had recently married a local Berber girl whom his mother had chosen for him. Maroum and his younger brother, Rafik, had always been tourist chasers, inviting people like myself up to their living quarters to see what they could trade. Far from being devout followers of Islam, scorning alcohol, they usually cadged as much as they could while offering hash or carpets in exchange for clothes, cigarettes or whatever else took their fancy. The third, eldest brother, was the straight one who managed the campsite, took the fees and slept in the reception hut, while his younger siblings did the deals.

Far from being reformed by marriage, Maroum invited me up for a meal made by his wife, though she stayed in the kitchen while he, Rafik and I ate together. After the meal Maroum served tea laced with the local brew as I had, disappointingly for them, not brought anything else with me. Their alcoholic offering was distilled fig juice, quite potent stuff as I found out the next morning when my head hurt.

Since my last visit the Falls, and the small village around them, had been connected to electricity by the installation of a town generator. Though the inhabitants thought this was great because they could now watch television and play their stereos without having to frequently recharge their 12 volt batteries, I found it detracted from the atmosphere. The most disappointing effect was the huge spotlight that was now mounted on an ugly pylon next to the Falls. Not only was it impossible to take a photo of the area without the pylon making its unsightly presence felt, but it was necessary to wait until the generator stopped at 11pm to view the Falls at night by the natural light of the moon. A truly beautiful sight, especially when it was full. Also the noise of the generator disrupted the peace of the village. Progress has its disadvantages.

I spent two days there though, pleased to be back amongst familiar faces. Rafik took me on a walk to a nearby community known as the Mexican Village and I played my whistle for some of the local women who were baking bread in the huge dark kitchen of Rafik's relatives' property.

Rafik and Maroum's family were well respected and comparatively wealthy. One of their ancestors had been a holy man and his marabout (shrine) was in this village. The large house adjacent was run as a hostel for all the pilgrims who came annually to visit the site. Built completely of mud, the house had three storeys and numerous rooms including two hammans, one for each sex. It was an amazing structure and I was lucky to be escorted round and offered tea on one of the balconies which overlooked the rest of the village. We wandered up the adjacent valley into which the Cascades tumble their waters. The women use the power of the flow to mill their flour. The grinding stones are situated in small huts straddled across streams diverted from the gushing water at the head of the Falls.

That night it was my turn to treat the lads, so Rafik and I went to the next village with an empty litre bottle hidden under his coat. When we arrived he made discrete enquiries and a young lad walked with us to the outskirts of the village where a track led up into the hills. The bottle went with the youth while Rafik and I waited. The moon was bright, the air crisp and still and the river valley spread out beneath us.

I told Rafik we were waiting for 'Moonshine' by moonshine and proceeded to play a few appropriate tunes on the whistle. After about twenty minutes the boy returned, money changed hands and we were on our way back with our booty hidden under my jacket. I saved a small amount for later consumption and took the rest up to Maroum's room where we played cards while he had one eye on his new television.

The next day was Maroum's turn to guide me. In fact we walked a track that he had never followed so far before and we were rewarded by sights of monkeys, wild pigs and goats. His recent marriage did not deter his usual propositions and I said sternly, 'Maroum, you are a married man.'

'Ah but Linda, that is at home. Here we are free in nature.'

I laughed and told him not to be so silly. I can walk quite briskly in the bush.

That night Maroum didn't stop talking about the place we had been, nature and friendship as he played loud Arabic music. Not feeling too good with a heavy period, I retired early to my tent but was awakened about midnight by Rafik outside saying he wanted to 'talk to me'. I told him, nicely, to piss off.

These Moroccan boys take whatever opportunity they can to get whatever they can, be it goods or sex, from tourists. However, few of them are actually aggressive or forceful and all that is necessary is a good humoured but definite 'No!' If you can laugh it off then so can they. Their philosophy is that you don't get anything unless you ask for it and they are not afraid to ask. I'm not afraid to refuse and can be very amused, and even sometimes flattered, by their methods. After all, it's not too often a 48 year old woman is propositioned by an attractive young man—not in my circles anyway. Next morning they gave me a great breakfast as a send-off and I left some of my socks and a pair of Georgia's cast-off sandals for Maroum's wife.

As I rode north the weather cooled and I need to put on some extra clothes. On a back road somewhere in the region of Casablanca I stopped to take them from my pannier and re-dress. I had first checked that I was away from a village and that no-one was in sight but as I was about to remount the bike two men suddenly appeared and, though I rapidly made ready to leave, they caught up with me. My engine was running and I wanted to move off but one positioned himself in front of the bike. The other, an older man, was carrying a bag of fruit. He looked crazed, with staring eyes and a dribbling mouth and he gabbled incoherently.

'Bonjour Monsieur,' I smiled politely, 'ca va?'

He nodded and indicated that he wanted to climb up behind me for a lift, pointing and mumbling 'Casablanca'.

'Non monsieur, pas possible, pardon.'

I didn't want anyone touching the bike, one push and it would be over, and I was incapable of picking it up alone. I kept on talking.

'Mon mari arrive toute suite et nous allons. Au revoir.'

But I couldn't leave because not only was the younger man blocking my way but other young boys had arrived. It was beginning to look like a very tricky situation and I felt panic rising but had to appear in control. It seemed that the group were watching the outcome between this foreign woman and their older compatriot. I didn't think they would hurt me unless he made the first move but I was sure they would take what they could, given the opportunity. The man was still gabbling and slathering, dirty torn clothing hanging on his skinny frame. He thrust out his hand, palm upward, toward me.

'Dirham!' he demanded.

Of course I didn't want to give him any money but I could see no other way out, but surely once the group saw me hand over the dirham to him they would realise my vulnerability and all want some. Most of my money was kept in my money belt but luckily I knew that there were two notes in my jacket pocket, one 10DH and one 50DH. I reached into my pocket and the old man's eyes followed my movement, I would not have a chance to see which note was which but pulled out one and threw it at him. I only had a second to act as his eyes left me and he jumped sideways to catch the note. The other boys moved away from the bike and towards him. Seizing the opportunity, I slammed the bike into gear, took a handful of throttle and shot forward. I felt hands reaching to grab the back of the bike but I accelerated and, though wobbling as their grip threw me off balance, managed to break it and ride away. I was trembling with terror, my heart thumping, and it took a few miles to calm down and feel safe enough to stop for a coffee. Luckily I realised that the aggressive man had not been normal and that, although these isolated incidents did occur, they were few and far between. These were the problems that tourists reported and put others off coming to Morocco. But what about the muggers in our western culture? Nowhere is one a hundred percent safe.

The November weather became worse and I was in cold, damp fog by the time I reached my destination of Kenitra. The BM had a hole in her exhaust which needed welding so I would have to stay to get that done. As usual Fatima's large family welcomed me and this time I took them up on their invitation to stay in the house for it was too cold and miserable to camp.

The two days I spent in Kenitra included my 49th birthday and, learning this, the family bought me presents and made a special dinner for me, then gathered around and asked, very seriously, if I would help them by marrying their then 21 year old son, Mohammed.

It was a tricky situation. Their idea is that marriage to a European means instant freedom to a country which has streets paved with gold. I had to explain in my very broken French that this is not so. Had they even enquired at the consul at Rabat what requirements were for Moroccans going abroad, married or unmarried? Of course not. In my circumstances it couldn't be done, I said, but I would take his photo and details of his qualifications (a fisherman) and past work experience and would ask about jobs for him and what immigration requirements were in Spain. That was all I could do. What a birthday present to turn down, a handsome 21 year old Moroccan boy and a warm, endearing and ever growing Moroccan family!

The following day on taking Hinde for a ride to the beach I spotted an Overland truck, and who should be driving it but Glen Bull, one of the bike riders with whom I had come to Morocco three years previously when we first met the Kenitra family. We greeted each other with surprise and delight and he told me he was now based in Nairobi and a tour leader for Trans-Africa. That evening he came to dinner with us and Hinde and Zohre cuddled up to him on the sofa, insisting I took their photos. Boy, did he have a big grin on his face!

And so to the last leg of my journey back to Spain. The bike had been welded in Kenitra and it was going well. The weather cleared and I decided to take a back road across the hills to Chefchaouen. It was a good choice, the road had recently been repaired, traffic was very light and the scenery stunning with its myriad shades of green and brown and winding silver rivers. On arrival at the Youth Hostel, waiting for Taieb to return from the village to open the door, I chatted to other tourists and shared my last drop of moonshine with a couple from Ireland whom I knew would appreciate it. I made a toast to Georgia's onward journey and the beginning of my 50th year.

Part Two

Diverse Destinations

CHAPTER TWELVE
Back To Base—First Letters

After all the excitement of the past few weeks in Morocco the homecoming to Castellar would have been an anti-climax if not for the distraction of Christmas looming ahead. This coincided with the arrival of a Scottish friend whose interest in a week's trip to the North of Morocco gave me the excuse to execute a quick turn-around.

Kate, another independent lady in her forties, was a small vivacious red-head. Her two grown sons now off her hands, she was spreading her wings and indulging in many new experiences. A trip to North Africa on a motorbike was one of them.

Kate and Hadja

Wrapped securely in the unfamiliar motorcycle clothing she braved the now much cooler weather to be transported to Chefchauen, where she also made the trek to visit Hadja, and then on to Kenitra where we spent an unusual New Year (94/95) with Fatima's family. For a Scot, not to be allowed alcohol on Hogmanay is almost sacrilege, but Kate managed to eat herself to sleep instead on the huge feast that Fatima produced.

With only a week's holiday, the time went by very quickly and, after taking Kate around the sights of Medhia and Rabat, it was back to Spain for her return flight to Glasgow. As a teacher, she needed to prepare for the new term.

On my arrival home I found a letter awaiting me, dated 28th November 1994, from Georgia in Mauritania. I excitedly read about her experiences since we parted in Agadir. The Moroccan boys had waited at the bus station with her as the bus to Dakhlar was delayed for (only) an hour then:

Luckily I was able to sleep most of the night and half the next day. The nine a.m. arrival turned out to be about 5.30 that evening. This was mostly due to me having to stop and fill out declarations for the road blocks. At one in the afternoon Hassan, the bus driver, asked me to sit in the front seat. We had become fast friends, joking with the police, who even gave us tea at one point. Sitting beside me was a man named Chisali. He and his sister, Thia, adopted me. They bought me a fish dinner, took me home and fed, lodged and clothed me for three days. These are Saharouino. The men wear bird-like brocade cloak outfits in blue or white. The women are wrapped into beautiful transparent cloth, similar fashion to a sari. You would have laughed to see me clunking around in this caterpillar garb and boots! I refused the high heels they tried to make me get into and vetoed their constant application of make-up after a while. One of the men asked me why I don't like make-up. I asked why he didn't wear it and pointed out that Allah had made me without it.

The women lounge around on cushions. pouring tea and spraying perfume on each other. This is partly due to uncleanliness. The women I was sleeping with seldom washed other than their hands for eating. Yes, I got doused, felt very ill and refused the next offer, much to their chagrin. In the evening I had interesting discussions with the men and one woman who was divorced – more worldly. The best night was when a singer came. A lot of percussion was got up on a plastic tub, the floor and hands. We sang a chant, he would answer. It was incredible.

I am trying to learn the mouth call the women make, without much success.

Their neighbour, Hassan, a military man from Marakesh, and Helena, as well as their three sons, had me for lunch twice and a shower once. They gave me a beautiful jalaba, sometimes it is impossible to refuse. (I sent it on to Craig to hold onto).

Helena took me to visit her friends, more like Berbers. So here I am hennaed again. This time it is beautiful. The process took three hours of dancing, singing, cuddling, applying, eating and drinking tea. None of them spoke English or French and we communicated with my few words of Arabic and the usual facial expressions.

On the evening of the last day the police came. The inspector took me on a long drive, buying me a fish dinner en route, explaining this was a political situation so I had to stay in a hotel, desist contact and catch the convoy the next day.

Arranging transportation was easy. I had a ride all the way to the Camerouns! (However) the police refused to let me go saying I wasn't on the list. They then proceeded to ask questions for about three hours. It was all ultra-polite. During the extra three days their constant surveillance wasn't even subtle. They would come and read pages from the book or the journal over my shoulder, making jokes, pretending they didn't speak English. It was comic and scary at the same time. What happens when they don't let you leave?

Friday was the convoy Exodus. Everyone was ready at 10 am.—we left about 3 p.m. Getting a ride with Alaine was easy: through a series of being in the right place at the right time it was arranged. Some day I'll give you the details over tea. Travelling through the desert was amazing. Two days turned into about five as we dug our way out of the dunes. The conditions are akin to Canadian winters except for the heat factor.

The beauty is bewildering: stretches of hypnotic sand and rock, with the endless night sky. I sing the song you gave me { 'Crusader') every day. I don't know if I'll ever get the sand out. I experienced an incredible burning itchy scalp for a few days due to the dryness and detergent in the shampoo. There are big circles underlying my eyes and I've lost weight, partly from fighting off men's advances and sleeping in a car. Alaine has been aggressively persistent. Last night a relative of the Saharouin family from Dahkla took me to his own vehicle and tried to convince me that molestation was O.K. Tonight is uncertain.

This is the land of papers and officials. I had to bribe my way into this country without a visa. Still, it was cheaper and less hassle than returning to Rabat. I thought of you and smiled; knowing we're of the same mind on passage blocks.

Tomorrow we can start again if Alaine will have me. He's yelled a couple of times. On the whole he's a nice guy as are his three companions, all in separate vehicles. As much as I love this desert I'm not fond of this town. (Nouakchott—I believe. L.B.) A lot of magical experiences, meetings with women have happened en route. When those times are current it's great. I'm invincible. Dealing with authorities and men, which seem to be one and the same, is more difficult. I ask the angels to get me out of there. They are quick to respond.

There were eight motorcycles on the convoy. One woman, Anita, from Germany is 29. We talk about being with men as the only female, self-testing, loneliness, aloneness, the differences. The men tease us because we hug each other at every juncture. Tonight I may have a chance to play at a restaurant and pass the hat around. Making music on the desert an hour before Sunset I was at home. Sometimes I want to walk away from the others and just keep going. I can feel camels under the saddle in my mind. This morning I was tired of being mauled and thought of running down to Craig, then I sang the song and the second verse about turning round to face the desert again made me laugh, knowing it's all written. Whatever happens, happens. There is a beautiful butterfly dancing around as I write.

Alaine has this fabulous collection of cassettes—everything from Billie Holiday to the Rolling Stones. He reminds me of a heterosexual Joe, if you can imagine. Friendly, talks a lot, old music. French men are always joking. The other three are all individuals, I like them. Two smoke a lot of dope, Joe included.

Today I'm by the ocean. For the most part I've been alone to renew strength, catch up on the harp playing and you. When I was entrenched in Dakhla police security I completed my Christmas cards. Another butterfly has zoomed by, this one white and greenish yellow. The birds are singing a hundredfold; I can see three men's faces in the clouds, a spaceman, one a Turk, and a baby monkey.

Today I met two nice Germans who are working here. One rode on the 2 1/2 kilometre freight train for 17 hours sitting outside on the stock. Today I ate the tuna bun with carrot standby. It tasted especially good as the food supply was running low last time out in the desert. There are boats going by . . .

So, she had made it O.K. I knew she would but was relieved to hear from her. I had written a letter to Dahkla before Christmas in case I caught her there before she moved on. (I didn't).

I could imagine the convoy situation and the hassles with men and border crossing. I had completed a Trans-Africa journey back in 1974, taking the Algerian route through the Sahara. I too had to travel in convoy and, when my bike collapsed all four of its shock absorbers, travelled with a group of Arab men on a date truck. There had been some uncomfortable moments when the men had eyed me and the other girl aboard in a speculative manner and we'd had to bluff it out. So, knowing the dangers she faced, my heart and hopes went out to her. This sort of experience certainly tests the inner strengths of mind as well as the body. I knew that you always have to be planning the next move, way before the other person or persons.

A song I heard on a Mary Black tape which I presumed to have been written about Robyn Davidson and her camel trek across Australia. I felt it also applied to any traveller, male or female, who was facing their own journey into a desert. I gave the words as far as I could remember them to Georgia to sing to herself in Mauritania.

Linda Bootherstone

'CRUSADER' Mick Hanley

There's a wilderness it's a no-man's land
Between Alice Springs and the ocean
Seventeen hundred miles of burning sand
And a silken thread keeps a hold on you
When the emptiness like a potion
Tends to thread your reason strand by strand
And there's no more need for the mask you wear
When the last good-byes have been said
So kiss the cheeks of your dearest friends
And turn to the desert ahead
Now you're on your own like a sailing ship
You're the captain, the crew and the sailor
Turn around and this is what you see

Chorus:
This is me facing me, all alone 'cos I choose to be
With the wind and the sun on me, only me

Now you dream so much about being lost
Your ghost by a coolabah sleeping
Haunts you and whispers in your ear
'Give up, give up this lonely road
No one knows the promise you're keeping'
You can touch the emptiness out here
But the grace that mends the broken wing
The blue sky to regain
Will lift those feet and raise those eyes
To face the desert again

As the dawn reveals the journey's end
In truth it's only beginning
And it's as big as your eyes wish to see

This is me, facing me, all alone 'cos I choose to be
With the wind and the sun on me, only me

Chapter Thirteen

Debby

No sooner had Kate left for the snows of Scotland when Debby, my friend from Louisiana, arrived. In true American style she swept up to my humble abode in a taxi. The driver pulled an enormous suitcase out of the boot while Debby and I gave each other a welcome hug on the patio. I hadn't seen her for 12 years!

We first met 20 years previously in Windhoek, South West Africa. I was working there, having finished my trans-Africa trip on an old R50 BMW and she was holidaying from her job as a lecturer at the University in Petermaritzburg. We had struck up an immediate rapport and, although our actual meetings had been few since that time, our correspondence had kept us in touch over the many years. I did spend a fun-filled two weeks with her at her home in Port Vincent back in 1983 while I was touring America on a 360cc Honda.

Debby is an amazing communicator. Although she has no languages apart from Southern USA drawling 'English', she manages to win friends in every country and social strata. She had followed many career paths, each one successfully, and dabbled in teaching, management and promotions. Currently she had just left a very high powered job with Wella Hair Care for whom she had organised modelling shows all over America and Europe. Before finding another career path she decided to 'rough it with Linda' for a while. I had warned her of the primitive quarters and the dubious delights of pillion riding but she was game to give it a whirl. A job interview in Barcelona was lined up in a month's time, so we spent only two days talking in Castellar before packing the BM once more to take the ferry on my now well worn path to Morocco. It was mid-January.

Whereas Georgia is slim and fair, Debby is pear-shaped and dark. Her looks are taken from her Haitian father and Cajun mother, who also has dark curly hair and an ample figure. Although about the same height as Georgia, Debby's legs are shorter and it was much more difficult for her to get on and off my bike. This made balancing the bike with our load more dicey and I had to brace myself for every movement. It also made it harder to plan a quick getaway in case of any harassment at the roadside. Fortunately her experience in travelling alone in many parts of the world meant she was an easy companion because she could quickly size up a situation and use her initiative. She also had a great sense of humour, which she needed on more than one occasion on this trip.

Debby was *not* a walker and declined to trek up to see the Hadja in the hills at Chauen. As I had brought some second-hand clothes and shoes for the kids, I inveigled Fued, the cheerful Moroccan campsite assistant, to accompany me carrying the bundles. Needless to say the family was pleased to see us.

The short walk into town Debby did manage and we came back laden with a kilo of 'cous cous' wool which I'd foolishly said I'd knit into a jumper for her. It is wool that is normally use for weaving into jelabas and has lots of small round stubs that resemble cous cous pieces. It is, I found out later, impossible to knit on its own as it breaks too easily. Months hence I overcame the problem by working it together with another stronger yarn, but at the time I thought I could knit it en route and we ended up carrying this kilo many hundreds of kilometres, cursing it every time we repacked. However, this was early in the trip and there were far more things to collect en route. Americans love souvenirs and 'experiences' but in some cases Debby got more than she bargained for.

Though I pride myself on my safety record and adept handling of my bike, Debby was treated to some very unusual experiences of me dropping it on this trip. I can only say that she was very good humoured about these unfortunate events. The first time was not long out of Chefchaouen. We were travelling in heavy rain and along a road close to which the soil was eroding and had washed across the tarmac in a sheet of mud. I was aware of the danger and had slowed down accordingly to a walking pace, but hadn't realised the extent of the mud patches and the fact that the surface had no traction whatsoever. Once both wheels were upon it we slid along as if on ice and I could not hold the weight. Moving at little more than walking pace, we toppled over. I extricated myself from under the bike and turned to help Debby.

'Are you OK?' I asked worriedly, very embarrassed.

'Well, Geez, Linda, my first fall on a motorcycle! Wait till the folks back home hear about this!'

There was no harm done to either us or the bike and some locals rushed to help pick up the heavy machine. We continued on our wet and windy way. We arrived worn out and wet at the family home in Kenitra but only spent one night with them before heading south through the still pouring rain.

With Georgia's and my experience in Casablanca still fresh in my mind, it was a place where I was not inclined to stop, so we paid a brief visit to the Hassan II mosque, which was too shrouded by mist to photograph well, then carried on to El Jadida.

In contrast to the sunny, colourful ride along the coast that Georgia and I had enjoyed, this time the route was fraught with traffic and adverse conditions, made worse by the fact that the setting sun was in my eyes.

It reminded me of a journey on this very stretch of road in similar conditions two years before. I was taking Sally (a girl on holiday from England who I had previously met on the 'boat project') on a short trip to Morocco. We were aiming for Ahmed's house in El Jadida and were about 50kms short of the town when I felt the back end of the bike begin to sway. For a moment I thought Sally had fallen asleep and was falling off but then I realised that it was a rear tyre blow out. Fortunately I managed to bring the bike to a halt in an upright position and we climbed off. After unloading we pulled the bike up on the centre stand and I began to unfasten the back wheel. All the while my mind was ticking over with the fact that there was *no way* that I could get the tyre off the rim to fit the spare inner tube. I knew I hadn't the strength even though I had the tyre levers. I didn't like to admit this to Sally, who was helping me remove the wheel and had full confidence in my abilities.

Just as the moment of truth was about to break, along came a Moroccan youth pedalling his push bike furiously towards us. He stopped, flung his bike on the ground and rushed over. Taking the wheel and tyre levers out of my hands he began exerting his strength on the problem. As he was puffing and panting over the difficult job, another, older, man arrived by foot, watching and joining us in shouting encouragement to our saviour. Eventually the reluctant tyre broke from the rim, I handed over the new tube and the exertion began again as he repeated the process in reverse.

Within half an hour the whole job was done, I put the wheel back on the bike, gave the lad 20 dirhams and a packet of Winston cigarettes, plus one to his mate. Our hero smiled happily, jumped on his push bike and rode off into the dusk. So did we and reached El Jadida shortly after dark. Yet another guardian angel had turned up when I needed one.

Fortunately, this time Debby and I had no such delays and we arrived in El Jadida late afternoon to try and hunt down a phone card to enable Debby to phone home. We had not been able to get a card, even in Casablanca. In their never ceasing attempts to earn a dirham, the Moroccan youths would buy up all the phone cards and then stand by the phone boxes offering to sell time on one of 'their' cards. Much as I admired their entrepreneurial enterprise, it was frustrating not to be able to buy a full card oneself as operator connected calls were exhorbitantly expensive and it was not always possible to make them. Debby finally handed over large amounts of dirham to an operator in a grand hotel and contacted her sister in Louisiana.

Ahmed and Nezrah were pleased to see us but the latter looked pale and thin. She had just suffered a miscarriage and they were both upset. However, they brightened at the news that Georgia was OK and on her way south.

I took Debby on the tour of the Portuguese city and then we left to visit the pottery town of Safi. This is the ceramic centre of Morocco and a museum housed in a beautiful old palace displayed work from many different periods. The amazing thing about the pottery crafts in Safi is that they are still worked manually in the same way as they have been for hundreds of years. No mechanised factory output here! We found the old area where individual potters have their own workshops and kilns. The area is hazy with the smoke of many fires stoked continuously to a white hot temperature by boys who sit outside all day feeding the flames with ever-green leaves. In the low mud buildings all kinds of pots and dishes are shaped by men who have been spinning a pottery wheel since they could walk. The area is alive with activity as clay is collected, moulded, fired and then finally painted and glazed. The sales houses are set in a street slightly apart and are full of tempting items. With our lack of space we managed only one star-shaped wall pot. So far so good.

At Essaouira Debby went on a spending spree in a jeweller's shop, adding two silver beads to the necklace that she was making by collecting various items and threading them on to a leather cord around her neck. She already had some interesting ceramic beads strung there.

Debbie and Brahim

Establishing our camp at Diabet, where Georgia and I had spent so many nights practicing, Debby and I rode back into town and ate in style at Sam's Place on the quayside. As well appointed as any international restaurant, this had a wonderful view across the fishing harbour and the lights of the town glittering in the background. The smartly dressed Moroccan waiter served us a sumptuous three course meal for only 60 dirhams a head and we had a bottle of good Moroccan wine to wash it all down.

While we were reminiscing about our past times together in Africa and good naturedly arguing about the exact circumstances of our initial meeting,

Debby said

'Hey Linda, honeychile, what are you going to be doing for your 50th birthday—it's only 10 months away?'

'Good heavens, Debby, I haven't a clue—I don't even know where I'll be then.'

'Well, I think you should be in New Orleans with me. We can go to Pat O'Brien's piano bar like we did in '83.'

There followed a sniggering session over how drunk we both were on Hurricanes that night way back when and how the drive home over Lake Ponchetrain was only possible after a long snooze in a comfort station to sober up. Although we didn't discuss the idea of my revisiting USA any further, it somehow lodged itself in my brain.

On our arrival at Imessouane we were greeted cordially by Abdullah, who enquired anxiously about Georgia and I told him what I knew so far. This time he arranged for us to stay in the VIP house—a traditional abode on the riverbank which had its own well and a roof terrace for sunbathing. As we had left the wet weather behind us up north, we were able to take advantage of this private spot and actually get into our bathing costumes to try for a tan.

By coincidence the house was situated next door to that of the fisherman Brahim and his wife Latifa who had the retarded child. When I called in to visit them Latifa said that her boy had seen my bike in the village that day and raced home shouting 'My hat, my hat!'. It took a while for me to realise that he was remembering the song that Georgia and I had sung for him and his mother, 'All around my hat'. I was amazed. This boy spoke no English, had obviously just picked up the sound, but it had made that much of an impression on him to connect the sound with the reappearance of my motorbike! It just goes to show how observant children are. I sang it again and 'My Johnny' for Latifa.

Debby and I went with Abdullah to buy fresh fish from the fisherman on the beach and we stocked up on vegetables so that Abdullah could cook us one of his wonderful tarjines, which we ate by candlelight in our little house. Our chef also entertained us with his tales of America as many years ago he held an art exhibition in New Orleans and was eager to reminisce with his 'native' guest. Of course we experienced the sunset and sunrise on the rocks at the water's edge and I was inspired to write a poem which I left in Abdullah's visitors book.

Dawn at Imessouane 24.1.95

Reaching high the peaks of spume crash upon the ragged rocks, and cascading water runs away
Relentless rhythm of the sea
Pink tipped waves swirl and fishermen cast their hopeful lines into breaking bubbles
Fingers of light creep gently down the curving hills, while fleeting rainbows play hide and seek amongst the spray
Nature provides the inspiration and I sing with the joy of living

Chapter Fourteen

Bad Brakes And Berber Banjos

On the road again to Agadir, we took a whirlwind trip to Paradise Valley; still beautiful despite the drought—palm trees grew wherever a suggestion of water occurred and contrasted their dark green against the red, gold and brown of the rocky hillside. Again I noted the layered colours of ochre in the rocks where the road through had been cut, reminiscent of Aboriginal paint sources in Australia.

We were lucky enough to find the family Georgia and I stayed with in Agadir, and Adbelmounin was there. He told us how he had taken Georgia to the bus station to see her off and he was also glad to hear of her safe passage.

Apart from the souk there is really not much else to see in modern, tourist ridden Agadir, so we stocked up with food and headed out of town on the road to Tafraoute. This was breaking new ground for me and proved an exciting change. The only fly in the ointment was that the front brake was beginning to fade and I wondered if I should buy a bottle of brake fluid and top up the reservoir. It was under the tank so I couldn't easily check the level. However, as the problem was only minor at this time I concentrated on finding the way out of Agadir and up into the mountains. The traffic in the immediate vicinity of Agadir and on the coast road was horrendous with scruffy looking trucks belching black diesel exhaust fumes and blocking the road, but almost immediately after Ait Mellal, where we turned inland, it cleared and we found ourselves on narrow roads winding ever upward. The many blind bends necessitated a slow pace and made overtaking almost impossible, but the scenery was stunning with wide open rocky mountains all around.

By late afternoon I was feeling the strain of riding and looking for a place to stop for tea. We came to a small village in a valley where an enclosed garden with car park heralded a tea shop. I pulled over and we thankfully dismounted and went inside. Obviously a tourist bus stop, the garden also sported a jewellery stand and a merry eyed Moroccan who greeted me in English. As we relaxed over tea, I pulled out my whistle and began to play. I was applauded by the other clients of the tea house and the jewellery tout, who had introduced himself as Ali, then another figure appeared on the scene in a brown and white striped jelaba. He was a young man, incredibly good looking with black curly hair and flashing white teeth. Hurrying over, hands outstretched in greeting, he introduced himself.

'I am Brahim and I am also a musician. Please come to eat with us. Ali and I have a house up the road. We are nearly finished here, let us pack up and we will take you. Please, *please* come with us; we can play music together.'

He was genuine in his approach and I'm a sucker for those brown sparkling eyes. Ali was nodding his agreement.

'What do you think, Debby?' I said.

I was quite happy to take them up on their offer but it was up to her. We finished our tea while the boys packed their stall away and managed to get the two of them on to a tiny moped which we followed about a kilometre up the hill to their house.

There were three more young men, all of whom we judged to be in their mid twenties. The 'house' was actually a health clinic, of which one of them was in charge. Looking at the grubby walls and very unhygenic equipment it didn't appear the ideal place to bring a young baby for its weighing-in and weekly check up—but Rachid was the closest the local mothers were going to have for a qualified health officer and he was proud of his job and the quarters which he shared with another boy, Ahmed.

Visiting his friends, the young village school teacher joined us. Ali and Brahim's quarters lay in a small room behind their 'shop' – a very small building a little apart from the clinic in which they kept their treasures and displayed them for the tourists not already caught at the tea house.

Brahim immediately brought out his Berber banjo, which he proceeded to play with great skill and gusto. He instructed the others to start making a tarjine while he and the school teacher took us on a sunset walk of their local water source. Near the village, it collected in a lagoon where rushes grew, fish swam and mozzies buzzed. Brahim sat playing his banjo by the water while Debby and I snapped away with our cameras. Then we followed the water up to it source, which flowed out of rocks made of a type of rose quartz or pink limestone. The effect of the evening sun reflecting off these rocks was amazing; we were all bathed in a rosy hue. Brahim's constant, lively chatter in his very good English kept us amused. He told us that he and Ali were students at University in Agadir where their families lived and that this was their holiday job, selling to tourists.

We came back to the 'shop' to sit in the tiny kitchen area in the back room where the boys also slept. The tarjine they prepared was delicious and we sang songs, watched them play a Moroccan game of cards and eventually, due to Brahim's amazing energy singing and jigging around while he played, we too danced in their tiny living quarters. It was obvious that Ali was greatly attracted to Debby and this was borne out by him continually knocking on our door that night once Debby and I had retired to a room in the clinic.

'Debby, you are beautiful—I need you' he cried. 'Go away, Ali,' I said 'she's not available.'

After about half an hour he gave up and went back to his own room to bed down alone—or rather with Brahim in their limited quarters. Perhaps I had ruined the chance of a wonderful romance. The next morning Rachid, who was married, apologised to us for Ali's behaviour—he was obviously embarrassed.

After a tasty breakfast of coffee, hobs and jam out in the open, watching the sun gradually light up the mountains around us, we swapped addresses and carried on to Tafraoute. The front brake was becoming worse so I stopped to buy brake fluid in Tafraoute centre and whipped off the tank to top up the reservoir. 'Good,' I thought, 'that's fixed it.' However, riding on I found no improvement and was somewhat perplexed as I'd spotted no leaks. The road out of Tafraoute lay in a wide, sandy valley and sported many palm trees. It reminded me of the countryside around Alice Springs.

Tafraoute is renowned for its embroidery with which the women decorate their dresses and shoes. Another thing we had noticed, and stopped often to photograph, were the gaily coloured and patterned iron doors on the houses. The houses themselves were often painted a dusky pink and the bright primary colours of blue, yellow, green and red stood out against them. Not only that, but it was almond blossom time and the trees were a mass of pink flowers. This is the best time of year to visit this area as in the summer the temperature is often around 50 degrees centigrade.

As we came out of the mountains and on to the flat plain of Tiznit I decided to stop and bleed the brake system. While Debby wandered off to get us a drink, I once more took off the tank and seat and set to work with my spanners. The locals hardly batted an eyelid at the sight of an irate woman muttering amongst bits of BM. Although I checked thoroughly for any leaks and had no air bubbles, when I'd finished nothing had changed. The front brake was non-existent after one pull. I couldn't figure out what was wrong.

Debby wanted us to get south to Goulmein that night as her guide book said there was a camel market early the next morning, so we headed off directly into the sunset of the now flat horizon. Fortunately the road was straight and good and we arrived just after dark. Debby treated us to a hotel as I was knackered. We walked over to the market before dawn. It was a mite chilly as we were now right on the edge of the desert, in fact there was an archway over the road with 'Gateway to the Sahara' inscribed on it. As I looked out across the flat, empty horizon, the sun gradually crept upward, turning the camels in the market enclave from dark shadows to brown humped animals, looking very at home in this arid landscape. I thought of Georgia's step across this threshold. We were one side of the desert and she now was on the other.

As daylight breaks the market becomes busier. Unfortunately there were few 'blue men' this week—the Tuaregs who come in from the desert—but the market is popular for the local people and we were especially impressed with the decorative camel saddles, hand painted in a variety of colours and ethnic patterns, and the selection of silver desert jewellery. I bought an Agadez cross from Algeria and Debby spent a wonderful hour bargaining for more beads and amber for her necklace.

Stalls here sell everything from oranges to West African wedding dress material (so the lady said as she draped some across me for a photo). It was at this instant that we experienced one of the less pleasant tactics that the people sometimes use to force tourists into a sale. After the woman had insisted on draping the colourful cloth around me, Debby took the photo and I smilingly unravelled myself and handed back the cloth to the saleswoman.

'200 dirhams' she said, not accepting the cloth.

'No thanks' I replied. 'It's very nice but I don't want it.'

Her face changed from the previous congenial smile to a look of fury as I re-hung the piece of cloth over another.

'But this is a marriage gown. Now you have worn it I can't sell it; it has been despoiled and you must pay for it!'

'No, that's silly—you shouldn't have given it to me for a photo. Look, here is 5DH for the picture.'

I held out the coin but she dashed it out of my hand to the ground and started screaming. Heads turned and people stopped in their tracks and stared. Before there was time for a crowd to gather, Debby and I turned and walked briskly away. Almost immediately a man came running after us. 'Oh no,' I thought 'there's going to be trouble now!'

As the western dressed Moroccan caught up with us I waited for another tirade but amazingly he apologised for the woman's behaviour.

'You were quite right to walk away,' he said 'she was just trying to embarrass you into buying.'

We felt relieved; that sort of situation leaves a nasty feeling and he helped dispel it. Not only that but he waved goodbye and did not trouble us further.

This was as far south as we were going. From now on our route would be a gradual return to the north, but we had more new ground to cover.

Chapter Fifteen

Into The Desert

Whilst in Tafraoute a few days earlier I had bought a guide book which told of a route I hadn't taken before along the edge of the desert in the Anti Atlas. It described interesting oases and agadir villages. Varying information sources had told me that agadir means stronghold or store house. The small, walled villages in this area it seems were used for keeping reserves of grain and were fortified against attacks from warring tribes. According to my new guide book, one such village lay next to an oasis about 20kms off the main road. Following my instinct to find hidden treasure, I asked Debby what she thought about taking the detour.

'I'm game, Linda, you're the driver.'

So I steered the bike off the well tarmacadamed road and on to a dirt track. With the heavy load I rode slowly and very carefully over the rough ground. In a small, dusty village a few kilometres along, we stopped amongst a crowd of inquisitive children to refill our water bottles and then continued. The track turned to sand and split, in a disconcerting manner, in varying directions. Sweating with effort, I picked the most major looking route and carried on, now down to a snail's pace. The fading front brake was not a problem for slowing us down but was more for balance. I was tiring with the strain, so when the front wheel jammed on large stones in a riverbed my aching arms no longer had the strength to hold us upright and we tumbled over. From her stony seat Debby quipped, 'Linda Honey, just give me a mite more warning if you are going to take a photo break.' Laughing, we picked up the bike and decided to call it a day.

This track was obviously not the right one, it was no more than a walking path now. Our belated lunch tasted mighty good, eaten under a small tree which provided a small patch of shade in the sandy, stony landscape. A jelaba-clad figure appeared from over a nearby hillock but passed us by with just a wave of his hand. We retraced our steps to the village where the correct track was pointed out to us, but by this time the sun was low on the horizon and I couldn't face another 20kms of dirt road. Discretion being the better part of valour, we returned to the tarmac but our day's adventures were not yet over. In the next town we enquired after lodgings but, as there were none, we set off once more into the gathering dusk towards a group of palm trees which might yield a camping spot. Unfortunately, it screened a very poor mud village where hoards of screaming, snotty-nosed kids swarmed around us and I had to keep the bike in motion to escape their grubby grabbing hands. Moving faster than I wanted between the houses and on rubbish strewn streets, I managed a wobbly U-turn and we returned back to a riverbed. Negotiating the large, smooth pebbles in almost dark conditions, we picked our way up the dry water course until finding another group of palm trees thick enough to hide us. While setting up camp two children appeared on the scene.

'Oh no,' I groaned, 'we'll be overrun by the whole village.'

However, luckily, these two urchins just stood and watched our evening routine and eventually, as darkness overcame us, they melted into the night. Brmm, chugger, chugger, brmm, chugger, chugger; we awoke the next morning to the sound of a diesel truck. The spot we had picked was next to an irrigation channel and was a water collection area. No-one hassled us but we packed up quickly and were on our way. Our guide book informed us of rock paintings in the area and, riding to the spot described, we searched the dusty hillside for about an hour, but to no avail.

On to Tata, where the guide book (I was beginning to think it was more trouble than it was worth) promised an ancient agadir about 4kms out of town. Eventually we found it and parked the bike outside a small shop where a group of jelaba clad elderly men were quietly taking tea. Up the steep, narrow streets we stepped as one by one a group of children gathered behind us. By the time we passed the last of the buildings and came out on higher ground close to the mosque at the summit, there were about a dozen of them, all demanding cadeaux, dirhams and stylos. Suddenly, I felt a movement at my back. I turned and half a dozen small boys were racing down the hillside. Foolishly I had put my wristwatch with its broken strap into a small pocket in the rucksack. A small boy had dipped his tiny fingers into the pocket and found his prize. One little girl shouted after the boys and pointed at them, but what could I do? The culprits had fast disappeared into the maze of streets. The remaining children watched us round-eyed in consternation to see what my reaction would be, but it was nil—until we returned to the bike. Then, in

front of the village elders still sitting with their tea, I turned to the children and said in my best French,

'Les enfants sont voleurs—c'est tres mal. C'est pas bien pour vous.

Allah est tres malheureux.'

Having vent my spleen, though the children looked totally nonplussed, we rode away. I hoped the elders might realize something was wrong and admonish them, though the true culprit was still in hiding. This was the first time I had been pick-pocketed and it was foolish of me to be so careless. The watch was of no real value; I'd long ago learnt not to take anything to Morocco that I couldn't afford to lose.

By the time we left Tata there was only half an hour of daylight left in which to find a camping spot. My Michelin map showed an oasis a few miles away and, sure enough, there it was. A track led down off the road to a flat area amongst the palms although, unfortunately, it was still visible from the road. Had my tent not sported trendy, purple panels it would have been less conspicuous but I was aware that until dark we could still be seen. The traffic was almost non-existent though, so we assembled our stove for the evening meal.

Just as the kettle began to boil, the sound of a car engine hummed along the main road then, to our consternation, a 4/4 turned down on to the track and pulled up beside us. Our concern increased when three Moroccan men, probably in their thirties and dressed in western style, emerged. One of them had a rifle slung over his shoulder, and as they walked towards us they were followed by two huge alsations with spiked collars. Debby and I looked at each other and gulped. This could be a dodgy situation. We wanted to appear friendly, but not too friendly.

'Bonsoir, messieurs, comment allez vous, bien?' I smiled politely as I spoke. They circled the bike, looking at the number plate and one of them spoke to us in English.

'Are you alone?'

Quick as a flash Debby answered 'Why no, monsieur, we are waiting for our boyfriends. We came ahead to set up camp while they were sightseeing in Tata. They will soon be here.'

I was busy looking for escape routes but said 'Would you like some English tea? We have no sugar though.'

'No sugar' is an instant deterrent to the Moroccan, their own tea is saturated with it. English tea is also not usually to their taste, but we had been hospitable.

'No merci' they answered, but made no move to leave.

'Is this the first time in Morocco?' the English speaker asked instead while the others looked on and the dogs sniffed around.

'No, we have been here many times and we like it very much. We have many friends here, some in Agadir.'

This was my way of telling them that we were known in the area and would be missed. We were both thinking quickly.

'And what do you think of Morocco? Are you not afraid?'

Debby's inspired reply came with a sweet, calm smile that belied her racing pulse.

'Allah watches over us and people are kind.'

The spokesman told us that they were from Agadir and had been on a hunting trip this weekend. They were now returning home as it was Sunday evening. They wished us a good journey and we shook hands all round before they and their animals re-entered the 4/4 and drove away. No cup of tea has ever tasted sweeter—sugar or no sugar. Debby and I breathed a huge sign of relief and had an early night. We didn't want the tent light attracting more visitors.

The next day's ride to Taroudant took us through hills that looked like the swirls of coloured sand found in bottles from the Isle of Wight, and the women walking along the road wore long flowing skirts, of which the deep blue colours stood out vividly against the ochres of the land. I was riding carefully, always aware of the lack of the front brake to balance slowing down and stopping, but a circumstance occurred in which I could not compensate for its absence. We had just rounded a bend and were riding uphill when Debby shouted for me to stop. 'Linda, the tent bag is falling off the back!' she cried.

As it was indeed dragging behind the bike by its remaining bungy cords, I had to stop at once. But on a hill! This, of course, is where a front brake is imperative and we didn't have it, so the bike began rolling backwards, momentum increasing. It was frightening not being in control. Before we gathered too much speed I shifted my weight in order to throw the bike down and stop it. This time we both fell heavily. Thank goodness it was just a case of bruised elbows. As I insist on my passengers always wearing full riding kit, even in warm climates, we had no further damage. Some local men rushed to our aid and soon righted the bike and retied the load.

'Poor Debby,' I thought, 'she's seeing a lot from ground level.'

We were rushed for time as we needed to cross the Tizi n Test Pass to Asni that night, so the tour of Taroudant itself was brief, though Debby bought yet more beads in the colourful souk. Her necklace was now looking splendid.

At this time of year this high pass over the Atlas is usually closed with snow, but the country was in the grip of a drought and not a drop of moisture had fallen, thus the pass was completely clear. It became colder as we climbed

but the vista increased and improved with altitude and we stopped many times for photos. At one point a young lad appeared abruptly out of the bushes, demanding money. I drew away fast and Debby dropped her gloves, which he quickly took. Never mind, now he has warm hands. Our descent toward Asni was a slow one, for now I was even more seriously missing the front brake. While the light lasted we enjoyed the lush vegetation on this side of the mountain with the almond blossom glowing pink in the evening sun. It was dark by the time we reached the youth hostel and we went straight into town for a coffee. As usual the bush telegraph had alerted Brahim of our arrival and he came to find us to take us home for tarjine and tea. He, too, asked about Georgia and was happy that I'd brought yet someone else to peruse his jewellery collection.

Whether it was a cold or an allergy, my nose was running badly and I need a Panadol to knock me out that night, despite my exhaustion. By now Debby was itching to get to Marrakech and I was desperate to find the solution to my bike problem. Hopefully I could find someone to help me fix it there. En route to the big city we called in at the Tanahoute market where Brahim was displaying his wares, and we lunched with him and his friends while Debby drove a hard bargain over the jewellery. I had a musical session with the tea house buskers and we left with the good wishes of our Berber friends ringing in our ears and yet more souvenirs packed on the bike.

Chapter Sixteen

Marrakech

In contrast to Georgia's aversion to the famous city, I could feel Debby's mounting excitement as we carefully entered the busy streets of Marrakech. From our approaching direction the first sight was the pink ochre walls of the old town. We rode straight into Jemel Afna Square to find the Hotel de France that Brahim had recommended. It is situated on a tiny street off the main square and, as Debby walked ahead to check out the hotel, I waited with the bike and its mountain of luggage. It was so wide that the rest of the traffic of taxis or horse-drawn vehicles could not pass. I was frantically looking for somewhere to park out of the way when a sooty-faced man flashed me a wide, toothless grin and beckoned me to bring the bike in behind a large steel door and into an area which stabled a mule. As I parked the BMW beside the hay bales, he waved me further into the yard and I saw another similarly soot covered man feeding a furnace. It was the fire for the hammam next door. Night and day these two men fed the flames to provide hot water for the bathers.

I was fascinated by yet another manual job that would be unthinkable in our culture where such heat is normally provided by gas or electricity. Here a man and mule walked the city streets with a cart everyday, collecting rubbish to be consumed by the ever hungry fire. Not only that, but during this month the local people brought soups and other various dishes which, for a few dirham, the stokers would heat. We had arrived at the start of Ramadan, the religious festival when Islamic people fast from dawn to dusk, then eat three times during the night. The hammam boys made sure the food was ready for the first meal at sunset – about 6pm. Although they could not partake of tea themselves at this moment, one of the hammam men ordered some for me so, in gratitude, I played him a tune on my whistle. Debby, following the sound, found me there and imparted the good news that we were booked in at the hotel. All was fine, except it was impossible to ride the bike in over the high entrance step, so I parked it in another place and paid for a guard.

The next few days were a mixture of pain and pleasure. My cold became worse, keeping me awake with a running nose and hacking cough to such an extent that Debby organised us separate rooms so that she could sleep. I also had a heavy period which exhausted me and made me ache all over, and I had the constant worry of trying to fix the bike.

On the first night whilst we were in Jemel Afna Square taking in the sights of the many entertainers in the lively, jostling crowd, I recognised a couple who I had met previously near Gibraltar. Frequent travellers from Northern Europe to Morocco, blonde, petite Canadian Margo and Peter, her older English boyfriend, were at present in Marrakech while taking a group of German students on tour in their van. Together we watched the witch doctors, jugglers and snake charmers and partook of the fresh orange juice squeezed by the young men who ran the many stalls around the square.

Fortunately, Debby needed no nurse-maiding in Marrakech, or any other unfamiliar city. Well used to finding her way around the world, she was quite happy to be left to her own devices while I enlisted the help of Pete and Margo to tackle the front brake problem. Debby soon had a handsome young Mohammed lined up as a guide and was disappearing into the Medina with a grin on her face while I took the tank and seat off yet again. Peter soon located the problem; one of the seals in the master cylinder was leaking.

Margo, to whom French was a second language, came on a search with me around what seemed like many hundreds of small parts dealers to locate a tiny rubber seal to match the one we had taken out. Every time we thought we had one which might fit Peter helped me replace the system, which we tested yet again with Fairy liquid, but to no avail. Three days and many frustrated attempts later, Pete and Margo had to leave to complete their tour and I was exhausted. I had even tried the Gendarmerie as I saw that the police had BMWs in their fleet and thought their workshop might help.

Despite my ill health and the bike problems, I managed to join Debby in some of the 'tourist' activities. One evening we walked out to the Menara, a folly built by an artificial lake which, when viewed from across the other side of the water at sunset, has its reflection as a base and the usually snow covered high Atlas as a backdrop. We also shared a Ramadan meal with Debby's friend Mohammed in his family's home, and enjoyed many delightful cups of tea with the hammam stokers, the elder of whom played the Berber banjo like I've never heard before. When he first disappeared into the depths of his dark corner and brought the instrument out covered in soot it only had two out of three strings, but we were impressed with his playing and searched the Medina for another. With this attached the tunes he produced from that battered instrument would put Bob Marley, Jango Reinhart and Eric Clapton to shame!

Hamman Blues

We enjoyed a few fruit juices in the Hotel Essouira where Margo and Pete were staying, which had a charming roof terrace bar with a panorama over the roof tops of Marrakech, the snow peaks of the High Atlas verifying the postcard views.

After Pete and Margo left, Debby's Mohammed came with us in a taxi to help find some motorcycle shops. Eventually we tracked one down who said I should bring the bike to them. I rode it carefully across town, dodging the many mad taxi drivers, and left it in the shop while I disconsolately went for a walk. Where would they find the correct piece to fix it when I'd been all over Marrakech and failed?

However, on my return two hours later it was repaired and all back together. I didn't quibble over the somewhat high price because I was so relieved to have it back in working condition. We were running out of time and had to leave the next day.

The idea was to ride straight through to Kenitra, so we took the fast road to Casablanca, only stopping once for tea. During Ramadan it is very difficult to get any sustenance whatever during the day and, having been turned away from one cafe, we were supping on our water bottle when a kindly bread delivery man freely gave us a loaf from his stock. It never ceased to amaze me how the Moroccans could feed others while they observed their harsh abstinence. They didn't expect us to starve with them!

By the time we arrived at Fatima's house Debby had caught my cold and both of us were grateful for a day's rest and the cosseting that the whole family afforded us. The girls took us to the hammam to scrub us down and Fatima made a huge tarjine and Ramadan feast. It is a very important time of the year for them and they were happy that we were there to share it. Nebil, the cousin, asked me to take him out to his aunt's place at 6pm so that I could join them drinking their harira soup as the sun set and the call from the mosque heralded the first meal of the night. Although Debby and I were both feeling very under the weather, she wanted to push on to see Volubilis and Fes, so we made our farewells to the family and rode out through the mist towards the Roman city nestling in the fertile valley. The best preserved Roman site in North Africa, its stately pillars and arches rise up from the open countryside so unexpectedly that it resembles a Hollywood film set. The mosaic floor designs are well preserved and reconstruction of many of the important buildings is gradually taking place with various monetary grants from Europe. It is a very photogenic and fascinating place but we only had a short time there as we wanted to reach Fez before nightfall. Here we camped in the modern campsite out of town and, despite her bad throat, Debby was all set for us to ride into the city centre to see the nightlife. Thank goodness the BM's light switch had a fault and were unable to go—I was more than happy to relax over a drink with two other English campers.

The next day, after fixing the switch in daylight, we were off into the city, making sure we employed a guide because the maze of streets can be a trap to the uninitiated. One street is full of workshops just dyeing clothes and there are separate sections for the many different crafts and trades. We, like many others, photographed the colourful leather treatment area where the skins are first scraped clean of wool, then washed in urine and finally dipped into bright dyes of red, yellow or ochre. The whole of the ancient part of Fez is designated as a National Monument because it is a city that has not changed for hundreds of years. There are many different areas where groups of artisans work, still manually crafting commodities that in our world became mechanically produced back during the Industrial Revolution. Children and adults together work at their family trades. There are metal workers hammering huge copper bowls or engraving brass plates and wood carvers who sculpt intricate designs on furniture or use their feet to turn chess pieces on a simple lathe.

The city resembles a termite mound with its activity from early morning to late at night. It vibrates with the movement of jelaba clad figures scurrying about their business. It rings with the cries of donkey men guiding their heavily laden animals through the narrow, cobbled streets to take their goods to the shops. It echoes with the attendants of these Aladdin's caves calling out to tourists to come and buy in any language that the punter might speak. A vast fruit, vegetable and meat market is located near one of the mosaic 'Babs', entrance archways to the Medina, and restaurants advertise evening 'Moroccan shows', but we had to forgo any exotic nightlife for, with our time limit catching up with us, we left Fez to ride the last 200kms back to Chefchaouen.

The road was good but there were a lot of animals, people and trucks and we arrived just in time for the 6pm call and were given a free bowl of harira by a stall holder while buying our veggies for the evening meal. Much to my disgust Taieb was not at the YHA so we couldn't get in to cook it. Tired and hungry we walked over to the Hotel Aasma where, fortunately, Mohcin, the artist, was on duty at the bar. He took pity on us and gave us his own evening meal of fish and peas. Taieb didn't arrive back until 8.30 and we, very disgruntled, crawled into our sleeping bags.

The campsite was full of camper vans as the winter migratory movement was in full swing. Taieb informed me that the people from Ireland with whom I had shared my moonshine last November had passed through on their way home just the week before. Just to take our trip full circle weather wise, the clouds gathered that night and by morning it was throwing it down. Debby was determined to buy a tarjine pot and burner so, in order to make room for this, I left my tent and sleeping bag behind with Taieb, thinking I would shortly be back. (As it happened it was 18 months before I could come back to collect it). In the pouring rain we left Chaouen and stopped at a ceramic sales stall just out of town. Debby began bargaining with the stall holder who wanted 50DH for the set; she tried 30DH and he wouldn't budge.

'For goodness sake, you are talking about a couple of dollars difference!

We've got a boat to catch—hurry up!!' I grumbled.

The tarjine pot was bought without further haggling and put in the tent bag. The bike was by now considerably heavier and the steering light on the front end. I didn't appreciate the pouring rain and muddy roads as we descended the Rif mountains towards Ceuta.

Relieved to be safely aboard and out of the rain, Debby and I toasted each other with a beer at the ship's bar. It was our first taste of alcohol for a month—apart from the wine at Sam's Bar. Although we were both tired and still suffering colds, we congratulated each other on a great trip and, on

arrival at Algerciras, headed straight for Continente supermarket to buy a stock of wine. Debby had a duty-free bottle of gin already in her bag.

It was dark but fine weather and we were on the very last leg of our journey. Just beginning the final 5kms climb up the hill to my house, the bike spluttered and stopped. I was amazed. I tried the starter and she was dead. No reason.

'Off you get Debby,' I sighed.

I pushed the bike into the driveway of the only house on that part of the hill. It had an outside light and I tinkered for a while with the points, checked the coil connection and everything else I could think of, but to no avail. She was still dead. I gave up. Knocking on the door of the house, I asked the occupant in my abysmal Spanish if we could leave the bike there. In his pyjamas and looking somewhat stunned, he caught on to my request and agreed. So we took off the panniers and, hitchhiking the remaining 4kms home, were soon rescued by a friendly Spanish family who squeezed us into their small car.

I had left the key to my kitchen with PC as the house he was looking after next door had no facilities and I said he could use mine while I was away. Fortunately that night he was in the room and had a roaring fire going—a very welcome sight.

'Where's the bike?' he asked, as Debby and I staggered in with the panniers.

'It's down the hill,' I replied, 'with the rest of our luggage.' 'Shall I go and get the bags?' he offered.

'No!' I said emphatically, 'It can stay there. I need a drink!'

While PC kindly cooked us a meal, Debby and I uncorked the bottles and spent a hilarious evening relating our experiences to him. Next morning, hangover throbbing, I went down to try and get the bike going in daylight. I fitted new points, condenser and plugs but that bike absolutely refused to start until Debby had left for Barcelona two days later; then it burst into life. I think it had decided that all of us needed a well earned rest. Debby was typically American and had to see and go everywhere, camera clicking. 19 rolls of film recorded our trip and it sometimes took us hours to cover a short stretch of road if there were photographic opportunities. The trip we made together was great but at a much faster pace than the one with Georgia; purely because Debby's time away from the USA was limited. I enjoyed both trips, and the harder pace of Debby's taught me that both I and the bike weren't infallible and I needed to take things easier on future tours for everyone's sake.

Debby's departure was a sad one for we were good friends and I wasn't sure when we'd meet again.

However, I was cheered to receive another letter from Georgia in Mauritania dated 7th December 1994:-

'Well, I've been across the desert twice. The first time was with the large convoy. Then I got lucky. Unable to find Alaine, Raymond volunteered to take me with him. He is a good man. We sang French songs and laughed a lot and spoke of personal moments. I was the lone woman with 7 Frenchmen, an Arab guide, then later a Swiss man we picked up half way.

Our party kept crossing over with another group I liked, including Anita, the German motorcyclist. Ahmed, the guide, took me under his wing. We slept out under the stars one night. The air is pure and haunting. The last day we drove along the ocean and saw the dolphins swimming. It was a jolly party reunited at the campsite at Nakashott, where I am now. The others left in spurts—the last to go were the *Germans yesterday.*

It's catch up time for me. I spent yesterday practicing the song I just finished composing. The next one's going to be in French. Unfortunately I have head lice so am battling that with medication and my dad is sending me money so I have to wait for that to arrive. The book is going well, though I'm anxious for the ending. No visa is required for Senegal, I double checked at the Embassy here. As soon as the money comes I'll get a ride with someone. It would be good to find a place I can work and rest for a while. Capetown seems so far away. Still, there are boats from Dakka, so you never know. The people at the campsite are very good, buying me free dinners and making sure there is nothing I need. They gave me a sleeping bag to use too.

There is a fishing village along the beach. The boats they use are adorned with flags. The long, narrow vessels floating on the glassy surface remind me of Viking days.

I want to post this letter today if I can get a ride into town. It's essential and I need more hair treatment. Yesterday marked 6 months on the road for me. It's interesting how fast time flies and yet each day is so long.

I miss the desert. Hopefully I'll get back to it one day. On camels? Are you in Morocco or Spain?

The three German, one Austrian motorcycle group were an interesting group. None of them felt they belonged with the others. Each was quite different from the others. Anita fell in love with a French lad and spent most of her time in their group. Still, if Michel had asked her to join them she wasn't sure if she would have said yes. I spoke to them individually; they were all fine with me on a one to one basis. Each said they wished I would continue with them. This was not possible. Aside from the lack of equipment for me, I wouldn't want to be in that group either. It was stiff, unyielding. An interesting psychological study from all points of view . . .'

In answer to Georgia's question, I expected to be in Spain for a while after Debby's departure on 14th February. The BMW was resting in the driveway. It had been a very strenuous trip and both the bike and I were feeling the worst for wear. I had to give the BM quite a bit of TLC to persuade her that she should keep on transporting me.

Chapter Seventeen

'Buy Them All, Dahling'

Little did I know at this stage but 1995 was going to be a very eventful year with many unexpected circumstances, both good and bad.

During Debby's stay a small derelict cottage directly behind where I was staying came up for sale. A few weeks before I left for Morocco with Debby, the owner had returned from America, evicted Geoff the junkie and put PC in as a watchdog against other squatters. PC had left his Winnebago parked in a field a few kilometres away and moved in with a few belongings.

At first Debby was offered the property as she was the 'Rich American' but she had other fish to fry in the States and said to me 'Linda, why don't you buy it?' It was an idea that hadn't occurred to me because the place was in such bad condition and I still had my house in Australia to contend with. However, the more I thought about it the more the idea appealed. It was time to make a decision about where I wanted to base myself. Although I had acquired a name for being a free spirit or wandering person, it was actually a false image. During my previous travels I always had a permanent base; either the parental home of my youth or, later, my own house in Australia. I needed a home to come back to. Unlike the boat or van travellers that I had lately met, my home wasn't with me. One can only live for so long in a tent, and rented property was insecure.

I had left my home in Adelaide under traumatic circumstances and it was now in the hands of an estate agent. They had lately written to inform me of its degenerating condition. Either I must return and spend a good deal of money on it or it would be advisable to sell it before it fell down. So did I want to return or should I try and start a settled life elsewhere? And was this else-where, a Castellar cottage, a good place?

Due to the depressed state of the market in Australia and the poor condition of my property, I did not expect to realise a great deal of money on its sale, but surely it would be enough to cover a ruin in Spain and renovation costs if I could do a lot of the work myself. The pros of the region were:

a)   It reminded me in climate, topography and vegetation of Australia.
b)   It was close to my family in UK, relatively speaking.
c)   It was easy to fly via London to other cities and countries I may wish to visit.
d)   It was very close to Africa, which I loved visiting as a place to regenerate and escape.
e)   Because of the variety of people and nationalities, life was always interesting.

The cons were that it was difficult to earn a respectable living, there were drug problems and, also, I was finding it difficult to find people I could really relate to. I'd met some nice people with whom I thought I could be friends with but they had usually been just passing through. But then, I thought, South Australia is also a depressed economic area, drug problems were growing throughout the world and Castellar was a lot less frightening than, for example, depressed areas in London or any other northern European cities. I'd lived on my wits in many countries for many years; surely I could handle this area? I felt that I would really like the challenge of rebuilding this house for I had already had experience in redecorating my own property in Adelaide and building a mud brick 'granny flat' in the garden. I knew about plans and construction methods and materials. As far as the people went, with owning my own property I would have control over who stayed there, which I couldn't in the property I was renting at the time, and once I was settled surely I would eventually find like-minded people and build up another group of supportive friends.

So I started negotiations for the property, which became complicated. PC was still living in the house and had also been given an option to buy it, which he had turned down due to lack of money, but in occupying it he seemed to have taken on a possessive attitude towards it and I felt some sort of power play taking place between the owner, her agent, PC and me. I wasn't sure who was manipulating whom but became very dubious of the whole deal and wondered if I should pull out altogether, but I had set things in motion in Australia, borrowed money against the eventual sale of my house and had become involved and excited about the project. I thought if I could work through this current unpleasantness I would benefit in the end. Finally I made a deal with the owner and was waiting for the money to come through when I found that another house, two doors away, was also up for sale.

I was in a quandary—I knew that the owner of the original house, a German girl, was desperate for the sale to go through in order to leave the country. I didn't want to let her down but the other house was in a more secluded position and, being in far better condition, was instantly inhabitable. I was tearing my hair out with the responsibility of it all and not knowing who to trust for advice when Roger from France arrived to hold an art and poetry exhibition with me in Gibraltar. He had spent much of his life wheeling and dealing in houses, seeing them as investments, and when I told him of my dilemma said the now legendary words, 'Buy them all, Dahling.' So, with more financial juggling, I did, forming the long-term plan of using one as a rental property at a later date. At least I'd know my neighbours! If he wanted to, PC could stay in the first house for the time being as I couldn't renovate it until I'd sold my Australian property and it was convenient for him to be in the area for the building work that he now had near the castle. Apart from my moments of worry regarding the house situation in which PC had played a somewhat ambiguous part, the month of March was filled with the entertainment of having Roger and one of his girlfriends, Malcy, around for the exhibition. It was a time of publicity and posing, which was good fun but dampened by the news that my mother was ill in hospital.

At 75 Mum was finally succumbing to the ravages of old age. Her petite figure had further diminished by spinal shrinkage to 4ft 10', her slim body thickened, although she still showed a well turned knee, and her once lush, dark curly hair was now thinning and completely white. Previously lively and active, she did not take kindly to the limitations that increasing physical problems placed on her. Her health had deteriorated further around Christmas and my sisters had kept me posted. As a heavy smoker all her life, she was now beginning to suffer lung problems; not cancer or emphysema but a blockage caused by the nicotine, exacerbated by osteoporosis. However, she had been at home until an attack of breathing problems put her in hospital. I phoned the UK nearly every night from the exhibition hall and was finally told she had improved and been sent home where a nurse would call on her every day. My sisters assured me that the danger was past, but I booked a flight to see her as soon as the exhibition was finished and my house contracts were signed, which would be early in May.

I made arrangements for a local Spanish motorcycle club to look after my bike while I was away and was also seriously considering looking into the possibility of something else connected with motorcycling later in the year. One of the other women bikers, Hilary Simkins, who worked in Gibraltar, approached me for some information on long distance touring as she and her boyfriend, Terry, had seen an advertisement in their Moto Guzzi club magazine for an event in Odessa, Ukraine. The thought of an excuse to travel to such a destination immediately caught my imagination but, as I was in the throes of the house business, I wasn't sure of the financial viability of such a trip. Keeping the details, I put any further thoughts on the back burner. The Rally wasn't until July but the project would need bike preparation, route planning and visa applications before then.

While all these thoughts and problems were going through my mind, another letter arrived from Georgia. She was now in Senegal and was settled there for at least 3 months. She wrote:-

'In Novakchoff I had $1500.00 stolen through the post. This was a blow that sent my confidence level plummeting. I lost more money to a slick operator in Dakar and was en train to fly to Cape Town. It was too expensive, the flight wasn't for 3 days and I met a man named Dousah. He is a 30 year old black angel. The room I rent is on Rue 3, he lives on Rue 4. The families in both establishments have adopted me. Yesterday Dousah said 'You will never leave Africa. You eat Choybugem as if you have always lived here.' He introduced a classical guitar player. Zale Seck has taught me 2 songs in Wolof. One has an English section. Also he's teaching me to play the Sabah. We will make our radio and TV debut on Saturday. Tita is his agent. He is also a fabulous artist and college professor. There's no money yet with all this learning going on. Possibilities are good. There's a rock band I've been singing with at the cultural centre. I will probably drop this as there's so much other work and Zale is professional. He has a friend with a studio and we're making a cassette. I finished the book and am in the process of editing. It's a learning experience. There probably won't be much left by the time it's red pencilled. No worries, pas grave, I have the outline for the next one. This is fiction. A better medium for me considering the world in which I live is somewhat

obscure. The Wolof language is easier than Arabic. Since a lot of French is in it, combinations of both languages work. The children love the harp. There are 2 babies and a toddler in this compound. Senegalese men are less sexually aggressive. Marriage is suggested occasionally. It's better than Morocco and definitely Mauritania.

This house is clean. Most have appalling living conditions. No one notices. Friends warn against eating the street vendors' wares, not knowing the conditions under which the food was prepared. These same friends live in houses with countless people. Snotty-nosed kids with dirty hands scoop handfuls of rice over to my side of the bowl.

We wipe our mouths on filthy scarves. I'm almost over head lice. Everyone has it. They told me I can pick them out. It's impossible to refuse their tiny hands. I'm still taking malaria tabs and weaning myself onto water. Pray for good health. Xmas and New Year were different. Quieter than expected. They invoked memories of last year. Was I really married and living in Canada?! This part of life is good. Not great, not bad. I miss country and coastal harmony. Dousah takes me to the sea every few days. When butterflies cross the path I think of you. 'I believe we are free within limits and yet there is an unseen hand, a guiding angel, that somehow, like a submerged propeller, drives us on—Rabindranam Tagore'.'

Then another letter followed not long after:-

Right now I'm in a bizarre situation. I've been working with Zale, learning Wolof and his music and doing TV and radio spots as well as promotion. Then a couple of weeks ago he started getting a big ego, cutting my parts. I'm not sure how that's going to pan out. Anyway, I'm working on a cassette on my own which will take a month, maybe 6 weeks. Honestly, do you think we can meet up? I'd love it. You too are the only truly musical person, totally committed. I love this part of Black Africa and want to see more of it. Still, if I know I can make money here and there, I can go and come back. My friend Lesleigh wants to meet me in Italy or Greece in September, depending on her money.

I'm sitting in my room. It's a typical concrete floor, plaster walls, eight by eight with a big, shuttered window. Today red flowers from the courtyard are peeking in and I have a baby on my lap. Her name is Georgia (Dio Dio/Jo Jo, they use both). She was born 3 weeks ago. What an honour to have a child named after you. This land is a land of contradictions, including the people. The family I live with are caring, gentle and, though Har warns me not to stay out too late, they respect my freedom. We have some hilarious meals together. I was given the gift of one bunch of broccoli grown at the Agricultural Development Centre. Har looked at it and was frightened. Finally convinced, he tried one piece then dipped his bread in the hollandaise sauce. It's a child's mentality where food is concerned. Another friend said he hates cucumber, he's never tried it. Bouillon cubes flavour everything. There's no point being insulted when they crumble it or squirt magi on spaghetti. My culinary expertise has been taxed to the limit. Cooking for eight to fourteen people, numbers vary, on a single propane burner in a kitchen without water or electricity by the light of a candle is something I wouldn't have believed possible and I've done it several times. I also make popcorn with sugar, which they love.

There is another Canadian on the scene. David is a composer from Hamilton. He is a great guy. It's been wonderful having someone to talk to in the mother tongue, share experiences and discover it's easy to lose your confidence in your own judgement and then rediscover that you were right all along. Sound familiar? I'm floating in the dilemma of honestly not knowing who I can trust. The couple of people I am sure of aren't around much. After everything that happened in Mauritania it took a long time to rebuild. Also, for a while my VISA card was dysfunctional and I was worried it would become defunct like yours. However, it was reinstated, tried and gave me some financial freedom again.

The mind set here is strange. One minute people are sweet, the next they are yelling about something ridiculous. Example, today I was eating lunch with about 10 people when a message came from another house that I should go there immediately and eat. I refused and later had a brief discussion with the woman who was angry. After explaining it would be impolite to get up and leave to join her, she understood. The point is you have to explain. It's uneducated Africa, land of rampant inbreeding. Today I received 4 more letters and the count of letters gone missing is enormous. It may be the fellow at the previous address. I'm going to ask my brother Dousah to look into it. He truly fits the role perfectly. There was one night when he tried to kiss me; somehow I successfully avoided it and acted as if it had never happened. Romance here is insane. The men for the most part are good about leaving me unmolested but I can't tell you how many have expressed undying love for me. Efou was definitely interested in sex only, so I called him on it in a room full of people and we had a good laugh and then he relaxed. The intelligent women are few and far between. Also they don't hang out with the others. Sometimes being with the former is OK, at others it's boring, frustrating and my heart is with the harp or sea. Yesterday a woman read my future in sea shells. The most fascinating bit of info was that I'm going to have a baby boy and love him to bits. I told her that it's impossible now but she assured me it's true. Actually she's the second one to say it. Funnily enough I believe her. Time will tell. Life is so bizarre. I am no longer surprised by anything. This moment is good. I jogged by the sea after sunrise, spoke to two most interesting and unexpected people, then the letters arrived, those magical pieces of paper that transport me to other worlds and dimensions. Sleep well my friend and dream of butterflies dancing in the sunlight—Linda and Georgia, they are playing our tune . . .'

Funny how in totally different worlds we were both going through a stage of not knowing who to trust and where we truly belonged. In order to finance these houses I was having to burn my financial and emotional boats in Australia and sell my house there. I didn't know if this was the right thing and whether I had made a good deal with the house: being very suspicious of the vendors and their agents. Anyway, another die was cast.

Towards the end of April—in fact 10 days before I was due to fly to England—I received the devastating news that my mother had suddenly died. I wanted to travel back immediately but my sisters said to wait for my booked flight as they would hold the funeral. I still hadn't finished my financial dealings over the house and could have lost the deal for no purpose, for I could do no good for my dear mother now. I suffered terrible feelings of guilt for not going over earlier to see her but I was assured by my sisters that her death was totally unexpected by them all. It was just such a cruel blow that I had missed seeing her by just a few days, but I prayed that she would understand and forgive me. I concentrated my distracted mind on finishing my business in Spain and preparing for the coming family reunion.

As soon as I arrived in England the weather put on its usual bad attitude. The funeral was held amidst thunder and lightning but the gathering of so many family and friends was heart-warming. My mother was a very well loved woman and over 100 people had come to honour her and toast her with a farewell drink at the wake we held in the church hall afterwards. At the crematorium service I read out a poem that I had written for her birthday the year before. It was the hardest gig I ever did and I only just managed to reach the end before my voice cracked on the last line.

WHERE ANGELS FEAR TO TREAD

FOR MUM

You saw the bombs in London's Blitz
Yet kept a smiling face when things were bad
And when the man you loved and thought had lost
Returned, once more your hopeful heart was glad

In post war years you ran a busy home
A working wife with children four
But despite demands on time and purse
You always found that little bit more

Your house was always open to
Neighbours, friends and family ties
So your children learnt to welcome all
To know friendship was the greatest prize

And within its walls they found out how
To sing and play and share their time
To discuss problems and events
And realize the mountains they could climb

Then the children grew and spread their wings
To lands afar or into hobbies strange
But as they went their various ways
Into your home more people came

For you and Dad ne'er ceased to be
A great example to your restless clan
Love and support was given to all
And 'there's no such word as can't—you can'

Then when he died you soldiered on
Hiding your grief as best you could
By helping others in church and home
Trying to ensure their lives were good

Linda Bootherstone

And though they did not mean to cause you pain
Your children sometimes fell along the way
But love and help you always gave
And the strength to face another day

And now in later years you still remain
A spirit bright to which we all turn
No better example can we have
Than our unselfish, loving . . . MUM

Chapter Eighteen

The Family

Our first family home was in Ruislip Gardens, Middlesex, on a small private estate just across from Northolt Airport. In my early years play days were spent with my friends 'over the fields'. A small river ran between the airfield and this arable land, which also encompassed a set of allotments. There were nearby woods and the whole area was riddled with mole hills and tunnels—a great playground for kids and dogs. There were three children in our family; myself as the eldest and Janet and Philip my younger siblings. We had a resident Grandpa from my mother's side of the family. Getting on in years, he mainly kept to his upstairs room until his death when I was about 9. My limited recollection of him is a smelly tobacco pipe and toe nail clippings.

Due to my father's TB weakened chest (contracted during the war), the doctors suggested a move to higher ground so, in the early 50s, we relocated to Sanderstead, near Croydon, in Surrey. Here, instead of Grandpa, we had 'Tante', a friend of the family who had been widowed early. She lived in a caravan in the large garden that came with our 3 storey building, the numerous rooms of which took my father the remainder of his life to redecorate. Shortly after our move, my best friend, Anne, came to live with us. Her widowed mother was in financial difficulties with two other children to look after and my parents, ever supportive, adopted Anne. I was always a little in awe of Anne; I thought she was good looking and clever. She always slept in rollers at night so that her hair would be curly and her handwriting was small and neat—I tried to copy both the handwriting and hair, but with little success. My writing remained a scribble and, as I couldn't stand the pain of plastic curlers digging into my head, my hair remained straight. Two years older than me, she progressed on to boys before I did and took all the ones I fancied from right under my nose! Anne and I went to Whyteleafe Grammar School for girls and she married, at the age of 21, a promising young horticulturist (who I *didn't* fancy) who later opened a chain of garden centres and became a millionaire! They had three children.

I had no such domestic aspirations for, from an early age, I became obsessed with travel and wanted to do it in or on my own vehicle. The jobs that I took, ranging from insurance clerk, salesperson and market research interviewer, were purely to finance my trips and I became interested in motorcycling as a mode of transport and, through one of Anne's early boyfriends, joined a local club which had overseas contacts.

My sister, Janet, four years younger, was more interested in the 'mod' clothes and Small Faces rock scene of the 60s. She also liked to travel and went to a variety of countries to work, including France, Germany, Italy, Canary Islands, Israel and America. However, she used public transport or hitch-hiking for her trips. The things I envied about Janet were her size 10 figure which looked good in her Mary Quant or Biba clothes, and the ease with which she learnt languages, something I find difficult.

The baby of the family, Philip, was six years my junior and also took to motorcycling. To this day he still prefers them to cars. He attended a boys grammar school in Purley but a bike accident during the GCE exam period set him back from his peers and he never caught up academically. Preferring self-employment, he worked as a motorcycle courier for a while and then, with his girlfriend Sally, set up his own shop, Spirit Games, for fantasy and war gaming enthusiasts. It had been a hobby of them both and he was keen to turn it into a business. For the opening of his new premises in 1988 Burton-on-Trent was blitzed by Bootherstones in fancy dress (me as a whistle playing hairy spider on holiday from Oz, Janet as a min-skirted witch and Sally as a glamorous vampire). Philip was besuited to greet the Mayor but his 'normal' appearance would have seemed like fancy dress to most people as his long, grey hair and beard lately appeared incongruous with his slim, youthful figure. Mum, though conventionally dressed, lived up to the family's mad-capped image by enthusiastically joining in with the pub games later.

At the time of Mum's death in 1995, I was the only family member living outside the UK. Philip and Sally were just about keeping their heads above water running the shop. Janet had settled down in Surrey with her boyfriend and daughter – with whom she'd surprised us all by having as a first and only child at age 40! Anne's offspring were now adults, she had been divorced for over 15 years and currently lived in Luton. We were all very different but followed our parents' lead in helping others and making new friends wherever we could.

For Mum's funeral, when my sisters, brother and I hired her local village church hall for the wake, it honoured both parents for, amongst the tables laden with food and drink, we displayed family photos taken over many years so that all the guests could identify the period of both Mum or Dad's life in which they were involved. Although Dad died at an early age back in 1973, Mum had never remarried. Though a relatively young woman, as far as I knew she had never courted anyone else but my father.

Whilst helping clear my mother's effects, I found in her writing desk a set of poems. These were written in my father's small writing in faded ink on a yellowed piece of writing paper. It was obviously penned while he was stationed with the RAF in Egypt during World War 2.

Linda Bootherstone

THE PRICE

These paid the price, that some at home might say
'Our troops advanced another mile today
And lost but twenty men'. So cheap a price to pay
For a few yards of desert. Yet twenty men
Will never tread on English field again,
Or homeward hurry through some busy street
And pause, some old remembered friend to greet.
For these no longer will the hearth fire burn
Or lamp be lit, and eager faces turn
Expectant gaze toward the door,
Hearing familiar footsteps. And nevermore
Will they return to those dear scenes
They dreamt of, dreaming on a foreign shore.
And yet in English hearts for them a lamp is lit
With bright undying flame; and fires will burn
Whenever English thoughts toward them turn.

* * *

Oh God, and I shall see again
An English Rose, an English country lane,
And smell again, on evening breezes blown,
The haunting scent of meadows newly mown.
And see familiar books, row upon row,
Reflect again the firelight's friendly glow.
And press with eager feet the velvet sward
Of English lawns, instead of this abhorred
Wind-furrowed sand. Oh God, grant me again
To breathe a garden's perfume after rain.

* * *

He spoke to me of old familiar scenes;
Fields, lanes, the windmill on the hill,
Deep pools beside the road; and Memory
Rushed in and drove the desert out,
And for a space she led me by the hand
And led me to a place where green
Lush grass grew underfoot, and where between
My feet white daisies peeped, instead of sand.

I was impressed with their style and sentiment and they prompted me to find out more about the history of my father and his family. His octogenarian sister, Joan, was able to help with information on his early life and I contacted some of his service friends for more details. The story I put together goes as follows:-

POETIC PILOT'S LICENCE

Arthur Royle Bootherstone (Roy) was not known to his family and friends as a poet but to be musically inclined, having been an avid chorister in his youth and a collector of classical recordings. He was also very clever with his hands, keen on DIY and tackling mechanical problems on his own, and later his offspring's vehicles. These skills were no doubt inherited from his father, Thomas Henry Bootherstone, a qualified engineer.

Originally from the north of England, Thomas Henry spent his early married life in Wales as a foreman of a group installing electric lighting in a cathedral. Here he and his wife, Maude, had a chance to practice their vocal abilities in the choir. Later, in the early 1900s, he was employed as a chauffeur and general engineer for the Earl of Clarendon at Watford. This job was well paid and included free housing on the estate and food from the dairy. Thomas Henry was able to pay for the schooling of his five children and, under his strict guidance in these cultured surroundings, they were taught to mind their manners and to appreciate the finer things in life. Later Thomas Henry took another chauffeuring job in Hampstead where the children continued their education.

Roy was the youngest of the Bootherstone brood and a delicate child. His mother had been advised against this final pregnancy but had no means
to stop it. His birth at Watford in 1920 nearly killed both of them. He was somewhat pretty and fragile in his youth and was bullied for this in his early school years. However, he was a natural learner and did well, gaining his London Matriculation and also meeting his future bride, Dulcie, at Fleet Central School.

When World War two broke out Roy had a clerical job with Westminster City Council. He applied for the Air Force, not thinking that he had a chance physically but he was accepted on educational standards and became a flying officer. His training was in UK and

Canada and, starting with a Tiger Moth, he learnt to fly transport, bombers and combat aircraft, including Spitfires and Hurricanes. As a fighter pilot in 213 Squadron he was stationed in Egypt, Cyprus and Italy.

On July 16th 1944, whilst in action over Yugoslavia, his luck ran out. The flight log reads 'Hit in engine whilst strafing railroad siding. Engine quit and had to force land in a small valley. Aircraft wrecked.' Although seriously injured, Roy managed to crawl away from the aircraft and hide in some bushes, not knowing if this part of the country was pro- or anti-British. The stricken plane had been spotted and was first reached by some young boys, who excitedly found their way into the wreckage. They located the gun and happily started firing it haphazardly, narrowly missing Roy in his leafy hideout. However, upon arrival of adults the children were dispersed, Roy was found and, fortunately, cared for by the local partisans. His back, which was fractured, was set on a kitchen table in a friendly farmhouse. From there he was smuggled across the border into Italy where he received hospital treatment in Bari and flown to a series of other hospitals in Biferno, Foggia and Naples before arriving at RAF Wroughton.

After two months in the RAF Rehabilitation Centre in Loughborough, Roy returned to flight training and gleefully followed the tradition of 'buzzing' the nurses at Loughborough. Unfortunately the powers that be had decided to crack down on illegal low flying and he was reported and confined to camp.

During his absence from the squadron and time with the partisans, Roy was declared missing in action and his family and girlfriend, Dulcie, feared the worst. However, on his return to UK the couple were reunited and married in February 1945.

Due to his injuries and sufferings with TB, contracted in service, Roy never flew again. Instead he became a devoted family man, bringing up his four children. His family remember outings to Biggin Hill and Farnborough air shows and the look of joy and remembrance on their father's face as the display teams flew overhead.

Roy was plagued by ill health for the rest of his life, which ended in 1973 at the early age of 53. He was well liked and respected, had a clever and enquiring mind and the ability to communicate on many levels with people from all walks of life.

WHERE ANGELS FEAR TO TREAD

My Father

* * *

Whenever I am questioned about why I'm so independent and not afraid of travelling alone, I look back on my upbringing and blame, or rather give credit for, my attitude on my parents. I've come to the conclusion that I was very lucky for, far from trying to mould me into being a certain type of person because I was middle-class and female, I was taught by them to develop my individuality, to mix with many different social groups and to try anything that wasn't illegal or immoral.

Some of my early memories are of being with my father in his work shed in the garden at Ruislip Gardens. He turned his hand to carpentry, when he would let me try to knock nails in wood (I still can't get them straight), and let me observe when he fixed errant electrical appliances by soldering connections. I watched, round-eyed with fascination, the small silver blobs of solder rolling into shining beads when they dropped from the iron. '*My* dad can make metal,' I would proudly tell my primary school friends.

It was also my dad's job to 'turn' the family sheets with the aid of the treadle machine which Mum couldn't handle. This, for those who don't remember such thrift, made worn out sheets last longer by cutting out the threadbare centres, sewing the two outside edges together to make a new, stronger centre, and hemming the thinner edges. Dad showed me how the machine worked while doing this domestic job and, years later, I still prefer a treadle machine to an electric.

Later, in our house in Sanderstead, I was handed the pasting brush for the wall papering and shown the tricks of pattern matching, hanging and carefully rolling the edges. When I was 14 my father was taken into hospital just after we had started to decorate my bedroom. The room looked a mess and I was disappointed because I was looking forward to sleeping with the new blue paper I'd been allowed to choose. Without Dad and with Mum *not* being DIY inclined, there was only one thing for it, finish the job myself. And I did. However, the ceiling paper was a different story, that waited 18 months to be finished. When, over the next 10 years, my father and I (plus other less willing family members) had covered every inch of our 3 storey home with wall and ceiling paper, I decided that a wallpaper brush would never grace my hands again. Although my brother seems to have taken over my father's passion for that medium, I prefer paint!

It was when I was about 14 that I fell in love with my cousin's best friend, who I met when he and my cousin were visiting. He was about 19 and lived over the other side of London. I began to think of ways I could go and see him and, having been brought up in a family with its own transport, my mind immediately turned to thoughts of a car. I dreamed of impressing him by drawing up outside his house in my own sports car; but I would have to wait until I was 17 to drive one. It so happened that at that time a small three wheeled car without a reverse, such as a Bond or a Robin, could be driven at age 16 on a motorcycle licence. By the time I reached that great age I'd forgotten the boy but not the idea of a car and, through holiday jobs and saving my pocket money, had the grand sum of £28.7s.6d. With this money I found a crashed Bond which had a sound 2-stroke Villiers engine and could be repaired. While we were supposed to be studying GCE's, a school friend, Lynn, and I spent hours working on this car. My father showed us how to knock out the dents and fill them in with fibreglass, prepare and treat bare metal and carefully hand paint the coachwork. This, Lynn and I brought to a high gloss finish by rubbing down the many coats with wet and dry paper between applications. This car was named Hiroshima II. I painted a large skull and cross bones on the bonnet and ban the bomb signs on the back. (Lynn and I, like the rest of our class, were into disarmament demonstrations.) The body was black, the wings red and a yellow pinstripe beading separated them. I now cringe at the thought of being so conspicuous but my parents were tolerant enough to let me paint the car my in own way and my father brave enough to teach me to drive it.

When I joined the local 'Saltbox MCC' in Biggin Hill my parents philosophy was to invite all my new friends to the house so they could get to know them. Then they would be aware of who I was mixing with and what I was doing. The same thing applied to my brother and sisters, thus my parents gained a great deal of respect from our friends. A point well made when our peers turned up in force at my father's funeral in 1973, and even 22 years later at my mother's.

My mother had also been independent in her own way. When my father asked her to become engaged before he went away flying during the war she refused.

'I don't want neighbours tittle-tattling about me while you're away,' she said. 'If I have your ring on my finger they will watch everyone I go out with and think I am betraying you. You know I have many men as friends and I want to keep them and be able to mix with them without anyone thinking it's wrong. Of course I'll marry you when you come back but I won't be labelled.'

This was a very unusual attitude for women in wartime romances to take, most married early to enjoy the partnership while they could, but for Dulcie and Roy it wasn't just a wartime romance. They had known each other since early school days and had a great friendship rather than a passionate love affair.

Dulcie was an attractive, very petite (just 5ft) brunette who loved cycling, dancing and singing. She had a good voice, as did Roy, and the choir was one of their shared interests. Being of a gregarious, friendly nature she had many friends of both sexes and, as she said, did not want to restrict her socialising.

Roy, slim and fair at 5ft 8', looked very smart in his RAF uniform but was normally dressed in casual clothes for he to was fun loving and enjoyed their variety of friends. He understood Dulcie's attitude and was prepared to wait for their engagement until after the war for, like most people, he though it would soon be over. Luckily he survived his wartime experiences and their wedding was a reality, although for a time it looked as if, like so many others, it would never be.

The family finances required that Mum work full-time for most of her marriage. My parents wanted a good house and standard of living and Mum needed to contribute towards this. From a very early age I was strapped into a seat on the back of her pushbike and taken to a baby minder on her way to work. Perhaps that's how I was initiated into my love of two wheels. Mum liked to pay her own way before and after her marriage and was keen we did the same and didn't rely on the whims and fancies of a man. However, I'm happy to say that during the 60s when I was courting age it was the done thing for a boy to invite a girl out for a drink or to the pictures, maybe buy her flowers or chocolates, and not expect anything more than a peck on the cheek at the doorstep when he escorted her home at night. However, with one of my regular dates, Barry (Tuesday night every week), we would take it in turns to treat each other to a dinner in a 'posh' restaurant (usually in the country) once a month. We both had well paying jobs and it was a fair deal.

My parents, by having a drinks cabinet which was opened on special occasions, taught me what to drink with a meal. They seldom went to a pub but we would have good wine and liqueurs at home at Christmas and birthdays. I never felt the need to drink to 'overcome inhibitions' to 'let myself go'. I always wanted to be in control of myself and this is probably the reason that I've never been interested in drugs. I learnt to sing at an early age and was never self conscious about it. Both my mother and father had good voices and we, as a family, would drive to Hampstead every Christmas Day to sing together in the choir of St Stephens Church. My parents were married there in February 1945 and tried to get back to it to sing when they could. (It's demolished now). I sang in school choirs, often solo, and never felt any false modesty. I used my voice for my own pleasure and other people's. Again, I had my parents' attitude to thank for that.

Anyone meeting any of our family recognises us as individuals (some say eccentric). We have led different lives but share the same philosophy of flexibility and positive attitude, and we all have our parents to thank for it.

Chapter Nineteen

Hekel The Flying Fiat

After the house clearing and financial business was over in the aftermath of Mum's death, I turned my mind to resurrecting my Fiat 127 which had been rotting in my brother's garden for the last 3 years since I had left England. My plans were to take it back to Spain to be used for collecting building materials for the house renovations. My sister Anne helped with this 'revival' project. First she drove me the 100 miles to Burton-on-Trent where Hekel (registration HKL) lay among the weeds. The first thing we noticed was that she was full of water thus out came Sally's Aquavac. My then 69-year-old car dealer friend, Don, back in London had told me that if she was worth saving he would help me make her road worthy again. We put in one of Philip's spare batteries and then managed to get the engine running. Also the lights came on and the radio worked! However, the bodywork was definitely suspect; a hole in the door where the side mirror had rotted away and dropped off, the door bottoms a lacework of brown rust and a similar affliction around the windscreen. Ever hopeful, for I *wanted* Hekel to be worth saving as I was fond of her, I dashed off to buy a new battery and arrange insurance. It was approaching evening by the time all this was done and we still had the 100 mile drive back to Anne's house in Luton. It was a Friday and we would likely be catching the traffic moving towards London. Tentatively, but thrilled to be back in my cute little car, I led the way out of Burton towards the motorway. Even before we turned on to it, Anne flashed her lights for me to stop.

'Lindy, for God's sake don't try and use your winkers—there is something wrong with the wiring. When you indicate right the left one comes on and your rear lights only work when you brake.' (We'd only checked the front lights!)

We were about to pull on to the busy motorway and be having to cross lanes all the time. It was definitely dodgy, I wasn't exactly fully legal and couldn't risk being stopped. What to do?

Anne said, 'I'll drive behind you and indicate to pull out when it's clear. You watch me in the mirror and when you see me indicating and moving over, pull out in front of me.'

By this time darkness was upon us. I moved on to the motorway with eyes in the back of my head. They flickered constantly between the view through the windscreen ahead and the action in the mirror where Anne was leading from the rear. As soon as I saw her indicator flash I knew it was clear to overtake and pulled out. She was having to see 'through' Hekel to judge when I had to overtake slow moving traffic ahead. It was nerve-wracking but after an hour's driving we had mastered the technique quite well until I took the wrong turn off to Luton and found myself in the middle of Dunstable, not knowing which way to go. Anne's indicators saved the day and I took my lead from her—hoping it *was* her as darkness had fallen and I couldn't distinguish one car from another. We were both mentally and physically exhausted when we finally reached her house. Some journeys, be they ever so short, test us the most.

To reach Don's workshop meant another nerve-wracking trip across London, but this time in daylight. Apologies to all the people who were expecting an indication as to which way I was turning.

Now Don enjoys a challenge and Hekel was certainly going to be that. Clapping eyes on her bedraggled appearance, he nearly reneged. However, as I'd made it this far and we both knew the engine was good, he pulled out his welding torch and the holes in the door sills and where the side mirror used to be disappeared. The lattice effect around the windscreen and rear boot hinges were filled with fibreglass 'pudding' and, after a going over with metallic blue spray, she looked as good as new. An auto engineer came to sort out her wiring problems, which of course were due to the damp, and she was given a full set of brake linings and pads and an oil change Finally, after a week of hard work, I booked her in for the MOT. Full of confidence I drove to the test garage and arranged to phone that afternoon. When I did so the examiner answered my query with a laugh.

'Yes, you'd better come and take her away to the dump.' The man must be joking I thought. 'You're not serious?'

'Yes I am,' he retorted, 'I can't pass this. There's so much rust on her it's like peeling an onion!'

'But we fixed it,' I said.

'No you haven't; come and see for yourself.'

When I arrived he showed me what he meant. With Hekel up on the ramp he poked a screwdriver straight through the wheel arches by the rear suspension units. I gulped; Don and I hadn't even looked there.

Dejectedly I took Hekel back to Don's yard. We pulled out the floor carpeting and there, in full, undeniable view, was the sight of two suspension units almost separated from the metal base. Don looked at me as I grimaced defiantly.

'No Linda, don't even think about it. You are *not* driving to Spain in this, it's dangerous. But I refuse to be beaten by a bit of rust—pass me my welding torch!'

What a saint! Another four hours welding and two large metal plates were tacked to the floor. I stood by with the fire bucket as the torch flame was mighty close to the petrol tank The plastic interior mouldings changed shape and smouldered at one point and I hurriedly splashed water about, not a little of it falling on Don. The poor man was bent double in the back of the car and said,

'I'm too old for this sort of thing. I should retire.'

'No you're not,' I replied with feeling, 'not 'til you've finished this car.'

Next day, within the 24 hours allowed for a re-test, I drove the car back to the test centre. The examiner watched me quizzically as I drew up.

'I just thought you may like to reconsider your decision,' I said smugly. 'We've been up all night slaving over a hot welding torch.'

With a flourish I flung up the boot of the car; the new bare metal sparkled—the weld clean and good. The man was speechless. I don't think he could quite understand why so much effort had gone into a cheap Fiat 127.

'Are you sure you are taking this car out of the country?' he said, as I had told him previously that I was en route to Spain.

'Yes,' I said, 'next week.'

'Well,' he admitted, 'Don's done a good job. Send me a postcard.' And the certificate was signed and safely in my hand.

I did a swift tour of England and Scotland in order to catch up with my many friends and relations and also made a trip to London to secure visas for Romania and Ukraine, having received my official invitation from the Strangers MCC, Odessa, to smooth my path in gaining these official blessings. I was also lucky enough to get to the annual BMF Rally in Peterborough where I bought a new motorcycle jacket, which was to prove invaluable on the coming trip. Hilary had asked me to find her a second-hand top box if I could and that too was packed away in Hekel for the homeward journey.

It was now mid-June and the time was ripe for the long drive back to Spain. Roger 'Dahling' had asked me to pick up some of his publicity cuttings from his English residence in Bath, so I detoured there on the way to Plymouth. Through a Daily Mail special offer, I had managed to procure a cheap ticket to Cherbourg. My plan was to stop over at Roger's French house near the Pyrenees to break the trip and to deliver his belongings.

The drive through France was trouble-free and I was surprised how easy it was to drive a right-hand drive car on the continent. Apart from having to lean across the passenger seat to see around the lorries in order to overtake, it was no problem. I was enjoying the drive for Hekel was going well, although heavily laden with goods from my mother's house such as tools, furniture, old letters and photos.

It was necessary to spend a night on the road and I had my tent and sleeping bag at the ready. Spotting a sign for an historic church and bridge, I found a small village, St Generoux, picturesquely set on a river and with a green, almost empty, campsite. Even better, the tiny community sported a bar by the bridge and it was here I spent a pleasant evening practicing my French by helping a holidaying English couple order their meal. The proprietor joined us in a few beers and I brought out the whistle to entertain the company.

Next afternoon I arrived at Roger's home, 'Lemoc', and met him coming down from his 'estate' and the goldfish pond he calls Lac Lemoc. The first impression of Roger is a man with white/grey hair, twinkling blue eyes and a face of smiling wrinkles. Despite his 66 years, his body was trim and fit and this was made all the more obvious by the fact that when he greeted me he was just wearing a plastic pinafore.

'Been doing a spot of gardening, Dahling,' he explained. 'It's good to get out in the sunshine.'

Roger is the archetypical artist. He trained at Slade and spent all his life painting. Of course this is a hard way to make a living and he supplemented the family income by buying and selling houses and also tutoring rich clients in exotic locations. He worked for an artist travel group for many years while his wife and children held the fort in their home town of Bath. Upon his divorce, after 40 years of marriage, Roger bought a typical Basque cottage which he renovated into a functional and charming home.

By this time Roger and I had known each other for a couple of years, for I had met him while he was touring Spain in his camper van. We had shared exhibitions in Salies de Bearn and just a few months previously in Gibraltar, and were good friends. His wit and love of life always gave my spirits a lift and I knew I would spend the next few days laughing.

Roger had certainly picked an interesting place to live, for Salies de Bearn is named for its salty history. Centuries ago a lord out hunting late one evening chased a boar into some marshy ground. Returning at daylight to claim his catch, he found the defunct animal covered in a white rime and thus the salt source was discovered. The town was thereafter built around the salt spring and the commodity was used as a source of income for, in the days before refrigeration, it was invaluable for saving food. In 1587 a guild was established, giving certain families the right to extract salt. These were known as the Part Prenants, and the terms of the guild in defining their rights was one of the earliest examples of sexual equality, since the heads of households, whether male or female, daughters as well as sons, were included.

At fixed times of the day a bell sounded and members of the elite band would rush to the waters edge, the source in the centre of town, fill hollow vessels and transport them back to their houses by means of a carrying pole. The strongest and most violent took the lion's share and this saline brew was put into drying trays built above open fires. The heat evaporated the water and left the precious salt to be bagged and sold. Every September the scramble for the precious water is re-enacted at the Salt Festival.

Unfortunately it was the wrong time of year for this event when I arrived, but I was able to swim in the therapeutic salt pools from which the town now makes its living. In the second half of the 19th Century, thermal pools all over the world gained popularity, especially with those having the means to relieve their various physical ills in style. The spa centre, built in romantic Moorish mode with a cool elegant interior, was completed in 1857. By the end of the century two ornate and splendid hotels were situated nearby to attract more well-to-do clients to the area. Now people can use the pools by doctor's prescription or pay a fee for the use of the modern therapeutic centre.

The old part of this medieval town is still much as it was. The streets are narrow and come towards the centre, previously the spring site, like the spokes of a wheel. The houses are tall with two or three floors and have steep, tiled roofs and large wooden doors and shutters. Basque red or blue is the favoured colour scheme.

The river provides a focal point as it winds through the town and in summer, when the flow is less, is contained in a channel that can be covered by boarding. This is effectively used as a central area for activities, such as bull running or the cooking of the giant omelette, which seems to be concocted at every summer festival.

Another remarkable thing about Salies de Bearn, and a place that should not be missed, is the town dump—or 'decharge'. Most of Roger's renovations were made using material from this amazing place. Windows, doors, baths, kitchen utensils, microwaves, heaters and clothes; in fact, anything you could wish for. On my previous visit with the BMW I had to rebuild part of the engine and needed to go for a test ride on completion of the work.

'I'll come with you dahling,' said Roger enthusiastically. I knew he was looking forward to the opportunity of grabbing me round the waist.

'No, you can't,' I said, 'you don't have a crash helmet.'

'It's OK dahling, it's Saturday, the decharge is open so we'll go and get one.'

Sure enough, the minute we entered the premises the first thing we spotted was a crash helmet, and it fitted.

'Cadeaux, cadeaux,' the decharge attendants shouted gleefully when we took it away.'

'Oui, tres bien.'

Fortunately Roger was so terrified by the short pillion ride he didn't wish to repeat the experience.

On this visit another situation occurred in which the decharge came to our aid. 'There's a vernissage on tonight for a local artist in the next village,' Roger informed me, 'and we are invited.'

'Well, I really don't have anything dressy to wear,' I replied.

'Don't worry dahling, it's decharge day, I'm sure we'll find something' he said confidently with his usual gleeful grin.

Sure enough, left there at the dump that very morning was a black crepe evening dress, complete with diamante, a perfect fit and just the thing for the occasion. Roger explains these remarkable occurrences as being part of the art of positive thinking.

'It's just a matter of having faith, dahling. Just put the thought in your mind and the object will be there.'

I have to agree the decharge always comes up trumps. I have since wished for new pairs of shoes and an Aquavac and it has provided, even within the limited time of my visits. I wish I had such a genie in Spain. There, a rubbish dump has rubbish.

On leaving Roger to his various activities in Salies, I fuelled up Hekel and skirted the Pyrenees by way of the road to San Sebastian, then took the route inland towards Burgos and Valladolid. The previous year, when I met Georgia, this area had been a furnace and so I was dreading the drive as I find it difficult to keep my eyes open driving in intense heat. However, this time the guardian angel smiled, for the sky was overcast and that night, when I camped up a small mountain in the Sierra de Avila, it drizzled and, with bagpipe music playing on a tape in my car stereo, I could almost imagine myself in the highlands of Scotland. The remainder of the journey was just as cool and I made good time to Castellar.

Stopping en route at the motorcycle club where the Spanish boys had been keeping my bike, I was somewhat worried to see it in pieces. Antonio, one of the non-English speaking members, told me in sign language that German, my mechanic friend, was in hospital. For one awful minute I thought he'd had an accident while test riding my bike, for Antonio was saying something about it. Had he hit some oil and fallen off? Antonio intimated that he was going to hospital to see German the next day and he would take me. At least I would find out what was really going on. Not only was I worried about German but I was supposed to be leaving for Ukraine in a week. Would my bike be ready?

I drove up the winding road to Castellar and turned into my drive. Blocking my entrance was a big blue bus, unfortunately full of junkies who were friends of the man who lived in the other half of my rented abode. I was not amused as they refused to shift the bus and spent most of the day sleeping off the effects of drink and drug ridden nights during which they ranted and raged, their noisy verbal tirades scaring me half to death. I lay behind locked doors, quaking in my bed. There was no sign of PC, who had agreed to stay in the recently bought cottage. It had been handy for his work and, in exchange for this accommodation, he had promised to keep an eye on my other house and this rented house where all my belongings were. Where was he? No-one seemed to know. When I saw him ride past a day later I expected him to call in to see me but he didn't. I went to his Winnebago, parked in San Roque, but it was locked up. Someone said they thought he'd gone to Portugal. Fine house watcher! I would have felt a lot safer if I knew he was next door to call on while these idiots were around.

However, the good news was that German was out of hospital, where he had been for some intestinal problems, not at all connected with my bike, and he was able to continue the work he had been kindly doing on it and get it running beautifully for my coming journey to Ukraine.

The pile of post awaiting me on my return included a letter from Georgia. Apart from her commiserations on hearing about the death of my mother, she had more news of her life in Senegal. The date was May 28, 1995.

My entire life has done a flip. I've stopped working with Zale, who became an egomaniac among other things. I'm still making a cassette and am working on the music for it now. It's almost ready. I've moved to Toubab Dialoa, a fishing village a couple of hours outside Dakar and am living in a single casque up on the roof of an art gallery. Since I want you to have this letter at the first opportunity, I'll save details for another missive. Yes, Dad sent cash through the mail in Mauritania. All I can say is I was very sick and we were both panicky about my health. It's over now. There was also an attempted attack on my person by three men with knives, one the size of a machete, on the beach at Tuegeiway. I called on the angels and was spared harm to my body once again, though the rigmarole with the police, watching them beat one of the perpetrators with a rubber hose and baton, left me shaken.

Mail takes a long time to arrive, Lesleigh's plans change with each letter. I honestly don't know about Spain in late August or September. At present I'm learning sculpture and lace batik as well as working on the cassette. All I can do at the moment is put my life in the hands of providence. If we are able to be together at that time it will happen.

Must go, I miss your beautiful voice, smile and tea in the morning. This is rushed, I can only apologise. 'Stay in the light'.'

This illness was a worry. Georgia had been having problems while we were travelling together but been able to cope. Hopefully it wasn't too serious if she said it was now over; or did that refer to the money situation? I wrote that I would like to try and get down to meet her, maybe in the winter. How was uncertain; maybe by air or boat, it would be impossible to take the bike for a number of reasons. Anyway, now I needed to prepare for the Ukraine trip and I wasn't too happy about the neighbours.

Not being able to get into the driveway, I had to park Hekel outside one of the 'new' houses and leave the key with some other friends. Kate was arriving from Scotland just before I left to spend her summer holidays house-sitting for Hilary and Terry, my riding companions on the trip to Ukraine. I said she may use Hekel if she could arrange insurance for her; I'd rather have Kate looking after the vehicle than leave it unattended in Castellar under the conditions that prevailed at that time.

When I left for Ukraine the following week the junkies were still in the driveway and I could only hope, given time, that they would go away—and without any of my belongings.

Chapter Twenty

Heading East

I first met Hilary and Terry when they were living on a boat in Gibraltar. Hilary was one of the women I interviewed whilst writing an article about a women bikers' charity run on the Rock. She was a delightful, pretty blonde, always bright and happy and usually in a hurry. During the few times she sat still long enough to chat, I discovered that she had a love of motorcycling which began at an early age in England, somewhat inspired by one of her uncles. She had owned several motorbikes before meeting Terry, a tall, amiable Moto Guzzi rider. Together they had ridden down to Gibraltar a few years previously, initially thinking of using his 30ft boat to sail around the world. However, as many people do, they settled into the Gibraltar Scene, making friends there. Eventually they sold the boat to move into a house just over the border in Spain. Since they both worked in Gibraltar, this was a handy location.

Hilary joined the Women's International Motorcycling Association (WIMA), to which I introduced her, and we had taken a couple of rides together. She had progressed from a 500cc Kawasaki to a 650cc Moto Guzzi, of which she was enormously proud and very capable of maintaining.

When she had told me about the Ukraine rally, although I am usually happy to travel alone or with a pillion, I thought it would be nice to ride with other people for a change. It would certainly be safer to be 'ensemble' through Romania and Moldova where military unrest and bandits were reported. Also, my bike was getting rather long in the tooth. On the last trips to Morocco with Debby the problems I encountered were signs of wear and to be expected in a bike that had been used so much in rough conditions. I knew that Terry was a capable mechanic too, and to have him around would give me an added sense of security. However, I did realise that he liked speed and wondered what the pace would be. I prefer to ride moderately, not just to look after the bike but also in order to see the countryside, notice unusual sights and stop or deviate accordingly. I know there is joy in riding a bike fast and smoothly on a good road, especially when the engine is sounding sweet, but I did all that on a race track during my leather clad racing days in Australia and now I prefer to be a dodderer and make lots of photo stops. Would this be a problem? We could only wait and see.

Hilary had sent off to UK for some parts for her bike and they hadn't arrived when I returned from UK. We were all hoping that both my bike and hers were going to be ready for our departure date, 5th July 1995. Two days before the deadline her parts arrived, she hurriedly fitted them and the boys in the Spanish club helped by welding an extra bracket for her top box that I had brought from England. It was real eleventh hour tension, but we all had our visas and maps ready for the great journey.

Our departure morning dawned warm and sunny with the promise of a hot day ahead and Hilary, Terry and I were packed and ready to leave their house near Gibraltar by 9am. Kate had arrived and took our farewell photos for us. We had until the 21st to travel approximately 3,000 miles. Although a rough timetable and route had been planned, who knows what would happen on the road? The carretera 340 that follows the coast from the south of Spain to the French border is tedious. It is a main route for trucks and tourists and at this time, the height of the holiday season, it was packed. We were forever breathing diesel fumes and Terry, with the largest amount of cc's and the smallest amount of patience, kept overtaking and was soon out of sight. In fact we didn't see him for two days, which tended to take the pressure off and left Hilary and me to relax and actually do some sightseeing.

We stayed the first night by a peaceful reservoir and the next by the Roman aqueduct outside Taragona; an almost forgotten relic, it lies hidden amongst trees just off the main road. There were no signs to it and we followed a dirt track to find an ideal camping spot beneath its stone arches, which glowed mellow yellow in the evening sun.

Where Angels Fear To Tread

Hilary, Tarragona

Barcelona is a sprawling city with a ring road lacking in road signs as to how and when to leave it for the correct direction north. We managed to partake in a scenic but unintentional tour of the old part of the city before finding the right road; more luck than judgment. The city has the reputation of being one of the nicest in Spain—but then they all say that.

Late in the afternoon we reached the Spanish/French border and there Terry was waiting. Oh well, the rest was great while it lasted.

Funny, how as soon as one crosses a frontier, the geographical features seem to change with the language. Suddenly we were in the wine growing area of France, riding through avenues of plane trees, vineyards on either side. Then the route took us into Italy, where snow covered Alps towered around us. The altitude meant cooler temperatures and some heavy rain showers and I was glad of my new water-proof jacket and visor. The scenery, of course, is spectacular but the severely winding roads quite exhausting.

Down on the plains around Milan the temperature rose again and Hilary had a frightening experience when some young men in an Alfa Romeo thought it might be fun to run her off the road. Fortunately she escaped them and alerted the traffic police but the culprits had disappeared.

The Moto Guzzi factory is in a small village, Mandello del Lario, situated by Lake Como. It is the Mecca for all Moto Guzzi owners and the setting is spectacular. The local campsite was filled with motorcyclists making their pilgrimage to one of the oldest motorcycle factories still in existence. For us it meant a welcome rest while the factory mechanics tuned Hilary's bike. I just cleaned the BMW's plugs and checked the oil.

One thing that had caught both Terry and me out in Italy was that petrol stations didn't take VISA or MasterCard – only Diners or American Express. This meant extra trips to banks to be sure that we had enough change for petrol, which was an added hassle. Travelling through many different countries using cash all the time is not only time consuming but wasteful. How many pocketfuls of small change in different currencies have travellers unintentionally collected? Would the Euro change all this? However, we survived by lending currency to each other.

The next few days provided more hard riding over the Tyrolean Alps into Austria. At one stop a local old timer rushed over and gave us some apricots. He spoke German and we understood that he had been a prisoner of war in Scotland and owned a military Moto Guzzi. He was grinning from ear to ear as he waved us goodbye. I think he was quite taken with the fair Hilary as well as her machine.

One morning, before leaving a wooded camping spot in the mountains, Hilary checked her carburettor settings and accidentally broke a piece of one of the floats. Fortunately Terry managed to tune the bike to compensate for this. I was impressed, with the bike that is, I don't know if the BMW would have been so forgiving.

Unfortunately I was getting more and more frustrated with our mode of travelling. It wasn't just the faster pace that Terry liked to set which made no allowance for territorial observations, but I am an early riser and fast packer which compensates for my slower riding during the day. Terry and Hilary woke much later and were slow at packing. While their normal riding speed was, as expected, faster than mine, I was spending hours waiting for them in the morning and then, when they were ready to go, both jumped on their bikes and rode off ahead at full speed without checking to see if I was behind. Hilary, I felt, was being rushed too. She had seemed a lot more relaxed and happier when she and I had the time riding without Terry in Spain. During my years in motorcycle clubs I learnt how to ride in groups, caring for other riders by compromise, to always be in sight of one another, avoiding separation and loss of contact. I had often led club runs with slower riders, whereas Terry seemed to have mainly ridden alone or with others who kept a similar pace. He expected Hilary and me to ride fast or be left behind. Hilary accepted this but I couldn't and was not happy. It came as a relief when one day the pair were too far ahead for me to catch them and point out that we were on the wrong road. I stopped, studied the map carefully to ascertain the correct route, and then turned at the next junction. Finding myself exhilarated to be on my own again and not under pressure to keep up, I assumed that Hilary and Terry would probably also feel relieved when they too realised our final separation. Our travelling mode was so different it was painful for all parties to try and stay together.

I was now on a small back road in Austria, making my way east to pick up the main route to the Hungarian border. Austria had so far been very interesting; coming down from the Alps there were many churches with inspiring spires, cows grazing in lush meadows and beautiful roadside shrines, rustically made in wood and painted with simple designs. Castle ruins stood romantically on the hills and then, suddenly, on this small road little wooden people appeared: tree stumps carved into faces. A roadside water trough was my first sighting of this phenomenon and then I turned downhill into a small village and stopped at a petrol station. Beside the forecourt and behind the building lay a whole hillside of them. A veritable forest of gnomes. Click, click went my camera; I was delighted.

Congratulating myself on my lone state and the ability to stop and look for a change, I was suddenly brought down to earth by the sputtering and loud back-firing of my bike, which ground to an ominous halt.

'Shit, BM, don't break down here. This is Austria, where everything costs a fortune. Why not wait until Hungary, it's a lot cheaper? OK Linda, clever clogs, you are on your own so it's up to you to fix it, there is no back-up. Terry, who you were recently cursing, has gone—it serves you right!'

Well, my lone state was no novelty but, being in the 'safety' of a threesome for the past week, I'd forgotten about it. I pushed the bike off the road and soon found the fault. With my comprehensive tool kit and some thread tape that, indeed, Terry had given me, it was soon going again. Phew! However, it was a timely reminder that I was facing many more miles alone and would have to use my initiative once more and hope for the best in the danger zones of Romania and Moldova.

The city of Graz proved another difficult place to exit. I kept my eyes open for motorcycle shops there in case Hilary and Terry had stopped to look for her carburettor part but, not seeing them, I pushed on through and over the border into Hungary. I had travelled this route before in '88 with another WIMA member en route to a rally in Budapest, and reminisced as I followed the straight, flat road to that romantic city on the Danube.

Suddenly, I felt an excruciating pain on my left ear. An insect had managed to get through my padded helmet and stung me on the fleshy lobe. I was frantic, not knowing if or where it might sting again. Erratically, I pulled over, ripped off the helmet and danced around on the hard shoulder of the motorway, cursing. All I could do was pop a couple of Panadols and wait for the pain to subside before replacing my helmet (having checked that the insect was no longer in there) and riding on.

The weather began to deteriorate until it was pouring with rain by the time I was skidding over the tram tracks of Budapest City, in the twilight, looking for a campsite. Some locals kindly guided me there with their car and my successful arrival was celebrated with a bottle of Hungarian Red, medicinal, of course, because of my still throbbing ear.

I love Budapest. It is graceful and full of interesting art galleries and museums. The music museum I found particularly interesting, with gipsy fiddles and flutes and bagpipes made out of all sorts of animal stomachs. I bought a tape of traditional Hungarian music which, on playing months later, I found quite boring but it *is* folk. A charming Hungarian man helped me buy a ticket and find my way on the metro and, as before, I was entranced by the paintings in the National Gallery. Hungarian artists are very expressive with their interpretations of the country's folklore and history.

It was possible to buy post-cards of the more popular paintings, so I have my own collection.

Romania was the next country through which I had to pass. Of course everyone has heard of Transylvania and Dracula but I had foolishly omitted to gather information as to where exactly his castle is located. My detailed road map was good but gave me no idea of the best route to take in order to maximise on my touristic inclination and music collecting opportunities. As luck would have it, there was a Dragoman Overland truck in the campground, so I wandered over to ask the drivers for their recommendations. To my surprise and pleasure I found the 4/4 Mercedes truck to be the responsibility of two women in their late twenties. They were en route to Katmandu with only eight passengers, who were at that moment engaged in 'doing' the town while their tour guides/nursemaids/mechanics/ drivers were indulging in a relaxing beer. The girls invited me into the truck to join them and there followed a mutual admiration session, during which we adjourned to a pizza bar. Over a delicious meal, with more Hungarian Red, we discussed the pros and cons of surviving in a 'man's' world, being responsible not only for ourselves but others, and swapped many amusing travellers' tales. They presented me with a copy of the Lonely Planet Guide to Eastern Europe, which gave me all the information I needed. Thank you Lindsay and Hannah. I hope you are still leading your flock through the trials and tribulations of adventure touring.

Chapter Twenty-One

Onward To Odessa

And so to Romania.

Many years ago I saw and old black and white film of 'Dracula'. The opening scene was of a coach and horses splashing through torrential rain over the cobbled streets of a Transylvanian village. The driver sat hunched on the coach seat, his cloak streaming water, cracking his whip to spur on the horses whose breath steamed in the cold air.

Yep, that's about it. The roads were horrendous, pot holes in the country and uneven cobblestones in the towns. The cold rain bucketed down for most of the four days I was there. However, I was impressed by Romania as a fascinating, picturesque and friendly country.

The first night I chatted to a local lad running the campsite who was interested in collecting crystals and was eager to obtain some amethyst. I later sent him some from Morocco. The museum in Napoca, near where I stayed, was closed but the staff sold me a folk tape anyway. On the main road east were many women in traditional long skirts, headscarves and shawls, selling lace tablecloths and runners and I bought some as presents. The delicate handiwork was excellent and my interaction with the women made me feel less of a stranger.

Singhdusa is the birthplace of Count Vlad the Impaler who was the inspiration for the Dracula story. Vlad actually had nothing to do with vampires. He just bloodthirstily impaled his enemies and displayed them as a deterrent to others who had thoughts of attacking his castle.

The Count's hometown is charmingly picturesque with multi-coloured houses and an interesting folk museum which exhibits more about Herman Obeth the Rocket Scientist than of Vlad. The castle had an overgrown verdant

German graveyard where I spent sometime playing my whistle amongst the mossy stones. Bran Castle, my next stop, is now known as Dracula's castle. But again, it is not historically connected with either Dracula or Vlad. It is simply a large castle originally built as a toll house on the road to the neighbouring region of Wallacia. With its many turrets and myriad rooms connected by secret passages it fits the bill as a Vampire King Transylvanian castle, so has been romanticised and kept in good condition. Before becoming a tourist attraction it was used as a country holiday home by many politicians. There is a folk museum in the grounds beneath the castle and the large car park for tourist buses is also a market place for the lace makers and wool workers. Many cherry-cheeked women, some knitting as they stood by their stalls, waved and cheered as I drew away on my bike.

In contrast a castle in Risnov, a few miles away, is a ruin but, in my mind, more romantic. I walked around this one with some fellow motorcyclists, a couple from Whyalla, South Australia, who were going home overland on their Triumph Bonneville, bought in London. They had a long way to go.

We had a meal together that night in a local restaurant. I had fillet of CRAP. I think it was misspelt because it tasted more like fish!

On my final evening at the campsite at Risnov I needed to re-set the ignition points as the bike had been running badly. A Romanian family camped beside me were fascinated by the sight of a woman tinkering with a bike. Later, when I was struggling to open my bottle of wine, one of the men came rushing over to help and invited me to join them. They were from the south, a large town called Galati, and were here on their annual holiday. Listening closely I found I understood quite a bit of their dialect as there was a strong Latin base with words similar to French. The more cheap white wine I drank the easier it was to understand them and by the end of the night I was being led in some pretty strenuous gypsy dancing. They invited me to stay at their house in Galati but, alas, I would be passing through while they were still away.

The road to Brailla was obviously used by a good deal of heavy transport and had recently been metalled to cope with this. However, the new stones served to cause a real hazard for I counted at least fifty broken windscreens, in the form of glittering piles of glass, over the same amount of kilometres. I was also wary of road stops as I had been warned that it was 'mafia' country; bandits and gypsies were rife in the area. I did have a worrying experience at one point. At Brailla I called into a petrol station for the somewhat scarce fuel. As I was being served by the young attendant another car pulled in jammed full of people. The driver emerged, a dark swarthy looking man. He came over to me, walked around the bike talking gruffly in his native tongue. I felt uncomfortable in his presence and glanced over to where the young attendant was standing. Having taken my money he was now keeping away. Not a likely ally. The dark man came closer, talking louder. He held out his hand and aggressively demanded kroners. I kept smiling; putting on my gloves and speaking pleasantly back to him in English. 'Yes, I'm pleased to meet you. It is a nice day', as I threw my leg over the bike and started the engine. I let the clutch out as he made a lunge at me and I just managed to evade his grasp. I accelerated out into the main road and sped away. It was a while before my heart beat came back to normal and I dared to look in the mirror to see if he had followed in his car. It was all clear.

I rode on for some time, not wanting to stop in this area in case of further hassles. I was well overdue for my lunch stop, and then saw two Swiss registered bikes pulled over on the grassy verge on the other side of the road. I stopped for a chat. Perhaps I could find out if I was heading for the correct border crossing for Moldova. Not all borders cater for international travellers and the maps do not indicate this. It was also necessary to check road and petrol conditions, and exchange rates.

Martin and Heinz, when they had recovered from their shock of seeing a lone woman on an ancient BMW, were very helpful. I offered them some of my usual stale bread and 'Vache qui Rit' equivalent and, on cutting the bread with my basic penknife Martin asked:

'Don't you have a Swiss army knife?' 'No,' I replied. I've owned two but lost them both.'

'Well, here you are,' he said, producing one from his bag and handing it to me as a gift.

He also gave me some extremely well-thumbed and tatty Ukraine 'kupons'.

'We left the country here this morning,' he informed me indicating the correct border to cross, 'and we won't be needing this money now.

We can't change it and it's only worth a couple of pounds, if that.'

I was very grateful for their gifts and the information. I doubt I would have found the crossing without their explicit instructions for it was not the one for which I had been heading.

In Galati where I became lost, a local van led me out of town onto the little back road to the border. Swiftly leaving behind the industrial city with its high-rise flats, I found myself now in gentle, rural landscape scattered with small villages of wonderful mud pise houses. Some were in the early stages of construction and others, more established, were decorated with carvings in the mud walls. There were donkey carts, mainly driven by women, and the people were not particularly curious even when I stopped at a roadside tea house for a cool Fanta and a cheap bottle of red wine. That day the rain had ceased, for a change, but I was still wearing my thermal underwear and thick rain jacket for the weather was cool.

The border between the two countries was designated by a river and at the Romanian exit post many trucks and cars were waiting this side of the bridge. As usual I was able to weave my way to the front of the queue and was soon waved out of Romania by a pleasant female customs guard. When visiting the Moldovan consulate in London I was told that I could only obtain a visa on entry and not beforehand so I was expecting some delay.

As I reached the other side of the bridge the Moldovan guards stopped me and I was told to report to a very officious army officer in the Immigration Department. He looked at my papers and brusquely indicated that I wait outside. An hour passed, which I spent talking to one guard who spoke some English and wanted to discuss topics ranging from Shakespeare to Margaret Thatcher!

I also played my whistle which drew smiles and comments such as 'Je vous admire.'

Eventually a woman drove up and I was beckoned into the small office. It transpired that as I was an international traveller she, the consul representative, had to be summoned to decide if I was to be allowed into the country. I was only expecting to be travelling in Moldova for two days and was granted a transit visa on production of $25.

As I drew away the friendly guard said 'Your back wheel is sick.'

Sure enough, the slow puncture I had been plagued with for some time was getting faster and my own pump wasn't working.

I found it hard enough to find petrol stations with petrol, let alone air pumps, so the problem was increasing.

As I don't have the strength to change tyres myself, I was hoping that some of the other rallyists in Odessa would help me but I was a long way from Odessa and the tyre was almost completely flat now.

I carefully rode through town on the look out for a garage. Sure enough the only one there was closed and had no sign of an air pump anyway. Then I spotted a Ural owner just about to ride off on his old-fashioned machine and sidecar. 'Aha,' I thought. 'he is bound to have a saddle pump'. Sure enough, when I flagged him down, pointed to my rear wheel and mimed the pumping action, he came up with the item which he used to good effect.

I said 'Spazebo' and waved goodbye to a somewhat bemused Moldovan motorcyclist. I was now safely mobile again and, after patiently producing my papers for an inquisitive local policeman, I found my way out of the attractive border town and on to the road east.

Evening approached and I hoped to find an inconspicuous camping spot but the road was lined with small, one-storeyed houses serviced by community covered wells, delightfully decorated with carved woodenshelters. Children goats and ducks ran in the earth streets and I had no chance of escaping notice camping by the road in the increasingly unlikely event of finding an unoccupied patch of ground. No, I would have to keep going and see what transpired.

It was almost dark when I reached the next town and concluded I would have to stop at some sort of hotel. This wasn't exactly a tourist area but, as a non-Moldovan, I knew I would be regarded as 'rich'. However, I had no Moldovan money. As usual my fairy godmother arrived, this time in the guise of a young man on a Jawa motorbike bedecked with BMW stickers. He pulled up alongside me and, despite our lack of common language, interpreted my need and took me to a boarding house, the location of which entailed riding through deep mud. I chickened out and he, very chivalrously, became covered in goo by pushing my bike through it. A gang of teenage boys appeared to view my bike, which was safely garaged, and my young guide puffed up with proprietary pride and even refused a packet of cigarettes I offered him for his help. My address was all he asked.

The room was sparsely furnished but comfortable. My landlady, Vena, provided biscuits, and tea from a beautiful silver urn. It tasted like nectar as I was desperately tired and in need of sustenance.

I was able to pay with American dollars and left early the next morning to reach the Ukrainian border.

The landscape was flat and open and there was a strong military presence. Control of this part of Moldova was very much in flux between Romania and Ukraine and several army check posts intervened before the real frontier.

'At last,' I thought, 'this is the Ukraine.'

Unlike the Moldovans who had been charmed by my appearance, the Ukraine guards remained stern despite (or perhaps because of) the whistle tunes and deliberately kept me waiting even though I had my visa and official invitation at the ready.

I kept smiling and waited patiently, though somewhat nervously, for my release. Many army trucks came through and I felt that I was being used as the local attraction for bored soldiers who dismounted their vehicles and surrounded me, gazing sullenly at the bike and myself.

At last I was waved on and soon after a huge, stately hammer and sickle sign appeared on the roadside and then a sign for Odessa!

Signpost Odessa

The weather, at last, was fine and I drove through a forested area, stopping briefly to buy honey for my bee-keeping friend back in Castellar to test. The young, bare-chested salesman didn't seem the least surprised to be bargaining with a female motorcyclist from the wicked west.

I made a short detour off the main road for a glimpse of the Black Sea at the fishing town of Kransa Kosa and felt elated. It was now only about 100 miles to Odessa and I would be there that night. I wondered if I had enough fuel for the distance and thought perhaps not. The problem was that I had not been able to change any money at the small border post but hoped my American dollars would suffice. I also had the small amount of 'coupons' that Swiss Martin had given me.

In a small town I saw a petrol station and, as these were rare birds, decided to take the opportunity to top up my tank. It was a simple forecourt with just one antique-looking pump. to which I drew up and dismounted my bike. There was no sign of anyone around so I walked over to what looked like the office. a small cabin, and peered in. I could see nothing although there did appear to be some sort of payment window. I shuffled around wondering where the proprietor might be.

Just then a small car drove on to the forecourt, stopped behind my bike and the driver emerged. He looked at my machine, then at me and began shouting and gesticulating, marching over to where I stood. I looked at him in bewilderment and he shouted again, louder, and pointed at the window.

Peering closer, I saw a little old, extremely grumpy-looking man scowling at me from behind the scratched perspex.

The driver shouted yet again and slapped the palm of his hand. Suddenly it dawned on me; I must pay first. But what? I didn't know how much fuel the bike would take, nor how much the petrol would be. In desperation I reached into my pocket and pulled out the tatty 'Coupons'.

I gave them triumphantly to the driver. He then threw another question at me which I interpreted as being 'How much petrol?'!

I held up five fingers—for five litres.

My money was pushed under the pay window and, incredibly, I was given some change. I then walked over to the bike expecting the little old man to emerge to and serve me. Nothing happened.

The other driver had walked back to his car after handing over money for his petrol. I stood there waiting. Suddenly the car driver strode toward me, red in the face and screaming abuse. I was fed up with this. I was obviously a foreigner, obviously didn't speak the language and obviously didn't know the procedure. So, I decided to retaliate. I jumped up and down, shook my fist and screamed back.

'Well, I don't f******-well know what to do. Why don't you f******-well show me, instead of screaming at me, you f****** idiot. Aaaaah!!!'

I rarely use such language but I knew he couldn't understand. Well it worked. He came over to the pump, grabbed the handle and pushed the nozzle inside my waiting tank. My money's worth of fuel emptied in and then he took the nozzle over to his car.

'Spazebo' I said and, mustering as much dignity as I could, replaced my gloves and rode away.

The incident kept me smiling for many miles. I now knew the ropes: decide how much petrol you want, pay for it and put it in yourself. The garage man never leaves his post behind the screen and never smiles. It proved to be the same all over Ukraine and I learnt I had been very lucky to find a petrol station with fuel and to have enough kopecks. Dollars were accepted, but usually at an unequal exchange rate. Petrol was remarkably cheap but poor quality, usually varying between 76-92 octane.

However, now I had enough fuel to make it to Odessa and it was a straight road into the city. My impression was of rivers and greenery and I was amazed to see telegraph poles and wires covered with some sort of creeper which engulfed the structures and moved in the air stream. They looked like giant green creatures reaching their tentacles across the road. Very surrealistic. Road signs were not helpful and after I had circled the centre a few times—dodging tramlines and becoming more frustrated with my inability to decipher Ukrainian hieroglyphics—I eventually stopped outside a tourist shop and managed by means of showing my invitation, to explain I wanted Pushkinstrasse.

'But you are on it', was the answer and indeed I was. Amazingly the guardian angel was working again.

The street was full of stately old buildings, many of which housed museums and art galleries. The two or three storey facades also concealed courtyards around which many offices and flats nestled. The OMK headquarters, a cultural organisation under whose umbrella the Strangers MCC functioned, was in one such office. I located it, was made welcome and, on request, was shown a tap and some soap. I immediately washed my hair and felt like a human being again.

The organiser, Vlad, was at the rally site about half an hour's ride away. In company with some other foreign arrivals I was escorted there and re-met Hilary and Terry who had arrived three days earlier and already knew the ropes. The one hundred or so participants were shepherded to a hotel on a very touristy stretch of road not far from the beach.

Having camped for most of the three week journey I was quite happy to stay in a hotel room which I shared with a Belgian lad. Other people preferred to pitch their tents in the grounds at the rear of the hotel. The weather was fine so there was no problem camping in that respect. But, it was difficult to say who was better off facility-wise. Our floor of the hotel was supplied with only one toilet (for male and female) to service 30 double rooms, and one cold tap. Needless to say, the toilet was blocked and stank. The campers located one outside toilet which was in the same condition. We found that this lack of facilities was quite normal for hotels in Odessa unless they were in the European top price bracket.

I started to meet the other rally participants. A group from Belgium, including two women riders, some Dutch, many Poles and an English couple on a trike. The European bikers were horrified at the unsanitary conditions but I must say, coming from my own toilet-less abode in Andalucia, I wasn't that upset.

That evening the welcome speech held in the hotel garden amongst the tents, was all we could have asked for—at least from my point of view. The smiling faces of the Ukraine club members who spread a table with caviar and other traditional tasties, the wine, beer and vodka they toasted us with, all made the long trip there worthwhile. Some southern members from Kransa Kosa, where I had first glimpsed the Black Sea, brought out a battered guitar and began playing and singing. I produced my whistle, a harmonica joined in and firm friendships were immediately established. Ena, Sergio, Nadia, Natalia and Uri were young, vibrant people dressed in leather gear, with shaved heads and bright lipstick. They were living up to their ideas of how modern western bikers would appear.

I felt quite tatty and 'eastern' beside them but was very glad to be there at last.

RIDING ON . . . AN ODESSA ODYSSEY

Andalucia—Ukraine July 1995

Preparation

Faxes flying, forms a filling
Visas chased and spanners turned

Planning, packing, maps consulted
Money changed and dates discerned.

Departure

Gibraltar fades into the west
As Spanish deserts breathe their heat

Roman ruins and tourist centres
Recede with Barcelona's streets

Riding on . . .

North to where lush French vineyards
Refresh the eye as wine does the tongue
Then Italian traffic leads to tempting toll roads
Timely taken around Turin

Riding on . . .

Past snow-capped mountains to relaxing lakes
Friendly faces and a well-earned rest
Mandello del Lario, Moto Guzzi mecca
Means a welcome pause on the eastbound quest

Riding on . . .

Linda Bootherstone

Where Tyrolean towns with inspiring spires
Grandly lie in valleys green
While awesome alps bedecked with rainbows
Complete the picture postcard scene

Riding on . . .

Into Austrian order, milch cows grazing
In flower strewn meadows green and lush
Ethnic chapels and ruined forts
Rise from midst surrounding bush

Riding on . . . humming

Hungarian rhapsody in the rain
Glistening tramlines weave the city lace
Danube divine with many bridges
Eastward flows at waltz time pace

Bumping along . . .

Lace-lined streets with working women
Heads bent intent on weaving cane
Then Transylvanian torrents . . .
Where the horror lies not in Dracula's castle
But in Romanian roads and rain

Riding on . . . remarking

Moldovan mud houses with exterior patterns
Covered wells and flocks of geese
While CZ riders with BM Stickers
Are all agog and keen to please

Stopped at . . .

Ukraine Border, stern with officials
Witholding passport to create delay
An anxious wait beside the BM
Nonchalantly whistling the time away

Where Angels Fear To Tread

Riding on . . .

Free to fly the final distance
Past honey pots amongst the trees
Fishing villages and hopeful signpost 'ODECCA'
To that gracious city beside the Black Sea

Riding on . . .

Through tree-lined boulevards that lead the traveller
To sun-drenched beaches where tourists play
Or where stately buildings in Pushkin Strasse
House museums to steal your time away

Arrival . . .

From many countries the 'Strangers' meet
And thus become no more
Talk and laughter fill the campground
Here and on the Crimean shore.
Vodka, beer and wine flow free
Language barriers are broken with friendship
And with tales of each, their own *Odessa Odyssey*.

Ukraine Bikers

Chapter Twenty-Two

The Black Sea Pearl

Vlad, the president of the Strangers MCC and initiator of the Odessa Rally, was a Stalinesque character who strutted around trying to keep things under control. He was doing his best to entertain we westerners by organising trips to town, discos and a bike gymkhana. To support his efforts, I joined in as much as possible but the motorcycle activities were of secondary importance to me. I felt privileged to be allowed into the Ukraine and its seaport of Odessa and wanted to soak up as much local atmosphere and culture as I could. After all, I can be a biker anywhere.

Important as a port, Odessa is also a holiday city. The summer temperatures are around 80 degrees Fahrenheit and the beaches attract tourists from all over Ukraine. There are fun fairs, coffee bars, ice-cream parlours, piers for fishermen, jogging tracks and beach chairs. On one of my early morning walks I saw many elderly men and women of all shapes and sizes exercising on the beach before the heat from the sun became too debilitating. The older Ukrainians didn't look too figure-conscious but the younger people were slim and attractive. Everyone appeared intent on enjoying themselves on their holidays.

Unfortunately a recent outbreak of cholera had been reported in the Black Sea area and I asked Lynn, the club translator, if it was safe to swim, especially as a large water outlet flowing near our beach spot looked suspiciously like effluence. She replied that for un-acclimatised foreigners it probably wasn't a good idea, but the weather was so warm and the sparkling sea so inviting that I risked a dip anyway, promising myself not to put my head into the water. However, this precaution soon went by the board for Sergio and co grabbed me for a ride on the waterslide and I was pushed, protesting and screaming, down the slippery slope to be dunked unceremoniously in the sea, whereupon every orifice was filled with water. 'Oh well,' I thought, 'if I get cholera, I get cholera.'

Vlad was keen to show us the state of the art deep sea Marine Centre at the port; a newly built terminal, it provides facilities, both military and commercial, for ships from all over the world. At that time there was an American battleship using its services and the sailors were promenading around town with a pretty Ukrainian girl on each arm and wide grins. Though the port complex is impressive, I told Vlad that I would rather explore the old part of town as it was of more interest to me to see something historically Ukrainian rather than a new western design. Old Odessa proved to be a gracious city with many beautiful statues and parks, onion-domed buildings and gilded memorials to state heroes.

I had left my bike back at the hotel and accepted a pillion ride with another Vladimir, a Russian who had travelled down from a town near Moscow to attend the meeting on a 200cc agricultural bike. He certainly set my adrenalin flowing, not only with the pleasure of grasping his slim waist but by riding full pelt along the cobbled streets trying to keep up with visiting Harley Davidson riders. He managed it too. His triumphant grin and look of disbelief and immense satisfaction brought it all home to me; that just a few years ago to be able to ride alongside this type of machinery was impossible because western riders were not allowed into these countries and Russians and Ukrainians weren't allowed out.

I bought a balalaika from a street stall in the park and was assured that it was hand painted by the vendor's mother. Later I wrote a song that its tuning suggested to me. As Odessa is such an important port for many nations, I made it a sailor's song.

Black Sea Pearl

By the sea Odessa, home to me Odessa
Though I sail away, I'll come back home one day to you
La la la la la, la la la la la, la la, la la
No other lady fair can unto you compare
Though I sail away, I'll come back home one day to you
La la la la la, la la la la la, la la, la la
My Black Sea pearl I find you're always on my mind
Though I sail away, I'll come back home one day to you
La la la la la, la la la la la, la la, la la

Boris, a local motorcyclist in his 50s, was most chivalrous and not only helped me fix my puncture but also presented both Hilary and me with an illustrated book about Odessa. He seemed very pleased that we had come all that way to visit 'his' city.

On the final night of the rally the awards were given. As I had made a more circuitous route exploring Romania, I gained the long distance award for 3,000 + miles, and Hilary received the 'best' female award. As she is certainly younger and better looking, I thought this was fair. After all, in east or west a pretty girl is appreciated.

For those of us with the time to spare, a five day tour of the Crimea had been 'arranged'. Vlad wanted the Ukrainian and Polish Strangers to lead the visitors out of Odessa in a grand parade to the peninsular in order to view the various scenic attributes of the area. We were under the impression that overnight stops had been planned at campsites on the tourist route, but this was not to be.

I spent the first few hours trying to keep up with our Polish leaders, who kept not only dropping their string tied luggage off their bikes but also themselves, as the city roads were greasy with oil and recent rain. Our wide variety of riding styles and machines was *not* conducive to group travel. I tried to find out from Vlad the evening's destination so that we could at least all congregate there after setting our own speed and schedule en route. However, it transpired that he hadn't determined one, so we carried on regardless in a general southeasterly direction, obtaining fuel where we could (or in some cases, couldn't). Finally, more by luck than judgement, we did all meet at dusk and camped at the side of the road. At the end of the following day, which passed in a similar fashion, we were at last on the southern side of the Crimean peninsular and found a pretty place to camp by the golden beach. En route I risked being shot when crawling through a hedge to photograph a field full of military helicopters that resembled giant, stationary mosquitoes. However, their drooping rotor blades were rusty and I doubted they would ever fly again. The nearby town had a very interesting museum displaying the life and work of the artist Ivan Aivanovsky, famous (at least in Ukraine) for his sea paintings. Unfortunately, the local police proved rather officious and asked to see all our papers. This was rather embarrassing for an American rally entrant, who, not being allowed more than three days on his visa, had already overstayed his time. We managed to smuggle him away from the danger zone and camped out of town.

Sadly there is always one lunatic who will spoil things for others. While we were chatting on another attractive beach site, someone noticed a black column of smoke drifting upwards in the clear sky. The cause was soon apparent; one of the Polish boys had indulged in too much vodka, overtaken at the wrong time, and ridden his machine into another vehicle. The motorbike had burst into flames and he was badly injured. Poor Vlad and his men had to find a local hospital and sort out the logistical problems of repatriating both man and machine. This occurrence rather brought the group trip to an end. Most people were beginning to feel that their sightseeing and holiday needs would be better achieved under their own steam and supervision, so we split into separate groups.

Hilary, Terry and I wanted to see Balaclava and Sebastopol which were both within a day's ride. We followed the coast road, which was urbanised with holiday houses at this point, and aimed in the direction of these famous towns but were abruptly stopped by police who told us to turn back for we were approaching an off-limits military zone. As a petty official brusquely investigated our passports and our bikes, I smiled sweetly and hummed a recently learnt Ukrainian folk tune in the hope we would appear a little less strange. Hilary, meanwhile, was inwardly panicking, wondering if we'd be taken for spies and shipped off to Siberia. After promising that we would retrace our tracks to the previous main town (which was too far), we immediately took another road and Hilary nearly had a heart attack when a figure at a road block waved us to a halt. However, this time we were allowed through. We were now inland from Yalta, riding up twisting wooded roads to the top of the coastal range. The views of the coastline encompassed sweeping golden beaches and a turquoise sea and, on dropping down into lush green valleys on the other side of the hills, we camped in a small glade which was so prettily overgrown with flowers and ferns we almost expected to see fairies around the lily pond.

Leaving early the next day, before Hilary and Terry rose, I had quite a hunt for fuel and only managed to find 80 octane. Fortunately my spare can contained 5 litres of 90+ from Romania, so I mixed the two and managed to cover the whole distance back to Odessa. I saw none of our group anywhere en route and no-one in Odessa either, so here I was, back on my own again.

Fill Up, Crimea

There didn't seem much point in staying around in the city with no contacts. The music clubs were closed for the summer and I had only 3 days left on my visa anyway, so I planned my northerly route out towards Slovakia. I did not have a detailed map of Ukraine, only one in Cyrillic Script with which I could roughly calculate which towns I should take for my exit point. There was only one main road north to Kiev, which another English couple on a trike, John and Ruth, had taken on their way down and pronounced it to be long, straight and boring and full of trucks and stones. I didn't have much problem finding that road but kept my scarf well up over my face to keep out the diesel fumes, stones and sun. However, the route required a turn off before reaching Kiev on to a minor road and from then on it was a case of matching the squiggles on road signs to squiggles on my map. It was no good stopping to ask as I couldn't pronounce the names and most Ukrainian peasants can't read.

Amazingly, I found the correct roads and travelled through rural countryside looking for a fuel stop. During my unsuccessful search I connected with Hilary and Terry, who were also on their way out of Ukraine. We rode together for a while and camped in a wheat field amongst the biggest marshmallow and cow parsley plants I have ever seen. I knew Ukraine's soil was rich but these were gigantic. Hilary commented that perhaps they were radio-active. I stopped to photograph the antique combine harvesters that were still in use everywhere. It was the height of harvest as here the summer is short and the fields are stripped by the end of July. Wanting to get a closer look at the work, I turned off the road and followed a track to where a group of men were having their tea (vodka?) break. It is in these situations that I wish a) I could speak the language, and b) that I was bigger and stronger and did not look so vulnerable. People watching me manhandle my heavily laden bike have been known to remark that they were *sure* I was going to drop it at any moment, I look so awkward. That's more positive than me—I only *think* I *might*. Quick get-aways are only possible if I'm already on the bike with the engine running. I approached these ruddy faced men tentatively, wanting to ask about their work but I could only smile and point at their machines. They smiled back and gathered round to look at mine as I walked up closer to take a photo of the red monster that spouted a golden shower of grain as it lumbered back and forth across the fields. I really wanted a picture of the men gathered in their faded blue overalls but nerve to ask failed me and I just wriggled back onto the bike and rode away—cursing myself for not trying.

I had been thinking about the famine of the 1930s when the Russians starved the Ukraine by taking away the entire rich crop for their own needs in Moscow. Whilst studying at University in Adelaide I had attended a meeting organised by the Aus/Ukraine Society. An American researcher was collecting information on the Ukraine famine and wanted to meet any of the surviving refugees who had emigrated to Australia. He had footage of the events, somehow taken from the Russian/UK archives; terrible pictures of emaciated people, mass graves and cart loads of the precious grain being snatched away from the producers by Russian guards. After the films came an appeal for any people in the audience who could remember the events to tell him their own stories. At first stunned silence prevailed then, one by one, little old ladies or gents, dressed sombrely in black, stood up and haltingly told personal experiences in their own tongue. The air was thick with emotion and the researcher had to take their names and addresses to continue his interviews later. I had been amazed and deeply moved. Afterwards I spoke to a Ukrainian man as we were eating and drinking our fill at a table spread for us all. He told me that the Russians were responsible for more deaths during that time than Hitler's extermination policy during World War Two. Little did I know that I would be viewing these fields first-hand a few years later.

The scenery changed from wheat fields to green pastures, rivers and ponds that were more reminiscent of Dorset countryside. I began to feel very tired. For the past few days I had been troubled by toothache and it was wearing me down.

Eventually I needed to stop for a while and sleep in a forest for a couple of hours. On resuming my ride I spotted some very interesting graveyards where metal crosses were decorated with tinsel and the entrance to the site was marked with a large, impressive statue. As I stopped for photos, Hilary and Terry once more appeared and we agreed to camp together. It was Sunday afternoon and, in the warm weather, many people were bathing and picnicking by a river in a small town. Terry led us down a dirt track to the river beach and, being hot and dusty, we immediately took a swim amongst the people, who showed no particular interest. I was keen to set up camp though as my tooth was aching, I was very tired and didn't wish to wait until the crowd left. So I left the area and rode around town to look for a less popular spot. For a short time I left the bike to inspect a watermill and when I came back for it a small crowd had gathered. Through sign language we communicated questions and answers. 'Where are you from? How old are you?', and from the women, 'Where is your husband? How many children do you have?' From the young men, 'How fast does your bike go? How many kilometres have you travelled?' They were a friendly crowd, the women just as inquisitive as the men, and I had no trouble communicating and leaving. I road back along the river but away from the beach and on to a green cliff edge. With no-one in sight, I began erecting the tent. Just then I heard the sound of an engine and a Ural motorbike and sidecar came chugging up.

'Oh no,' I thought, 'will I be moved on?'

The two young men approached me smiling and I recognised them from the crowd earlier. It transpired that they had fallen in love with my motorbike and really, really *needed* to ride it. They insisted that I had a ride on their Ural—a slow, lumpy contraption which, of course, I praised, but then it was time for me to offer the BM. I protested that it was very valuable, I was a long way from home, etc, etc, but they pleaded. Then one produced his police badge. At first I thought it was a threat but then realised they were telling me he was a respectable man and I could hold on to his papers as security while he rode my bike. I relented, saying he must only ride it around the field, not on the road. In first gear he bumped around in circles over the uneven grass, grinning from ear to ear, obviously in ecstasy. His mate was jumping up and down with excitement. Of course I let him have a turn and, watching their enjoyment, I was so pleased I had relented. To them a BMW is the ultimate dream machine. Their Urals are poor copies. Had I been feeling more compus mentus, I would have taken a photo for them of their grand moment. However, with the toothache increasing, I just wanted to crawl into my tent and dose myself on wine and Panadol. For a while they just sat and discussed every part of my engine (I thought they would never leave), but eventually they bade me goodbye and good luck and chugged off into the sunset. I took my 'medicine' and collapsed.

Ukraine Police

The ride next day over the hills towards Slovakia was very picturesque. The houses in the villages of the foothills sported decorations of ceramic plaques painted with rural scenes, and I photographed an impressive mural depicting music and peace on what appeared to be a school. The houses changed from brick to wood as the altitude rose and these were brightly painted in deep yellow hues. I espied the golden tower of a church and, riding off the road to find it, discovered that only the spire had been completed and painted – carpenters were still working on the wooden structure beneath. The air was crisp and clean, and on the top of a pass a smiling peasant woman sold carved wooden plaques, boxes and, of course, Russian dolls.

At the Slovakia/Ukraine border I met Hilary and Terry again and, after we passed through, we said our final farewells for they were riding on to a rally in Austria whilst I aimed to explore as much as possible of the Czech Republic/Slovakia. My last time here was in 1967 during my trip to Moscow, and I wanted to see the changes.

Chapter Twenty-Three

Slovakia And The Tooth Fairy

Slovakia is the poor relative of the once combined Czechoslovakia but nevertheless, the roads were still markedly better than anything I had traversed further east. It was a relief to be able to view the scenery rather than dodge potholes, and this is worth viewing for it shows a country of steep mountains, fertile valleys and wild rivers.

After two days of 'civilisation', staying at a campsite in Kosice and exploring the town's museums, I headed for the Tatry mountains in the hope of leaving the bike for a while to go hiking. Unfortunately rain set in again and I was riding once more in full wet weather gear with a visor. Out of the mist of low cloud loomed the towers of Spisske Podhrad, the largest castle in Slovakia.

I turned towards it and, as I rode up the small winding road to the ruins, the BM spluttered and stopped. The road was on a steep slope and I couldn't dismount. My visor was misting up and I was stuck.

'BM,' I pleaded, 'please don't stop here.' I tried the start button and she spluttered and choked but wouldn't take. 'Now come on, BM, this won't do, just make it to the top of the hill and I promise I'll give you a rest. You can't stop here.' If another vehicle came up or down the road, there would be trouble for I was blocking it.

There was no turn off.

I needed to roll backwards to move to the side, a difficult manoeuvre even when it wasn't raining and I could see.

Now it was impossible.

However, the angel smiled again. I pushed the button: the BM grudgingly came back to life and we reached the car park.

The castle was founded in the thirteenth century and used as defence against the Tartars, then as the administrative centre for the Spis region until it burnt down in the late eighteenth century. Its ruins are spectacular and at that time, 1995, had been partly restored to house a museum. There, among the armour and the cannons, I found a young woman playing classical guitar.

After a tour around the remains of the castle walls, which afford panoramic views of the surrounding open countryside when the clouds lift, I returned to play a few tunes with the musician. She was a music student in Kosice and we exchanged addresses to keep in touch.

The pine clad Tatry mountains have hidden lakes, cable cars and many marked and unmarked walking tracks. They straddle the border of Slovakia and Poland and their beauty attracts hikers from many countries, especially in the summer. Finding a campsite in the foothills, I entered the office to book in for the night and, to my horror, was unable to find my passport. I searched my bags and panniers and tried not to panic. Where did I last have it?

I had needed it to change money at the tourist bureau in Kosice the previous day. The campsite proprietor was charming and rang the tourist office immediately. Yes, it was there: what a relief!

I had never mislaid a passport before.

After an uncomfortable night, during which heavy rain flooded the site, I found a workshop to weld my pannier brackets. They had been broken for some time and the bike was wobbling in an alarming manner. The repair effected, I rode back towards Kosice but by a different route.

About 30 kilometres out I passed a few very slow-moving vehicles on a hill and, in doing so, crossed a continuous centre line, but I could see well ahead before the brow of the hill and took no chances.

Over the hill the road swooped down into an open valley and I was riding at an even pace when I reached the flat plain. A police car parked at the roadside had beside it a uniformed officer who waved me down.

'Passport please,' he spoke a little English.

'No passport,' I said, wondering what difficulties this might cause. 'It's in Kosice.' I pointed ahead.

'At hotel?' he asked. 'No. Bank.'

'Problem,' he said, walking around me, looking at the bike.

'Oh,' I murmured, keeping as calm as possible and waiting for the next move. He pointed back along the road.

'You pass on the line there.' I was gob-smacked. It had been about 3 kilometers before and I hadn't seen any police vehicles or personnel. How did they know?

'You must pay a fine.' he said. I gulped. There was another policeman sitting in the car and he produced a selection of bank notes which the first policeman brought over to show me. 500 crowns, about £20: in Slovak terms a lot of money. I had just 500 crowns on me, but I wasn't about to admit this.

'Problem,' I said. 'No passport – no money.' 'Where is your husband?' he asked.

'Problem,' I said again. 'No passport, no money, no husband.' This last piece of information must have at last struck some chord of pity in him for he rolled his eyes, waved his hand and said: 'Going.'

I 'goinged' as fast as I could.

In Kosice I retrieved my passport and retraced my route, but this time turned off to find something I had never seen before. I love display caves and have visited many in different parts of the world, but have never entered an ice cave. Instead of passing the usual surrounding limestone formations, the route in this case ran through a tunnel of ice which glowed blue and yellow in the guide's light. Obviously the temperature was low. The caves are created by water flowing into natural limestone cavities in parts of the mountain ranges that have frozen and never re-warmed sufficiently to melt the ice. Unfortunately, as the guide spoke entirely in Slovak, I could gather little else of the cave's history, but it was obviously a popular tourist attraction and permanent, as the usual show cave trappings of postcards and souvenirs surrounded the well-demarked entrance.

I abandoned the idea of hiking because of the poor weather and my lack of proper equipment to deal with it. Also, my toothache was getting worse so I became increasingly anxious to arrive at Uhersky Brod in Czech Republic where a friend from the UK was teaching English. Just before crossing the border between the two countries, I stopped for lunch by a small dam in which a man was fishing while a woman and child looked on. The mother and daughter smiled at me and threw out a few tentative words in English. We managed to make ourselves understood and they told me that the husband was only fishing here for fun, throwing back the fish that he caught.

'Why don't you eat them?' I mimed and learnt that the water was badly polluted by the factory upstream where the man worked. Regulations and controls on industry were not very strict here so many fish were poisonous.

The mother had learnt a little English many years ago at school and was clearly fishing in her brain to draw out the few words she could remember. As I spoke she nodded with delight on recognising a word. She was very interested in my travels, told me in which part of Slovakia her family originated and described their simple life. She said that they didn't have much money but were reasonably content. The husband came over, smiled and nodded and helped me turn my bike around when I left.

I had to endure more rain, thunder and lightning before I finally pulled up outside my friend's house in Uhersky Brod. During the four years since I'd last seen Andy he had settled in Czech Republic, marrying Stanya, another teacher, and was well-established among local artists and musicians as well as the teaching fraternity. We celebrated our reunion with bottles of good wine which helped to deaden my pain. Stanya arranged a dental appointment for me at 9.30 the following morning, a feat impossible in the UK.

That night I slept in a huge antique Czech marriage bed. As is normal in Czech culture Stanya, on marrying, had inherited her family house complete with family—in this case her father and grandmother. The grandmother now lived in the top floor of the house which comprised a huge bedroom and a kitchen/dining room. Since the death of her husband a dozen or so years previously, the old woman no longer slept in the bedroom, but on a sofa in the kitchen. The bedroom was reserved for visitors. I almost needed a stepladder to climb up onto the tall wooden bed, beautifully covered with embroidered pillowcases and counterpane.

Stanya's father, an accountant, had a separate room on the ground floor next to her and Andy's apartment. The basement was a neutral zone where various community possessions and the washing machine lived. It was obviously an upper middle class household and though Stanya wanted more space for her expanding family (she had a 6 year old son from a previous relationship and was pregnant by Andy), by Czech standards they all lived well.

Andy took me to the dentist in their Lada and came into the surgery to translate. I explained that the tooth troubling me, a rear molar, had already been crowned and was obviously bad beneath the capping. Would Andy, I asked, please translate my preference to keep the tooth, if possible, in order to avoid the 'saggy jaw' look?

I 'opened wide' and the middle-aged, craggy-faced man at whose mercy I found myself, tapped various teeth with his metal poker. He found the one I had already pointed out when I jumped about two feet in the air. Somewhat gung-ho, I thought.

He and Andy exchanged words and my friend explained that the dentist wanted to remove it. Of course, I nodded; he would have to take off the crown to investigate the extent of the damage.

'I need an injection,' I said. 'I'm very sensitive to pain.' 'Yes, it's normal,' the dentist replied.

'Make it a strong one,' I gurgled as the needle came into view. For about 5 minutes Andy and the dentist chatted in Czech while my gums went numb, then I lent back. A large pair of pliers was inserted into my mouth and I felt a strong pulling sensation. 'Gosh, I thought, 'this crown is on tight.' Then a wrenching feeling and the pain. I gurgled and screamed in the back of my throat, grasping the chair arms, my knuckles white.

Andy said—'Hold onto my hand, Linda. It's okay!' I squeezed his fingers tightly. A further wrench and then, to my shock and horror, I saw my whole tooth, roots dangling, pass by my astonished face. *The whole tooth!* The dentist hadn't meant removing the crown at all.

'Rinse out, please.' Shaking like a leaf and bleeding like a stuck pig, I lay back in the chair trembling while the dentist smiled and wiped his hands. 'No tooth, no problem,' he said. I wasn't sure whether to agree or not at this stage.

With a prescription for antibiotics and painkillers I left the surgery in a daze. Having been instructed not to drink alcohol or eat peanuts for a while. I meekly followed Andy to the chemist where we loaded up with my drugs. Andy said cheerily:

'I'll take you to visit my artist friends.' Well, I'm normally the most social and gregarious of people, but I must say, at this moment I was literally speechless. A mouthful of blood and frozen, immobile lips didn't bode well for holding sparkling conversations. I managed to persuade him that I needed a lie-down first: I felt completely shattered.

That afternoon I rallied and was taken to meet Lubja, a cheerful chubby lady, and her family. On hearing of my recent dental experiences this friendly bunch insisted that I need slivovitch. I protested that alcohol was off limits whilst I was taking the antibiotics.

'Ah, but it's medicinal, slivovitch; it's made with herbs.' It seems that to obtain the full curative effect it's necessary for you *and your friends* to take several glasses full. The formula was a success: the dull pain where my tooth used to be subsided, my whole head became lighter.

Live folk music is very popular in Czech Republic and in the summer many festivals are held in the numerous castles around the countryside. Lubja and her family were attending one that night, so we all squeezed into Andy's car and drove to the event. Parking about two kilometers from the castle we joined many other people converging on the various performance areas. In one, a country group played from the back of a truck singing 'Country roads' in Czech. Many young people sat around listening, drinking beer from paper cups and eating hot sausages. Most of them were dressed in casual clothes, with walking boots and some carried sleeping bags.

We also indulged in a beer, then walked further uphill and entered inside the castle walls to the main stage area. There followed one of the most friendly outdoor castle concerts I can remember, for the P.A. wasn't too loud and the crowd was attentive and appreciative. The audience were mainly young people but nevertheless, there didn't seem to be any marijuana smoking and drinking was minimal. No fights, no abuse and the folk artists performed brilliantly, encouraging the audience to sing with them. After their separate spots all the performers came up on stage to sing together in a finale that had everyone on their feet and belting out obvious favourites. I joined in too . . . I can 'la, la, la' in Czech with the best of them.

I stayed with Andy and Stanya for several days, not only because I enjoyed their company and the interesting area around, but because the tooth business had weakened me and I needed the rest. Moreover, it was possible to buy tapes and songbooks of traditional Czech music. With Stanya's help I was able to obtain translations. I also wrote 'Odessa Odyssey' out in full from my notes along the way.

On feeling a little stronger I made a trip to Zlin to see the shoe museum. How many people know that the Bata shoe shop, seen in almost every high street in the western world, had its origins in a little Czech family firm of shoemakers? I didn't. It's certainly a rags to riches story. The family business survived the war and the loss of one of their directors (a brother) in a plane crash. His sister carried on, to turn the company finally into a multinational corporation which even has outlets in China. The museum showed examples of shoe fashions from all over the world and many eras.

The Czech people I met in this part of the country were musical, artistic and well educated. Although through the new capitalist system consumerism, drug culture and other vices from the West are filtering in, at that moment (1995)—at least in the country areas I visited—it appeared to be a gentle, friendly and open place; I never felt threatened. It seemed to be at the point of having enough wealth not to need to steal from, nor aggressively sell to tourists—as in Morocco—but not too much to be paranoically protective as in the USA.

My last day in the Czech Republic was spent crossing through Bohemia where I unexpectedly came across a castle which housed a motorcycle museum. I was the only tourist there at that time. My attractive English-speaking guide informed me that the museum was there because the local town, Pacov, had a race track and one of the first motorcycle races held there in 1904, gave birth to the FIM (Federation of International Motorcyclists). I excitedly told her that I attended an FIM rally in Moscow in 1967. She was very impressed and even let me take photos, a practice that was usually prohibited in the building.

Emerging from the castle into the sunshine I spied two GB-plated motorbikes in the car park alongside my BM. When I connected with the riders I discovered one was another WIMA member, Audrey Amson. She and her partner kindly shared their lunch with me in the castle gardens and told me they were on a touring holiday, taking in a Grand Prix in Prague. It was a very pleasant meeting and I rode away thinking how nice it was to meet other motorcyclists on the road and to feel part of a family. Audrey and I had never met before but we had an immediate rapport as women motorcyclists.

That night I camped alone by a lake. It was a local fishing spot and the lights of a campsite twinkled from the opposite shore; little boat houses and fishing ramps were on mine and the sunset was calm and rosy. There was a full moon and I was in a reflective mood. I felt that the end of my eastern trip was nigh, for the next day I would be in very civilised Germany. I had many friends to catch up with between here and Spain, but it was now back to familiar ground, however, my foray into Eastern Europe and Ukraine had been most enjoyable and I hoped to return once more, before it was too spoilt.

As the guide books said, facilities and commodities were lacking in the East. The shops and roadside markets were desperately short of food; restaurants had very limited menus. Not being a fussy eater, this didn't worry me, but I could see that these shortages must be frustrating for other tourists, and perhaps unhealthy for the locals existing on a limited diet. However, there had been many interesting things to see, and people still knew how to communicate with each other, especially through music and dance. Technology hadn't taken over and a woman on a motorbike was not too far out of their reality to appear either too rich or threatening. People's reactions and behaviour had been interesting in comparison to that of Morocco: in the latter, when I stopped, children would appear out of nowhere to crowd around the bike, hands held out for dirhams or cadeaux. Adults too were not backward in coming forward, always looking for a chance to engage a foreigner in conversation, or make some money from them. In the eastern countries children were shy and wary, often running to hide behind bushes on my appearance, rather than jumping out from them. The adults were also slow to communicate, with a wariness that had no doubt been born of previous propaganda against 'wicked' westerners. However, once I broke through the wall of suspicion, they proved friendly and helpful.

Chapter Twenty-Four

Ja, We Have Ways Of Fixing Your Bike

Another mountain range delineated the border between Czech Republic and Germany. Leaving the eastern country the objects that caught my eye were row on row of garden gnomes. The Germans must sneak into Czech Republic to buy them. Does a Czech gnome have more magical qualities, or is it just cheaper? (like the dentist).

Arriving at my first German village, Fuhr in the Wold, I stopped to change money and, in exploring this picture postcard town, found a dragon workshop. Every year a traditional dragon-slaying story is re-enacted here. The star of the show was undergoing a re-spray and general tart-up for his appearance the following week. I wished I could stay for the spectacular, but time was running out.

The route to my friend Heiner's house appeared to be simple on the map and not too far, but I had forgotten to take into consideration the volume of traffic in West Germany so the journey took far longer than I had anticipated. However, Heiner wasn't due to finish work until 5 p.m. and I arrived shortly after his homecoming. We shared the traditional beer in celebration of our reunion. Heiner is another touring motorcyclist that I had met in Faro, Portugal, the previous year at the rally. When I had rung him from Czech Republic he was delighted to know I was in his part of the world and invited me to stay.

Heiner, Germany (at rear and following page)

During the next few days my host and other members of this Haefale MCC, Elmar and Rudi, took me around their local scene and, most

importantly, checked over the bike. We found the pannier brackets to be broken again, but worse, the frame had fractured too. The Eastern roads sure were rough. No wonder the bike had been handling awkwardly. Not only did Heiner organise the welding but he gave me a set of larger and newer panniers to enable me to cope with my ever-growing mass of souvenirs and music tapes. He also typed up Odessa Odyssey on his word processor and we faxed it to friends in many countries.

At the end of my stay Heiner, Elmar and Rudi rode down to the south of Germany with me, in pouring rain to deliver me to another friend near Lindau. This was a woman whom I had met in Australia many years previously because of a Harro tank bag. This is the story:

I, riding the same bike, and Coral, another WIMA member, were travelling from Adelaide in South Australia along the Great Ocean Road into Victoria. We were taking a week's holiday just to relax among the rock pools. On stopping for fish and chips we noticed a 250 Yamaha parked nearby with a Harro bag on its tank.

'They must be Germans,' I said of the momentarily absent riders, for Germany is where this make of tank bags originates. I have one myself. Sure enough, when the two riders, a man and a woman, came back to their bike, we found out they were indeed from Germany, touring Australia. As they were heading toward Adelaide I told them not to bother with a campsite but to go to my house and camp in the garden. My boyfriend Bill would look after them. So they did and a week later, when I arrived home, they were still there, having a great time because the annual beer fest in the village of Handorf in the Adelaide hills was on. After her return to Germany the girl, Pia, had kept in touch and offered me hospitality whenever I was in her part of the world. This time round Pia had a new boyfriend, Marcus, a young carpenter (Zimmermann) just finishing his apprenticeship and about to go on his 'Wanderschaft'. This is a journey into the unknown for young tradesmen and women proving themselves to be not just good trades people but also able to survive in a world away from their own environment. Indeed, they are not allowed to return to within 50 kilometres of their home town for three years and a day. Traditionally they must walk or hitchhike, carrying their 'Charlottenburger' rolls and tools on their backs. They work for their keep, or whatever arrangement can be made to include accommodation. Their dress is traditional: black serge trousers and waistcoat decorated with white pearl buttons, and a white shirt. They carry only one change of clothes which are similar. A wide-brimmed hat, often decorated with a feather, adorns their heads. The idea began in the eleventh century when manual workers and craftsmen joined brotherhoods, mainly for their survival. They aimed to ensure their income and keep, to improve their social standing and free themselves of dependence on authority.

During the twelfth and thirteenth centuries construction increased throughout Europe and, as most houses were built in wood until the eighteenth century, the carpentry section comprised a varied range of jobs. Not only did the carpenters construct the houses, but also designed and decorated them. As they were responsible for so much, the carpenters' guilds were held in high esteem. To keep their good reputation, many regulations were enforced, but it was not until the fourteenth century that 'footing it' (Wanderschaft) was construed as a duty. This was done to broaden the intellectual and vocational horizons of the journeymen on their way to becoming master carpenters; they travelled not only in their homelands but also internationally. However, the tradition of 'footing it' gradually came to a standstill after the mid-nineteenth century. Industrialisation, new building materials and the construction boom not only ousted the carpenters but also altered their outlook. Tradition was no longer in vogue.

But, with the rediscovery of wood in recent years, carpentry has regained its importance and the journeymen are on the road again. Depending on the possibilities and fancy of the journeyman he/she can travel anywhere. Use of public transport is frowned on but not forbidden in certain circumstances.

Their travel book, a kind of passport, helps them to find work and obtain permits. Some journeymen belong to large guilds and participate in their activities at certain times during the year.

Others prefer to be more independent. However, all are aware of each other's guilds and keep in contact. When they meet on the road there is usually great celebration and most of them are familiar with the traditional songs and the carpenters' hand clap and chorus. Following the walking out period, the journeyman becomes a local outsider and continues to participate in the activities of the guild. He/she can now go on to become a master carpenter with his/her added international knowledge. Any building worker can become a member of the guild as long as he/she is unmarried and not more than 30 years of age.

Marcus filled these requirements. He was an attractive and enthusiastic Bavarian, keen to see the world. As I was talking about the two ruins I was now the proud owner of in Andalucia, his eyes lit up. It was proposed that he talked to his fellow Zimmermann and maybe make a plan for them to come and work on my house in the coming winter. Pia, who has her own landscape gardening business, was keen to come too as winter was a quiet time for her business in Germany. I promised to send some photos of the houses so they would know what they were letting themselves in for.

The area around the lake at Lindau was packed with summer traffic and I threaded my way carefully between cars and was relieved to pick up the motorways in Switzerland. I was now on my way to find Peter and Annemeike Salzgeber, a couple I had met on the campsite in Spain in 1993. They had then been about to embark on a trans-Africa expedition on their Yamahas. They had celebrated the completion of their trip by marrying in Cape Town. Now back in

Switzerland, Peter had taken over his father's steel working business. I was looking forward to hearing all about their adventures in Africa.

The town in which Peter and Annemeike live, Davos Dorf, is high in the mountains, set in a wide valley. Its clean fresh air attracted many physicians trying to find a cure for TB in the early twentieth century. Sanatoriums were built, patients often being wrapped in blankets and put up on the flat roofs, specially designed for this purpose. Brrr. Sounded a bit kill or cure to me. Now it is mainly a ski resort and a tourist town, very clean, expensive, with many hotels and shops full of exquisite art and handicrafts, not to mention watches, music boxes and Swiss army knives!

I arrived at Pete's steel works on the same day he took delivery of a new twenty thousand pound sterling steel cutting machine. We drank champagne, pouring some over it and then christened it 'Linda'. Now that beats having a mere baby named after you!

Peter and Annemeicke are both tall, making me feel a real midget, both fun-loving and caring. Annemeike has a wide collection of folk music. She is Dutch but speaks English, French, German and Swiss German so was able to tell me of popular songs in many different languages. We sang some together and I took photocopies for my collection.

As it is an early start for the working day here, the family custom is to have lunch from 12-1, an enormous meal including wine. I usually felt like collapsing afterwards, but everyone went happily back to work. One afternoon after such a meal, Peter took the car to drop me off some miles outside the town for a guided tour of an historic silver mine. With my tummy full of food and wine I wasn't expecting to climb a kilometre up a steep hill in order to gain access. The mine was worked in both the fourteenth and nineteenth centuries in a search for silver and zinc, but was very low yield. It was in a deeply forested area high in the mountains—very scenic, but not a particularly hospitable spot for the two hundred workers who lived there summer and winter.

On another occasion Peter gave himself time off work to escort me up the mountain, in the cable car, so we could enjoy the walk back down. The views were stunning, snow-capped mountains, rainbows arcing over the valley's lake and a real bird's eye view of the flat roofs of Davos Dorf. I didn't spot any frozen TB patients. It gave me a chance to stretch my legs after many miles of motorcycling and increased my appetite for the evening meal!

When the time came for me to drag myself away from their excellent hospitality, Peter rode his XT600 Yamaha fifty kilometres with me along my southerly route. I was aiming for the Chamonix region of France. The BM was going well but I was battling to keep up with Peter who knew the roads. After we said our good-byes it took me the rest of the day, with one stop to refuel the bike with petrol and my body with Swiss chocolate, to reach my destination of Pombliere, in the Savoie district. I found myself riding along a scenic valley floor, somewhat spoilt by industrialisation, whilst looking for the home of Kheira, an Algerian woman married to a Frenchman. I had met the couple in Chefchaouen at the Youth Hostel a few years before. Kheira, though only French-speaking, had befriended me and had wanted me to visit her in France if I could.

When I arrived Bernard, her husband, was away. Kheira had an Algerian friend, Omar, from the Sahara desert, visiting. During the course of the evening he played an Algerian instrument and Kheira donned her black traditional dress. With her head and body totally covered and only her dark, flashing eyes visible, I was aurally and visually transported from France to the south of Algeria. I had to use my rusty French again and bedded down, Arab style, on a carpet on the floor. A great contrast to the duvet covered bed in Davos Dorf. Having travelled over four hundred kilometres and wound my way over three passes that day I slept soundly anyway.

Kheira, though quite heavily pregnant, took me on a walk to meet Jaques, a friend who lived in the village. He worked in the local sodium factory and explained that the main product was used for explosives and medicines and the bi-product, chloride, for bleaches and disinfectant. As he worked in temperatures of 600 degrees, he could only do so for fifteen minutes at one time and then had to rest for one hour. Very stressful work and, now in his late forties, he didn't know how much longer he could cope with it. Also, a lone traveller, he was feeling the urge to move on again. He lent me his beautiful Ovation guitar for the evening so I could sing and play for Omar and Kheira, which we all enjoyed.

Kheira piled me high with more food parcels (Peter and Annemeike had already given me a large box full of goodies) and I rode out into a cool and misty morning, leaving the mountains behind me to find the Ardeche valley. Through the lush vegetation I spied a huge iron bridge and, on turning off to explore, found it was the Pont de Airun, built at the beginning of the 1900's. It took seven years to build and is one of the chief metal constructions in France, along with the Eiffel Tower.

To shelter from a heavy thunderstorm I visited a horse museum. Funny to think that all the motorised vehicles we take for granted today, fire engines, buses, combine harvesters and so on, once all used horsepower. The number of connected trades such as wheelwrights, blacksmiths and coachbuilders who had to adapt their skills or perish when the engine took over, makes one realise that progress forces us to be flexible. It's the old 'If you can't beat them, join them,' attitude. After all, the Luddites didn't last.

My route to the French/Spanish border was through Toulouse, an impressive city with canals and art galleries, but I didn't stay long. The road into the Pyrenees climbed up into mountain scenery and through a long dark tunnel. Road works hampered my progress, but it gave me a chance to catch up with an English motorcycle group of about fifty riders touring the Pyrenees area. Their bikes were all gleaming, their leather and Goretex jackets smart: they were staying in good hotels and dining in expensive restaurants. Quite a different type of trip to the one I had just done. The BM looked very worn and tatty against their mounts—no doubt I did too!

As I rode over the high passes and down into Spain, the weather immediately warmed and the landscape suddenly appeared Spanish. I rode through colourful gorges and, despite a few thunderstorms with heavy rain, the terrain was generally parched. It took me a long time to find a camping spot. Though far from ideal, it was off the road and I settled down to munch away at the contents of the box of goodies donated by my kind friends.

Down on the Spanish plains, the road was straight and fast. I was attracted by the sight of a hillside fortress, Medinaceli, so turned off to investigate. The small village had been a Roman settlement and still proudly retained an archway from that period. Bypassing Madrid, which stank of rubbish, I went to look at Toledo. The weather was very hot by now and I needed a beer. I liked the hilltop town and spent some time wandering around its narrow, cobbled streets that were filled with people in holiday mode.

That night I found a camping spot amongst eucalyptus trees by a dry creek bed and really felt at home—it could have been Australia. However, although feeling safe initially, I slept badly as there were strange noises outside the tent. It may have been a wild pig, but there were no animal tracks visible next morning.

In heat which was typical of Spain in August, I followed the road to Cordoba. I had eaten all my chocolate and cheese the night before so that it wouldn't melt. The shade of Cordoba's famous mosque was most welcome. I stood within the mixture of Moorish and Spanish architecture at last, gazing in awe at the decorative arches and ceilings: it had long been on my list of important sights to see.

Nearer home, it was with difficulty that I found the minor road from Antequera to Alora, then the further track to Marbella. When I did eventually locate the correct route it was worth the trouble, winding over dry hills and past villages where Spanish peasants were pulling water from wells and using donkeys for their transport. The poverty level was astonishing. Only a few kilometres away is the affluent tourist region of the Costa del Sol yet these local people are living in third world conditions. I thought back over my trip, of the poverty in the east, but realised that some Spanish are just as badly off. We live in a strange world, often not looking outside our own social and economic circles to see the inequalities around us.

I visited friends in Estepona on the last leg of the journey to Castellar, stalling, not too happy to be finishing the trip. It had taken seven weeks, covering over seven thousand miles. The BM had done very well as usual; the only problems I'd had were with the points corroding, especially in bad weather, then the pannier brackets and frame breaking on the exceptionally bad roads in the Eastern countries.

The bike deserved a rest and would soon get it.

Part Three

Closing The Gap

Chapter Twenty-Five

Castellar Again

The south of Spain in August is hot and sticky; I hoped the next month would bring cooler weather. More importantly, I was praying that the junkies on the doorstep had left. Slowly I rode up the hill towards my house, the air becoming hotter and thicker as I rose.

To my relief the driveway was empty on my arrival, but my enthusiasm was soon dampened where I saw who was inside, sitting grinning on the patio. It was my landlord, the errant owner, PW. I had last heard that he was on the run from both the Spanish and Gibraltar authorities. While he was impounded in Gibraltar on his boat, awaiting the case for his extradition to Germany, I had not needed to have any direct dealings with him, other than handing over the rent once a month in Gibraltar. But later, his solicitor advised him that he would lose his final appeal and face imprisonment. So, just before I went to Ukraine, he and his British girlfriend skidaddled, living wild in the campo. After two months, tired of this rough life, they had decided to risk coming back to his Spanish house and, without keys to enter, they were sleeping on the roof of the other half of the building to my area. Wonderful!

I did my best to be polite and hide my distaste for their habits of drinking and dope-smoking themselves silly morning, noon and night, and for their constant arguing. It had been my intention to stay in the rented house for a while in order to take stock of what needed doing on the two cottages and, over two or three months, to make the better one liveable. I had thought there was no rush and also delaying an immediate move was a school show, planned for the autumn: a money-earner that took priority. However, finding a wanted criminal on my doorstep, it became immediately obvious that the best thing to do was to get out as soon as possible. I had to abandon the plans for the show and work all the daylight hours on my number one house.

Where Angels Fear To Tread

The little house was of indeterminate age, as in Spain the paperwork often comes many years after the construction. It is very hard to prove any dates on deeds much before the 1980s. The previous owner, Rafael, thought it was at least 40 years old. It had initially been built as a single oblong structure, 7 meters long and 3 1/2 wide. The sandstone walls were half a metre thick, with only two small windows in the front. The roof was made of eucalyptus beams covered with fibre board and tiles. Onto one end, however, two other rooms had been added in brick at a later date: a bedroom, access to which had necessitated making a doorway in the previous outside end wall, and a kitchen. This was tagged onto the outside of the bedroom and not connected. To this day in winter I still have to run outside, along the patio, in the pouring rain with wellies and raincoat to make a cup of tea. The original kitchen was also separate, but on the other end of the house, little more than a lean-to shed with a low asbestos roof. Rafael called it the Rat House, as it was indeed riddled with them.

The first thing I would need to do was clear the house of all the rubbish inside, then put down a proper tiled patio outside to stop all the dust being blown and trodden into the house while I re-decorated. The walls were just covered inside and out with cal (lime whitewash); I wanted to do a proper paint job. But before even that was possible, water needed to be piped down from the communal well, about 100 metres away in the rocks above and behind the houses. So, whilst still in the rented house amongst the druggies, I ordered pipes, sand, cement and tiles and looked for a Spanish workman.

Unfortunately, far from being able to concentrate on this house there was an unexpected problem with the other, more derelict one. As previously agreed, PC had stayed in it for the summer, but had now moved back to his Winnebago a few miles away, leaving a great deal of rubbish and personal effects in my house. Whenever he came to Castellar I was expecting him to empty the premises and to hand back the keys but he ignored me, seemingly very involved with PW and between them there appeared to be some sort of skulduggery afoot. On his next visit I asked him to remove everything that was his and clean up the house: I'd been back two weeks and he'd had plenty of time to do this. To my utter astonishment he flew into a rage, dragged everything out of the house, including some of the original furniture I'd bought with the property, and left it in a heap on the front patio.

'But, P——, when are you coming to take your things away?'

I couldn't understand what the problem was, but I was beginning to get some very nasty vibes from this man.

'I'll come back and set a match to the lot of it,' he snarled at me as he jumped on his bike and rode away.

I was confused and worried. What had got into him? We had discussed his occupation of the house months before when I bought it. He had been looking after it for the previous owner but had been prepared to leave when I took over. As he had work in the village and I had had no immediate need for the property, I had no objection to his staying on for a while. In fact, it was preferable for me to have someone in it that I knew, rather than it remain empty and a target for squatters. The previous year a fire had been started in an empty house when careless travellers had not fully doused a barbecue fire. With the tinder-dry conditions and a strong wind, the flames took hold, swept up the hill and threatened the whole village. It took seventeen air drops, using water from the dam, to quench it. As I was to be away for most of this summer, it had seemed preferable to both Peter and I that he stayed on until I returned in the autumn. This was all fully discussed and agreed to. Why then had he turned aggressive, and why was everything in such a mess?

I continued work on my house—hoping that Peter would explain and remove his rubbish given a little longer. I waited four days. Nothing happened. I felt embarrassed that my property resembled a junk yard. Something had to be done. I rescued the original table which now had its legs falling off and, after mending it, stored it to use as my writing desk. Peter's personal effects and other furniture he had collected I gave to PW to look after as it seemed that PC was likely to move into my old living area—if and when PW had to move on. The rest of the rubbish I loaded into Hekel and took to the tip. At last, after two days of hard labour, the place was cleared and I could resume work on my own accommodation.

I found the whole situation strange and disturbing. Whenever I saw PC he was unfriendly and would not tell me what the problem was. I could not understand what was going on and wondered what I had let myself in for, buying two properties in this area where such crazy people lived. Was I one myself? How I longed for some moral as well as physical support in this job I had ahead of me. At least on my return from Ukraine there had been a letter from Georgia, but it had been written in Senegal back in July and contained very worrying news. She had been seriously ill with hemorrhaging, followed by anemia and infections. All this was caused by internal cysts and she wanted to return to Canada, leaving Senegal early in September. 'Near-death experiences have made me long to return home,' she wrote.

Georgia assured me in the letter that she had been well looked after and now felt on the road to recovery. She asked if I could come in August to see her, gave a phone and fax number in Senegal and sent her love. Of course, by now it was too late and I couldn't get away. I had known something had been wrong; she was lucky to be alive. I was glad she was going home, at least to be in a clean hygienic environment for a while. Georgia said she wasn't sure how long her stay in Canada would be, as her intention was to leave there when in better health, perhaps to visit me again in Spain. Well, at least someone loved me. I needed the positive thoughts and good wishes to keep me going amidst this strange atmosphere of hate. Suddenly I had an idea—I could try ringing this number: it was early September and maybe she was still there. I rushed to a friend's house to find a phone, dialed the number she had given me and an African male voice answered.

'Est-ce que c'est possible parler avec Georgia, s'il vous plaît?' I nervously asked.

'Georgia?'

'Oui, Georgia. C'est Linda.' 'Un moment s'il vous plaît.'

I heard the man call her name and mine. There was a squeal of delight increasing in volume as she rushed to the phone.

'How are you, Georgia?'

'I'm fine; it's wonderful to hear you.'

'When are you leaving for Canada?' I asked hurriedly—just how much was a phone call to Senegal? I had no idea.

'Next week,' she replied.

'As soon as you get back give me a telephone or fax number and I'll try and make a plan to get over to see you in Canada.'

'Oh I will, I'll write straight away.' 'Good luck and take care, Georgia.' 'Goodbye my sweet sister.'

Amazing, the wonders of modern science. Over all these miles we could speak to each other. I felt better, although I didn't know if could go to Canada, I'd bloody well try.

Sand and gravel were delivered to cement the outside area so I could park the BM, Hekel and the caravan by the house. The delivery truck could not fully negotiate the narrow driveway so all the materials were dumped one hundred feet short. In the first two cool hours of the morning I would fill a wheelbarrow and push it up to the house. Little by little, bit by bit, ten spadesful of gravel at a time, I moved the pile until there was enough to start the mix. During the heat of the day I attacked the inside of the house, one by one bringing thirty eucalyptus logs stored in the lounge, filling black plastic bags full of remnants of old papers and clothes chewed by the rats. After ferrying all the rubbish to the tip I found a young Spaniard to mix the concrete and lay tiles for the patio. His first job was piping down the water so we could mix the cement. I acted as navvy to speed up the procedure as I was keen to move my caravan away from its present position, to start painting inside the house and to put in another window though the 1/2 metre wall. This last job was a bit tricky. It seemed better to have the Spaniard help, but he disappeared, so another girl and I took a sledge hammer to the area and, when large sandstone blocks fell away producing a huge gaping hole, we were committed. The window went in and the painting was completed. Knowing the rains were due in October, I found two more village lads to help fit gutters to collect the rain water in a barrel. By the middle of the month I was ready to move in. The night I did so, Foster and Allan in concert on my radio lent a friendly, familiar tone to the occasion as I sat in my hastily painted bedroom by the light of a kerosene lamp, toasting myself, my new house and Georgia with wine. The name of the paint colour I had used for the bedroom was 'harp' and I knew Georgia was thinking of me, as I was thinking of her. I prayed that she had completely recovered and that I could somehow get to Canada to see her.

A few weeks later, a letter arrived with her new address, phone number and an article written for her local church.

MUSINGS FROM OUR WANDERING MINSTREL

On a Sunday October morning in Canada I'm missing Africa. Looking out from a tenth floor apartment I see trees in gold, brown, the maroons of Autumn, the Thames river tranquil, rows of pristine houses on paved roads and I wonder what makes me long for that other world. Upon entering third world countries I was struck by poverty and its dominating presence in the city, country, on street corners, hungry hands pounding buses. Poverty in their faces, eyes and hunger in their bellies. Hunger changes perception it becomes the only priority. It was depressing to feel one person's powerlessness at dealing with it. Knowing there are limits on our financial contributions and also that it is not always the best answer, rarely a long term solution. Kindness worked and encouragement. We both got something out of that.

There were many levels of poverty to look at. Young African boys born of extremely poor families are often placed in a teacher's guardianship. This teacher of religious studies provides the boys with shelter. Twenty to thirty youths live in one room, perhaps they have a mat to sleep on. The boys are equipped with a tin can. They walk the streets accumulating leftover food or begging for coins. At the school which is usually a patch of dirt outside their sleeping quarters the children are instructed in lessons of the Islamic faith. Unfortunately there is an accent on corporal punishment. It is thought that a lesson beaten into a young mind is not soon forgotten. This reminds me of an African tale which addresses the subject and ends with 'if beating was a way to learn, asses would be the most intelligent animals'. These boys walk in small groups in torn, filthy clothes from dawn till dusk and yet when they were together I often saw them laughing, joking and communicating on a boy's level. One time a child came to our house after a meal. I gave him oranges, something he didn't normally get. He turned to go, the people who owned the house shouted at him, angry. The boy was supposed to have given me a blessing.

Imagining the hopelessness of his lot in life I wondered if in the same circumstances I would feel anything more than resentment and bitterness.

Abandoned women and children also fill the ranks of the impoverished. They line the streets seated on a four by four mat on the ground. Women cross-legged, their children close at hand. Passers-by toss down a coin or two. At the end of the day maybe they have enough to eat, maybe not. These are women who end up having children with or without marriage. The other party leaves and often the woman will return to her parental family because she has no other choice. If the family is poor, departed or rejects her she must live on the street. I thought about viewing the world through people's feet as they passed by, looking up, making eye contact, imploring for mercy, the kindness of strangers.

On that same level were crippled people. I use that adjective because it is appropriate. These people are not crippled by their disabilities so much as by the conditions in which they live. To be without limbs or with gnarled bodies, crawling along filthy roads with animal excrement was unfathomable. Dragging useless legs behind strong arms, choking on dust and sand. And yet in Dakar I met one such afflicted man who smiled at me and said 'Have a great day'.

Linda Bootherstone

The man without a nose stood outside the rapid cars, small buses, staring into the windows. People dug into their pockets quickly so they wouldn't have to look at him any more. He was in good company—many of the unseeing at his side. Two of my favourite blind people were women, older, seated on a rapid car singing in rounds, clanging their coins in rhythm. They did well, people were uplifted by the music which inspired generosity.

I walked through shanty towns and saw families with multiple children living in shacks of cardboard with a corrugated tin roof if they were lucky. No water, no electricity, no toilet inside or out. We label poverty and filth as being synonymous with one another. Without water how do you stay clean?

The majority of families consisting of parents, adult children with spouses, grandchildren, cousins and friends lived together in compounds. A family of four plus would have one room. The entire household shared common cooking facilities, usually one propane burner, one toilet, one shower. Those who worked contributed their wages for food.

It was a well known fact that the woman of the house given money for food would put a small portion of it aside. For one or two days weekly the family would have more rice, less fish or meat. Eventually the savings would accumulate and she would buy new clothes. My friends in Canada didn't understand this concept. The thought of a woman taking food from her children to clothe herself was unthinkable. The situation was more complicated than that. An African woman at home had very little self-esteem. Her life of drudgery, service to others and continual childbearing day in and day out seemed at once infinite and hopeless. A treadmill, an existence of unvaried physical labour for life. Women were never without children, theirs or somebody else's. On a typical holiday a woman was shipped off to her mother or mother-in-law with the children while a man visited friends or family on his own. Men were good about caring for infants when they were home. Unfortunately their absences were numerous and lengthy. Work could be responsible for this dilemma. Often in a compound there was only one breadwinner for the entire clan. At other times these departures were a result of escapism. Unable to contribute on a financial scale men felt inadequate, incompetent, eventually abandoning the situation completely rather than having to face it. Returning to the earlier theme of a woman taking from the family coffers to dress herself is more comprehensible when her position is understood. Wearing new clothes netted her compliments which made her feel better albeit temporarily. It was considered a reflection of her husband's ability to provide for her. It's easy for us with closets full of clothes, surrounded by stability to be critical. Living with these people, sharing their lives gave me a greater insight into their behaviour patterns and our own. How many of us have squandered large amounts of money on something frivolous for momentary self-gratification and struggled to make ends meet afterwards? Africans don't expect to live a long time. Young and middle-aged people die daily, victims of disease, poverty, childbirth, lack of medicine, ergo they take pleasure in this moment.

The relationship between parents and children is confusing and contradictory. A couple is praised for having many children, considered blessed. A baby spends almost the first three years on its mother's or another woman's back. From the time a girl is seven she is often carrying and caring for a baby sibling.

As soon as a child can walk and understand commands they are instructed in service. Girls hand wash laundry, carry hot tea and water, begin to cook. Boys fetch, make fires. Everyone sews. Children are discouraged from displaying emotions. Criers are exiled from the room expected to solve their own problems. The role of older children as caregivers for younger brothers and sisters is unquestioned. Sharing is automatic, not thought about.

I was living in a compound with seven adults and three children. My room was small. It had a concrete floor, one window, a metal door and there were bars on both. Furnishing consisted of a bamboo mat and a single foam mattress. No matter which room you went into in any house there was usually a bed. Space was a precious commodity. Kine was a three year old girl who befriended me. She was a smart child. I taught her to sing 'the itsy bitsy spider' in English when she didn't even speak French and few words in Wolof. Kine was under the rigorous eye of three women and her training was severe. She quickly learned when it was safe for her to show her pleasure with me and when it endangered her position. I was frequently invited to join the families for dinner. We would sit on the floor on small benches and eat tiay bougin, rice and fish. I sat on a bench and gestured for Kine to join me. She sat down smiling proudly to the others. The women were severe with her, criticising her eating, telling her to clear things away better, almost bringing the child to tears. The next time we were together Kine sat beside me but now she was careful to guard her emotions, keep a straight face and act as if she wasn't enjoying herself. She also learned the moments she could visit me to laugh and sing when the others were too busy to interfere.

Another similar situation occurred in my next compound with Anta also there. Her nightly visits were in the courtyard where I cooked over a furneau, a charcoal cooker.

Anta sat at my side fanning the coals of the burner smothering me with hugs, kisses and laughter. When one of the other of the women came she immediately walked away from me and acted as if I didn't exist. Anta needed affection and knew the parameters of where and when to get it. Her parents Rochi and Har were good people, they simply instructed their children the way they had been *taught.*

When the new baby arrived I was greatly honoured as she was named after me. A week later as is the custom we celebrated the child's baptism. During this event a sheep or goat is killed and over the course of the day about three hundred friends and well-wishers stopped by to eat and congratulate. From sunrise to sunset people came, sat on my floor, filled the house and spilled onto the street where Sabah players beat a rhythm and women danced. At the end of that day Har, the man of the family, came and said, 'We are so pleased with you. We hope you will always come and live with us.'

As much as Africans are strict disciplinarians with their children, they have a camaraderie, respect and a way of greeting that I find sometimes lacking in our culture. Perhaps this too is a result of living in the present, making each moment count.

Conversations about God are ongoing daily as phrases are integrated into the language. 'A sahla mae lay koom?' Are you in peace? 'In Chahala,' God willing. If someone dies, it is God's will, one human's poverty, another's riches are all attributed to Divine intervention. Being taught from the cradle to hide feelings, deaths are buried quickly. Those incapable of suppressing sadness are considered mentally unstable. No one wants a reminder of what might happen to them. This also allows for blossoms of gaiety, a counteraction to the reality of mortality and suffering. Which brings us back to the importance of greeting. When entering a room under any conditions it was important to salute each person individually, to shake hands and offer words of welcome and gladness at meeting. In our hustle bustle existence this may seem time consuming, tedious but it allows each person recognition, a salutation that says, 'We acknowledge your presence and are glad to be in the world with you.'

On any day I could walk into a stranger's house and be given food. A place of honour would be set and I could return again and again. There were times when I was in the most deplorable living conditions, filth, intense heat, seated in a room with twenty others, talking, eating and somewhere in the middle of it all a person would get up and start dancing. Everyone else would clap, sing and take joy in the moment. Happiness erupted like a spring from the earth

Drums are in integral part of African life. Djembai and Sabah players pounded rhythms, filled the air waves, exciting people. One evening I was in a cultural centre with friends watching dancers portray a tribal ceremony depicting black magic, voodoo. Suddenly the rains came, monsoons. The djembai players rushed to one side under cover, the dancers followed suit. A single light bulb made a spotlight and the drummers continued to beat. The lead dancer stripped down to underwear the colour of his skin. He moved to the open courtyard and danced *while lightening flashed behind him, illuminating gyrations, creating an otherworldly effect as the rain streamed down for a full hour. My friend Kare turned to me and said, 'Georgia, this is Africa.'*

I walked through enchanted forests of BowBon trees. Deciduous relics old enough to make our trees look like saplings. African law protects them, wherever they grow they are never cut down. Bark, leaves and fruit are used for medicinal purposes but the trees are left standing, rooted to the earth perhaps since the beginning of time . . .

When I was sick with fever Dousarr took me to his sister Asu's house in Smona. She bathed my head with cool water and stroked my hair until the fever broke. Another time when I was ill for three months Kare took me in, stayed by my side, took me to the hospital and doctors. He told me I could not leave until I was well again. It was his responsibility.

Africans want change. Women spoke of abolishing polygamy, gaining rights for their children and themselves, having a voice. Men also want change, better and more ways to provide for their families. They too have been victims of polygamy and a system that leaves too many children uncared for with little hope for their future. It would be too lengthy to delve into the medical system. Suffice to say a lack of hygiene is a main contributor to many illnesses.

In every case, no matter who I talked with, the consensus was a need for education.

Canada is much respected for the amount of aid it sends to African countries. I had more than one occasion to be proud of my citizenship. However large sums of money don't always go to designated areas. Unfortunately corrupt governments line their pockets. The library system was inadequate, inaccessible and costly.

Answers, are there any? We do what we can. At home we form food banks, cook meals for our underprivileged, we donate clothing and used goods. We extend hands across the water and continue the effort. Some of us have foster children in countries worldwide. It is something. Each act is important.

Memories: Massaging Har's back when he was sick with fever, the Tuculeur woman who rubbed ashes on my throat and spat in my face to remove a sore throat, placing a new born babe in her mother's arms for the first time, sitting in a house with twelve Arab women who hennaed my feet into beautiful patterns, spoon fed me while they dried, we sang danced and communicated without a common dialect, teaching Africans to say Grace before meals, Holy men who prayed for and blessed me, children of every age calling Dio Dio (Jo Jo) my African name as I came onto the street. Introducing the harp, a musical instrument they had never before seen or heard. Throughout these experiences I realised there is no right or wrong, we learn from each other. Sometimes we have the opportunity to share a better way of doing things and sometimes not. Customs dictate what has been done for centuries. It's hard to break the mould.

On a personal level I feel we are all in the world together needing each other's help and perhaps more importantly compassion, understanding where we come from.

Will I return to Africa? Yes, there is much left to discover. I feel it is possible to make changes in small ways that are lasting. When I drift off to sleep at night I remember the children of Guegeway singing with me as we walked along the sandy road, 'Freedom, oh freedom, freedom is coming.'

Reading this article helped me get my own problems into perspective. At least I was in a situation that ultimately I could escape or change because I had the capital to do so, whereas, as Georgia pointed out, in Africa things are very different. I needed this perspective for I was feeling very much alone and even quite frightened at times. I felt very uncomfortable whenever I came into contact with PC, and had found, on going to move my caravan, that it had been ransacked and several items taken. No-one in my old lodgings, which now included PC, would admit to having anything to do with it and I wasn't sure how to take this latest occurrence. There was a general feeling of antagonism against me and I was almost afraid of coming home at night.

To try and alleviate those feelings and celebrate the fact that I was now in my own home at last, after three months hard work, I threw a housewarming party and invited people from many different places – but *not* my closest neighbours. The party was great but as soon as it was over the idea of getting away for a while took on more of a hold. I began to seriously consider what Debby had suggested when we had been wining and dining together eight months ago in Morocco.

Chapter Twenty-Six
A Judas In The Camp

'Linda, honeychil', what are you going to do to celebrate your 50th?' Debby's words, lightly spoken over our meal at Sam's Place in Essaouira bobbed often to the forefront of my mind. After all the work and hassle I felt I deserved a holiday and when she had suggested that we went on a Rage in New Orleans I couldn't think of a better place to celebrate my half century of survival. The way things were in Castellar at the moment it seemed a good idea to escape.

The snag was that I hadn't heard from Debby all summer and the last short letter in the spring did not mention anything about my visit. But, if it was still OK with her then perhaps I could kill three birds with one stone: spend my birthday with Debby in New Orleans, Christmas with Georgia in Canada, and get away from Castellar for a few weeks and hope things settled down. At least both my good friends were on the same continent, even if at latitudinal extremes. Come to think of it, I had other friends in America and it would be great fun to catch up with them too. I warmed to the idea very quickly.

There wasn't enough time to write, I had to phone. I rushed to Dave the Bee's house, a neighbour on the other side of the hill who had a satellite phone system. There I put a call through to Port Vincent, Louisiana.

'Hi, Debby. It's Linda. How are you? Would you still like me to come over for my birthday?'

'Why sure honey. You know you're welcome any time. Just let me know the flight and I'll be there.'

Great, and now Georgia. She was staying with a friend in London, Ontario and I was lucky to reach her too.

'Georgia, where will you be at Christmas? London? Well, I'll be there!'

'Wonderful!' she cried.

It was great to hear her usual positive adjective again. And now to arrange the flights! Good old Bankcard. It had to be done through a travel agent in the UK and the phone lines were hot for a few hours while they checked times and dates before getting back to me. Then suddenly it was all arranged. I'd be leaving Spain on Tuesday 12th November on a flight to Gatwick to stay two days with my sister, then flying out to New Orleans on Friday 16th to arrive that evening. My birthday was on the 21st so we'd have time to organise the Rage. One of the girls in the castle suggested we have a pre-birthday get-together in the Castle Bar on the Saturday before I left. Fine with me, any excuse for another party.

I began packing. I'd only be taking a rucksack so would have to choose carefully which clothes I needed for both warm weather (in New Orleans) and very cold weather (in Canada) and, of course, my glad rags for the Rage. The house needed cleaning and tidying and I had a pack of bulbs to plant in the garden so I could look forward to a flower-filled springtime. Thinking everything was under control and feeling happy about my departure I was kneeling, trowel in hand, by the flower beds when I saw P. C. walking up my drive way, bottle of wine in hand. I stood up as he approached the gate with a smile.

'Hi, Linda, I've heard you're going away and thought we might have a drink together.'

'Great', I thought. 'This is wonderful, we can sort all this misunderstanding out and be friends again.'

'Oh thanks, come in.' I opened the gate and led him through to the patio table, drawing up chairs for us both and fetching glasses, a bottle opener and cheese and biscuits. I asked him how he was, chatted about my flight plans and generally made small talk as we drank the wine. It was a pleasant interlude on this sunny mild day. What a nice farewell.

After a couple of glasses I was feeling a little tipsy as I am wont to do when drinking at midday. Suddenly PC's genial attitude underwent a dramatic change.

'Right, now Linda, it's settling up time. You've had your parties and your fun and it's time you paid for it.' I sobered immediately. The ambience of this warm sunny day took on a menacing feel. It was as if the birds had stopped singing. The look in his eye was one of pure hatred and I was suddenly aware of the huge bulk of his figure and my own vulnerability.

'What do you mean? Please explain to me what all this is about.

What have I done to upset you?'

'You know very well what you've done. You are a nasty selfish lying bitch and the time has come to settle up the account.'

'Please, P——, I don't know what you mean. What account?' 'You've stolen my things and I've come to get them.'

'I only have what is mine. I think you'd better leave now,' I answered warily, standing up and moving to my doorway to block it, but he came towards me. I put out my arm to stop him. He grabbed me, forcing me back into the room and onto the lounge seat, my head jammed back against the wall. It was like being up against a steam roller and I was pinned down.

'Now, you selfish bitch, you've been fucking me around and if I'm going to be fucked I might as well get some fun out of it.' As he spoke he was ripping off my shirt and bra. He bit at my nipple as his grip was tightened on my arms.

'P——, you are hurting me. I don't know why you are doing this. Please let me go.' My right arm with the weak elbow was being strained back, his fingers digging painfully into my wrist.

Both my body and my mind were writhing. Was this the same man who had previously been so helpful and caring? My mind flashed back to 18 months before when I had knocked at his door at 2 a.m. in tears after I'd fallen off my motorbike. He'd wrapped me in blankets, given me a stiff brandy and walked out in the night to push my bike a mile back to his campervan. On another occasion I'd cried on his shoulder when a letter from Australia had painfully reminded me of the life I'd lost. But now this man was a monster. He was undoing my trousers, pulling them down, his fingers poking and groping.

'Please, P——, this is crazy.' I was struggling but his enormous bulk and strength were too much for me. 'Well,' I thought, 'after all those miles, the places and dangerous situations I've been in and I'm about to get raped in my own house by someone I once thought of as a friend!'

By now I was naked on the floor and Peter was struggling with his own clothes while he held me down and I had realised that this man was on a power trip and was capable of violence. Just how far would he go? I was still talking, trying to reason with him but he wasn't heeding my pleas.

'Force is the only way to deal with you,' he said. 'It's the only thing you understand.'

But I couldn't understand and was about to give up the struggle to save more damage.

Just as he was moving himself into position above me I said:

'Wait, P——. Yes it's ok but please use a condom. I'll see if I can find one; after all you don't know where I've been!' It was a last ditch attempt at some sort of joke.

But miraculously he stopped and shifted. I squirmed out from beneath him, rushed into the bedroom and grabbed a dressing-gown then headed for the door.

'P——, wait. I have to go to the toilet!' My bladder was indeed bursting. I rushed outside and relieved myself, but what to do now? In complete bewilderment I stood on the edge of my patio gazing out across the hills, clutching my dressing gown tightly around me.

Where could I run to? Who could I call for help? My little cottage was in a hamlet of only eight dwellings. Two were mine, three belonged to Spanish people who only came intermittently at weekends, one was a bar that was now closed, one the smuggler's house that PC was guarding, and the last cottage occupied by Sam, the English girl.

There was no hope there: she was in Gibraltar with her boyfriend for a few days. PC had obviously chosen this opportunity while I was alone. The nearest people were either 3 kilometres up in the hippy village or 5 kilometres down in Nuevo Castellar where English was rarely spoken. The dead end road between the two which ran by my house was infrequently used other than at weekends. I did not relish the idea of running semi-naked in any direction. The situation was dangerous, embarrassing and unreal all at the same time but I felt I must be able to talk my way out of it.

In the open and away from him my confidence came back. He had let me go. Hearing movements, I cautiously walked back to the doorway. He was dressed and standing.

Relieved I stepped inside. He grabbed me by the scruff of my dressing gown and pointed to my desk.

'I want this back, and this. You are a thief.' He was pointing at a cane carpet beater I had brought down from my mother's house that summer. A common style, it did resemble the one in the house next door where he was staying, but it was mine. Suddenly I was furious, incensed by the fact that something that had been my mother's should be involved in this filthy scene.

'How dare you say I'm a thief! This is from England, and this table is mine from the other house. None of these things are yours.' But he snarled at me:

'I'll give you 24 hours to bring these items back otherwise I shall take them myself. You are going away on Tuesday and I'll take whatever I want. If things get damaged it's too bad—these locks won't stop me; you'll have to do better than this.' Then he turned and walked toward the gate.

'If I give you these things, P—, will you promise not to come near me again?' I shouted after him. He grunted as he walked away.

I was shaking all over, and my mind reeling. Would it be better to sacrifice a few bits of furniture to stop further attack? But why should I be threatened like this? I'd done nothing wrong. All these things were mine—I'd returned his belongings to him when I could have thrown it all away: they had been lying around my property for weeks when I'd asked him to move them. No, there was some hidden agenda that I didn't understand. Maybe he was now on drugs and paranoid. Something must have make him crack. I'd realised that he was a depressive, but this was something else.

I couldn't handle this situation alone. I had to get out and talk to someone away from this village. The first people I thought of were about 10 miles away, in Campamento. I'd get dressed and drive there. I badly needed a shoulder to cry on and the motherly woman there would at least be sympathetic while I tried to work things out.

So, still trembling, I put on my clothes and went to lock the door behind me. No keys. In my tidying up session before PC had arrived I had hung both my main and spare set of house keys on the hook by the door so, for a change, I knew where they were. Nothing now: both had gone. There was only one explanation: during the time I went out to the toilet PC had taken them. Now the house couldn't be locked. Just to make totally sure I didn't have them I searched my bag and pockets. No, they had definitely been on the hook and now they were gone. He must have them. With more bravado than I felt I marched down to his house and shouted over the fence, 'P—, where are my keys? What have you done with them?' He came growling out.

'I don't have your keys. I don't have any of your property but you have mine! I've changed my mind and if you don't return it within 12 hours I'll come and take it'. Then he turned his back and walked inside.

I could hardly turn the key in Hekel's ignition my hands were shaking so much. Mercifully her keys were always kept separately. Even though the house was open and vulnerable I had to get help.

I drove to Campamento in a flood of tears. What had I done to deserve this? Nothing.

The situation was entirely illogical. Unfortunately Annette, the mother figure, wasn't there. Her husband and daughter let me in. Tears flooding my cheeks I told them I had been attacked and threatened by Peter whom they vaguely knew. What should I do? I was certain he had my house keys.

'There is nothing else for it, Linda, too much has been going on lately: your things have been stolen and now you've been attacked. You must go to the police,' Alan said. He had helped move my caravan to my new house after it had been ransacked. But how could I explain it to the Spanish? How I wished I'd studied the language. And I baulked at describing the sexual attack, even in English.

'I'll come with you,' Lee the daughter said. 'Not that I speak Spanish, but we'll find someone.'

En route to the police station I thought of my Spanish biker friends who ran a workshop at nearby Estacion de San Roque. Some of them could speak English and they could vouch for me being a respectable person. I was so relieved to find some of the men working on their bikes. One of them, Angelo, could speak enough English to get the gist of my story and agreed to accompany us to the police station and to translate. Antonio and Jesus came too. They were keen to help. With names like that I couldn't help but feel that God was on my side. Antonio drove the others in his car and in convoy we reached the police station in Nuevo Castellar where Angelo translated my statement that Peter had physically threatened me and I had reason to believe he had my house keys.

What else could I say?

'What do you want us to do?' the police asked.

'I want you to speak to him and see if he has my keys.' Not really knowing what my rights were, I wasn't sure what this would achieve other than show him that I could and would call the police if he tried to break into my property and molest me again. I explained that I was leaving the country in 3 days and was under threat. If anything happened to my house he had to be the first suspect.

Angelo translated this and the police said they'd have to wait for their next shift to come on in 1 1/2 hours before they could do anything! They told me to go back to my house and wait until the new shift arrived; when arrived we would all go and confront PC together.

I wasn't sure if he'd still be at home then—what would happen if he'd left? We had to wait and see.

The boys decided to come too—they didn't want to leave me alone. It was getting more and more like a Laurel and Hardy cops and robbers chase. Lee came with me in Hekel and the boys followed in their car. Then we began the long wait for the police. I gave the crowd coffee and brandy while the sun sank and time ticked by. Eventually 2 hours later the police car drew up and 4 uniformed men with guns and coshes emerged. We were really in a movie now.

Angelo briefed them on the situation. Fortunately PC was still at home having a tête-a-tête with another English woman, from the village. They were drinking wine on his patio.

When the police approached and called him out he immediately put on an aggressive front.

'What right do you have to come in here?' he demanded. The police moved inside the gate and an interrogation began. It was slow as everything had to be translated. I said nothing, standing to one side in the shadows and listening. It was like being in the wings off-stage in a cops and robbers play, watching the players act out their part. PC was frisked and his bags searched. He denied attacking me and said we were having a glass of wine together on a friendly visit.

'What's this, Linda? What are you doing to poor P—?' The woman turned on me aggressively. 'You don't treat your neighbours like this. In this village no-one calls the police. A single woman needs a big man like this on her side. You should be friends with him like I am.' I wanted to throw up.

'Keep out of this, it's nothing to do with you. This man has attacked me and I have reason to believe he has my house keys.' It's all I could say and I kept repeating it. I could feel PC's anger at the humiliation of being frisked and I dreaded to think about what would happen when everyone left.

Eventually, as they found nothing, the police left him with a warning. The Spanish boys told him curtly that he would have to answer to them if there was any more trouble. I hadn't mentioned the attempted rape—I was too embarrassed and could prove nothing. I didn't then know the legal system and that I could have made a denuncia (denunciation) through the Guardia Civil – not the police (a fact I learned much later). Now I was emotionally and physically exhausted. After thanking the police and the Spanish boys for their help I took Lee home. I had to face returning alone, keyless, to my house knowing full well the Monster was still next door.

With planks of wood jammed against the handle I barricaded the door. Then began one of the longest nights of my life. Not much chance of sleep, but nothing happened and I rose nervously the next day waiting for Lee's father to come and change the locks. What a job to do. It was supposed to be my pre-50th party tonight, at Mara's bar in the castle, and I was leaving in 2 days. I would now need window bars (rejas) fitted in order to counter PC's threats of a break-in.

By midday Alan still hadn't arrived and the shops would close at 2. I went out searching for Dave the Bee on the other side of the hill. He and his wife were driving back from the village. My story sounded incredible but Dave said he'd come and look at my locks for me and see what he could do. What a job it was going to be – I groaned inwardly. While waiting that morning I had tried to take off the lock and had met problems. However, as Dave was bending over to look at the handle for some reason my eyes tracked up and over his head to the ridge on top of the partition to my office. I saw two small mounds there.

'Wait, Dave!' Jumping onto a chair I reached up and there they were— my two sets of keys. 'They are here, Dave!' We looked at each other in silence, Dave's eyes owl-like behind his glasses.

For a horrible moment I suspected he thought I had been joking with him and put them there myself. What could I prove? PC had been very clever, the whole story was my word against his and I could only look stupid, having the keys myself all the time as if I'd misplaced them. But I hadn't put them there. It was a horribly devious way of making me terribly afraid and pointing out my vulnerability.

'He may have taken and copied them, Linda,' Dave said practically. I didn't think PC would have had time to do that. I had to take the chance and stick with these locks, the shops were closed now till Monday.

'Thanks anyway, Dave,' I said. 'I'll just get the rejas (window bars) fitted as soon as I can.'

That night at the bar I drank every birthday drink that was offered me and had to be driven, legless, home. Boy, was I glad to be getting away for a while. I still didn't know how to solve this problem but for now I would forget it. On Monday morning I managed to locate some second-hand rejas and employed a young Spanish man to fit them while I packed my bags, gave my few valuables to someone else to look after and made final arrangements to store the bike and get a lift to the bus station to connect with the plane from Malaga.

Fortunately the Spanish boys said I could leave the BMW with them again at the motorcycle club, but Hekel had to remain in my car port. I could only hope that she wouldn't be interfered with. There was nowhere else I could take her to keep her under cover. At least here she would be protected from the winter rain. Dave the Bee said he would pass by occasionally and check on things.

When I finally reached my sister's house in Purley the shock really set in and I spent most of my two days there watching videos and sleeping.

'Well, you're an easy person to entertain, Lindy; all you want to do is veg out,' she laughed. Too true. Give me a motorbike and a continent to cross or a floodlit stage and an audience to face any day, but an unbalanced neighbour—phew!—now that's something else . . .

Pre-50th at Mara's Bar

Chapter Twenty Seven

<u>Way Down Yonder</u>

The in-flight magazine 'American Way' had a horoscope section called 'Cosmic Laugh'. My reading for this birthday month was:

'Scorpio (October 23-November 21)

For years you've been held like a toothpick in the teeth of an invisible, hungry lion who, lucky for you, for some mysterious reason just didn't feel like swallowing. Although few people knew how tense the situation was, it provided you with your favourite thing: something to fight for. Now that it's over, bow nobly; tip your top hat to the crowd and say, 'And now for my next trick . . .'

For once I agreed with it.

After an uneventful flight the plane landed at New Orleans airport and I rushed out after collecting my back pack to find Debby waiting for me—but she wasn't.

'Oh well,' I thought, 'perhaps she's been delayed. I'll change some money and give her a ring.'

However, as I was picking up my collection of greenbacks I heard my name over the tannoy system. 'Ms Bootherstone, your party is waiting for you at the baggage check out on the lower floor.'

'Wow,' I thought, 'a party already and I've only just landed!'

Funny the way these Americans talk. There was Debby, beaming from ear to ear and we walked out to her car.

'Gee, Linda, you smell great!' she enthused.

'Hang on.' I figured that after seven hours on the plane and a whole lot more bus and train travel before that, my personal hygiene was somewhat lacking and to smell great was hugely unlikely. On investigation we found an oily streak down the back of my rucksack, seeping into my jacket.

'Oh no!' I cried. 'It's my anti-menopausal oil!' Specially blended for me by an aroma therapist in Castellar, it contained essential oils of geranium, rose, lavender and clary sage. A broken cap had allowed the bottle to empty the fragrant (and expensive) mixture to seep through the contents of my rucksack. No wonder I smelled great.

'Well Linda,' Debby admitted laughingly. 'You don't look too good but your rucksack is looking younger by the minute'. As she giggled I ruefully thought of all the washing I'd have to do before I'd wear the clothes. Never mind, a few G-and-T's would soon brighten the outlook.

Debby has a 'camp', a small house on stilts by the Amite River, one of the many tributaries of the Mississippi Delta. Port Vincent, her local community, is more *in* the river than *on* it! Every year the residents battle with floods, which is why few houses are built on the ground. On my previous visit in summer '83, it had rained heavily for several days and Debby had pronounced that we were evacuating to her mother's house in Baton Rouge. Everything looked just fine to me, but we left. Three days later we literally swam back to her house!

On my exploratory walks this time I found more stilt houses in an assortment of styles. Some were at the river's edge with their own boat decks, like Debby's. The inhabitants of other houses, further inland, kept their boats beneath the stilted structure when not in use. As boating is a way of life here it's just the thing one looks for and asks after: 'What sort of boat do you have? What size engine?' is the conversation opener.

I had to learn to handle Debby's craft to be able to take it shopping. The first lesson is: Don't cast off until the engine bas been started and warmed up. It's a bit worrying to find yourself taken away with the current when the motor won't start. Yes, of course I learnt the hard way. Once I got the hang of it and did my first solo, one mile downstream, I felt quite the local 'River Rat'. So, taking that competent crew course in Scotland all those years ago didn't go amiss after all. And rivers don't make me seasick like a rolling sea.

It was a novelty to park by tying up to a tree trunk beside the town bridge and then jumping ashore to access the supermarket and video shop. Of course the pubs are on the river too. Sunday drivers take on a new meaning when they are lads who've been bar hopping, sped up a bit after one too many and are now rocking your boat with their churning wake. The riverside bars quite often double as general stores and have their own character and style. A sign in one which was run by a particularly heavyweight barmaid said: 'Grow your own dope—plant a man'. It made me think of Castellar.

Many of the riverside houses were like Debby's, converted from weekend 'camps' to full-time homes. These were well maintained. However, I found one backwater that was full of run down shacks and trailers. There were pieces of junk and scruffy barking dogs. The residents looked at me suspiciously when I snapped a few photos and one asked me what I was doing there.

'Rednecks,' said Debby contemptuously when I told her. In my wanderings I also found 'My Happiness Lane' which was more positive photo material.

Debby's house is set amongst cypress trees with hanging moss. Why they call it Spanish moss I have yet to find out as I haven't seen it in Spain. Its curtains of green create a very special antebellum atmosphere. The cypress trees grow along the riverside and have 'knees' which are parts of the root that double back up to the surface to collect more oxygen. Various trips in Debby's flat-bottomed boat took us out exploring the beauty of these and other plants in the bayous. As autumn was in full colour the reds and golds reflected in the calm waters, only rippled by the wake of our outboard motor.

Debby was hosting a Portuguese teenage Student, Rui, for a year and while Debby was at work in her new job as an insurance consultant, Rui and I spent time in the boat cleaning up our patch of the river. Fishermen's lines with polystyrene floats caught the rubbish that thoughtless people pitched overboard and these also snagged and jammed floating logs. Rui would navigate the boat up close to a log, I lassoed it with our tow rope and we dragged it clear of the others to take it further downstream, pushing it safely over to the shoreline with our wake. As many teenage boys tend to be, Rui was a touch throttle-happy. There were times when we narrowly missed capsizing as the logs built up too much momentum behind us and almost ran us down when we slowed for their release. But Louisiana in November is relatively warm so a dip in the water wouldn't have been too serious.

Another inhabitant of Port Vincent flood zone was C.W. (pronounce See Derble Ya). A man in his forties who worked as a welder and wore J J Bean shirts of colourful cotton plaid. He also had a stilt house and a boat. We spent a pleasant evening round his huge log fire, drinking mulled cider and 'shooting the breeze'. On his day off he showed me a deer feeder in the forest nearby. Used by hunters for locating the animals, a large metal can with a broom handle loosely fixed in a hole in the bottom is hung in the trees. The can is filled with grain and the deer find that if they nudge the handle a stream of grain will flow out onto the ground. The animals come back again to the place to find food and then are an easy target. A sneaky trick, I thought.

The 21st November, my 50th birthday, fell on a Tuesday and although Debby had to work in the morning she took the afternoon off and we celebrated the big event by having lunch on her patio overlooking the river. We watched the white heron perch on Debby's landing stage and the sun sparkling through the trees. Champagne flowed as we ate the typically southern food Debby had prepared. It was just the two of us, enjoying each other's company and many miles and space from the terrifying situation I'd been in just two weeks earlier. It was a laid back happy day but we did plan a more up-tempo outing with some others in New Orleans the coming Friday.

Thursday was Thanksgiving and the whole family – mothers, fathers, sisters, brothers, aunts and Uncle Tom Cobbley and all – congregated at Debby's brother's house to sit down to the biggest spread I'd ever seen. For a start it had to be served in the carport because it covered four tables. Turkey, ham, stuffing, sausage rolls, pies, trifles, cheesecakes, shortbread... my eyes ogled and my mouth watered. Even the paper plates looked good enough to eat, decorated with turkeys and fruit. I saved one for a souvenir. It was a case of eating until you were as stuffed as the turkey. I did borrow a guitar and make a musical contribution though. It was as well my fingers could still move; my gorged body certainly couldn't.

Luckily I had the following morning to digest it all before Debby, her sister Janet, Rui and I drove into New Orleans for the official Demi-Century Rage. We began the evening by cruising Bourbon Street with its Spanish style iron-laced buildings housing many antique shops and art galleries. We visited the Voodoo Shop where I placed a few well-chosen curses and bought a voodoo doll which I could later stick pins into if necessary. The street was alive with tap-dancing buskers, some really young coloured boys whose footwork rivalled Michael Flatley! Smiling po-boy and hot dog vendors in striped aprons were so rotund that I presumed they must eat as many servings as they sold. Everyone seemed to be in a holiday mood and the streets were crowded. I could imagine the hype and excitement and potential crush factor during Carnival. We called into Pat O'Brien's, the famous piano bar where two grand pianos play in shifts and will perform any tune of your choice if you send dollars up on stage. The drink of the establishment is the Hurricane, well named as the rum-based pink cocktail has a reputation for knocking you flat. I'd been caught once before so indulged in only one 10 ounce glass this time.

Bourbon Street

Next port of call was a jazz club where we stayed for a set of traditional tunes. The band included a huge brass horn and a tubby man with bulging cheeks to blow it. On enquiring if I could play my whistle we were directed to O'Flaherty's where a variety of musicians performed with Scottish bagpipes or sang ballads. I was just about to slip out my whistle and join them when Debby grabbed me and dragged us all out to move on to the House of Blues.

Anyone who has seen the Blues Brothers film would appreciate this joint. The building incorporates a concert hall, where blues bands play late into the night, and a restaurant adjoining which has the performance piped through on video so the diners can also enjoy the show. It was almost 11 p.m. and our hunger took us straight to the restaurant for a delicious jambalaya in true Southern style.

The Americans are so O. T. T. but I must admit it's nice. When a handsome young man comes up smiling and says:

'Hi, my name's Andy' (or Wayne or Sam) 'and I am your attendant for the night. Just call me if you need anything, O.K.?' it really sounds so personal and it's fun. Better than a bored, gum-chewing waitress, pencil poised saying:

'Well, what do you want then?'

After all the food and merriment I was asleep on the front seat of Janet's limousine even before we had left the car park to drive home. Being 50 can be hard work.

A day of culture was arranged for me. I was to be taken to the Baton Rouge with another friend, Connie – a lively brunette – to view the State Building and the Rural Life Museum. This started off as planned and I took in the Assembly Hall and tower of the State Senate and the timber-built simple slave houses and sugar boiling pots at the Museum. But after that our cultural cap slipped when Connie suggested we met another friend on the casino boat.

Now, I'm no gambler and am always a touch wary of such establishments, but I thought it would do no harm to see the riverboat. As gambling is illegal in Louisiana the law is bent by the Casino being 'off-shore' in the Mississippi. Sometimes the boat actually chugs up and down the river while those on board try their luck. The decor is sumptuous like most casinos, and it transpired that drinks were free. I ordered a beer but then we met Wayne, Connie's friend. He was dressed in jeans, high-heeled cowboy boots and big buckled belt. Lined up by his one-armed bandit was a row of Pina Coladas, so we helped him out with those and ordered a few more. A rosy glow came over me. I slipped into the swing of pulling handles and watching oranges, lemons, pigs or frogs spinning round. They occasionally even lined up and sent tokens tinkling into the payout bowl. I was getting sucked in. I could understand how men and women suddenly found they had spent their whole pay packets on these things. It's a painless thing to do at the time, especially with a free drink, and it's fun. Deciding that my downfall should be recorded I pulled out my camera and asked Wayne to take a photo of Connie and I leaning drunkenly against my favourite Froggy one-armed bandit.

Before we could say 'Legs eleven', a security guard appeared out of nowhere and swept the camera out of Wayne's hand. I sobered immediately; there were irretrievable pictures on that film. However, the guard was quite polite and said she would just look after the camera while I was on board, here was a receipt for it and please call at the cloakroom to pick it up on my way out. Okay, no problem, but I was curious as to why there should be this security limitation. Could one photograph the machines and somehow work out their secrets? Or maybe in the background there might be an important public person whose image would be damaged if seen in a gambling place. It may be cause for blackmail. The mind boggled.

So, I have no proof of my own fall from grace, but I did stop playing and came out $8 ahead which paid for my theatre ticket that night, so it was a case of culture winning over debauchery after all—or, was it?

My time with Debby was coming to an end. Our last night at her home was spent decorating the Christmas tree and when a friend came round to borrow a dress, Debby delved into her wardrobe and brought out an array of fancy clothes which she had worn in her last job, promotions manager for Wella Hair care. Based in New York, she flew all over Europe organising hair shows. This entailed hiring models, planning the catwalks, the music and the lighting. In all the razzmatazz of modelling she had lived the high life herself to keep in the swing, and these clothes reflected that style. Glittery, shimmery, velvety, clinging or flowing, they were evening clothes like I never wear. So what a great time I had trying them all on. Debby and her friend lavished the make-up onto my face, back-combed my greying hair and found wobbly high heels for me to pose in. Flash, flash went the camera to record a 50 year old Linda that no-one has ever seen before—or since. Funny what a difference clothes and make-up can make, never mind Old Father Time. 'And now for my next trick'.

Chapter Twenty-Eight

<u>The Wild West</u>

It was time to leave the mild climate of Louisiana (although it was now turning cold at night) and head out west to Wyoming to visit Jim and Paige Farby. These were contacts I had made just two years ago in Gibraltar. A couple in their early thirties whose cherubic looks made them seem years younger, they had been touring Europe in a VW combi van. American Paige hailed from Sheriden while British Jim was a Derbyman. They had found work in Gibraltar for a few months and parked their vehicular home in La Linea next to PC in his Winnebago, about the time when I first knew the burly Scot. After their sojourn in Southern Spain the couple continued their travels, sold the combi in London and went back to the USA to earn money for their next exploratory trip. I'd phoned them from Debby's house and was now on my way for a reunion.

Having checked out all the travel possibilities, I found the most direct and cheapest way from Baton Rouge to Sheridan was by Greyhound bus. The fare for the journey of approximately 1,500 miles was a mere $120.00. It was more or less non-stop travel, all I had to do was make sure I had enough warm clothes and food. Although the bus stopped at restaurants and main terminals, it was cheaper to have my own food and drink with me for the duration of three days and two nights.

After a few farewell Margaritas with Debby and Connie, I caught the afternoon bus to Houston and on to Dallas. By positioning myself in the front seat I was able to talk to the drivers. They worked eight hour shifts and changed personnel in the main cities. The first driver was a big fat Texan who chatted to me about the area in an almost almost incoherent drawl. The leg from Houston to Dallas was capably driven by a coloured woman who was less communicative, probably due to the darkness and heavier traffic.

The buses usually have all mod cons, power steering, automatic gears and a driving seat that has its own independent suspension. It can cause motion sickness to someone like me, just by looking at it bouncing up and down with the undulating highway.

Coming into Dallas at night was spectacular. Skyscrapers were brightly lit, especially as Christmas was approaching and every town was burning extra electricity in fairy lights. I slept, and on awakening the next morning found we were crossing the Texan plains. Wheat, cotton, cattle and signs to 'adopt a highway', for clubs and associations kept their own part of a highway clean. There were many steak bars advertised. In some cases if you could eat the complete 5 lb steak all by yourself in one go, it was free! No wonder there were so many fat Americans. It was really cowboy country. Ranches, wooden houses, 'southern cross' style windmills and 'grasshopper' oil pumps.

During the cool hours of the night I discovered, to my horror, that I'd left my thermal vest behind in Connie's car. I donned my wincyette pyjama top instead, but was worried about how I would survive in the freezing conditions further north.

Unfortunately it was evening as we approached the Rockies and therefore impossible to appreciate the scenery in the dark, but Denver was a picture. The pine trees lining the streets from the suburbs to the town centre were decorated with white fairy lights which twinkled in the cold clear mountain air. It was 9.30 p.m. and the night life was beginning in the Colorado capital. The place was alive and interesting but we didn't stop long. Just after we left I took the sleeping tablets Debby had given me in case I couldn't get enough rest and slept all the way to Cheyenne, South Wyoming. Being small has its compensations in being able to curl up neatly on a double bus seat if it's empty.

The bus company from now on was Powder River Trails and the number of passengers had diminished. At the next stop I had breakfast with a guy from Cheyenne who was on his way to meet his daughter in Canada. Apart from chatting intermittently with the drivers, I'd had little conversation for two days. Now there was John to talk to, a video to watch, plus the fact that we were in Indian country where the scenery was captivating. I found myself torn between looking out of the window, up at the movie screen or chatting to John who was a very intelligent and interesting person. Drought or plenty, even on a Greyhound bus! I was quite sad to wave John and the Powder River Trails bus good-bye at Sheridan, even though Jim was waiting at the depot.

Sheridan is what might be called a one-horse town. It has a small airstrip, the bus station, plenty of video shops and, thank goodness, a diner/bar which sold the most amazing selection of beers. Far from having to swallow weak, fizzy Budweisers that night, Jim, Paige and I drank jugs of 'Avalanche', a heavy dark beer that gave the impression it could well put hairs on your chest. Good stuff for fighting Indians – or at least tracking them down, for we were within a stone's throw of Montana and Little Big Horn: Jim and Paige had Sunday off to take me there.

Driving through the Crow Reservation (which now sports a casino) it was easy to imagine herds of buffalo roaming over the wide open scenery and young, befeathered braves riding down from the snow-covered mountains.

We drove to the Little Big Horn National Monument and were shown a video in the information centre, then directed on a tour of the battlefield. It had the same eerie feel to it as Culloden and Glen Coe in Scotland. Interested in the history of the Indian wars, I took a few notes on the battle of Little Big Horn and Custer's last stand.

There are many different versions of the circumstances of this battle: history is written by mere mortals whose perspective is coloured by their own beliefs and circumstances. It appears that the American Government had a treaty with the Sioux Indians. Under this, the Indians were allocated the Black Hills in Wyoming as their territory; no white men were allowed there. However, gold was discovered in the area and, of course, prospective miners, thinking they could become rich overnight, were prepared to risk a scalping for a fortune. The US army were supposed to stop the prospectors, but they hardly put up much of a fight. Although the Sioux did not start killing right away, when these people invaded their lands they started to lose patience and the scalping began. So, with lives being lost, the general consensus of opinion amongst the whites was that mining was progress whereas scalping was savagery: right was on the white man's side, never mind about the treaties.

Then came Spring, the Sioux Indians gave up trying to defend the Black Hills and moved up to the Powder River area in Montana. Other Indians from different reservations moved there too, it was good hunting ground and the native place of many tribes. However, groups of Indians, still defying the whites, resumed raids at settlements and attacks on travellers along the fringes of the Indian domain.

In December 1875, the Commissioner of Indian Affairs ordered the tribes to return to the Black Hills before January 31 1876, or be treated as hostiles 'by the military force'. Many people were getting sick of 'uppity redskins'. It was, after all, the one hundredth year since the Declaration of

Independence and it seemed illogical that a country holding expositions of wonders of inventions such as the typewriter and telephone, should be defied by a bunch of primitives.

So, to save political face, President Grant okayed a campaign against them. Leaders such as Sitting Bull and Crazy Horse, with a few thousand of their followers, were already in the Powder River region where the buffalo that had not been killed by the white man remained. In May 1876 a large campaign was planned to herd the Indians together from the West, South and East. General Custer, in charge of the 7th Cavalry, approached from the mouth of the Powder River and, as they left their last encampment there, rode forth to the tune of Garry Owen, Custer's favourite march.

The Powder River is one of the tributaries of the Yellowstone River. Others running parallel are the Rosebud and the Bighorn. The eastern branch of the Bighorn is called the Little Bighorn. It was this point of the campaign area that Custer led with the 7th Cavalry, while other divisions were approaching from different directions.

To cut a long story short, the white soldiers were unfamiliar with and unprepared for the terrain – which the Indians knew inside out. Custer refused to believe what his scouts told him about the location and size of the Indian villages, splitting his troops in such a way that when one division was attacked the others could not help. On Sunday 25th June 1876, Custer and his men were attacked by thousands of Indians and killed. The most famous Indian leader involved in the battle was Sitting Bull. The army was soundly defeated, but it was to be the last battle the Indians ever won. From then on the American government systematically wiped out the possibility of any more resistance: they killed all the buffalo, took away the Indians' rifles and confined them to reservations by force.

Both Custer and Sitting Bull have been immortalised in many ways. I think one of the nicest poems that I have read about them is this:

Two Trails to Destiny by Jack Lines - 1995

Two lives, walking, rustling, predestined paths
Through tall and sundried buffalo grass to questionable glory

Two leaders . . . each seemingly righteous
cause, whose spirits, and those of the ones
they led live on, here, near river shores
Whose remembered sights are lost in the mind-drift passing of time

Jim, Paige and I paused for a while by the small sectioned-off area on the hillside that marks where the soldiers fell. A little group of white plaques, amongst which one stands out in black – Custer's last stand.

My hosts were out working during the week so I hired a car to visit Cody in the Big Horn mountains. Instead of the small Toyota I'd anticipated, only a bright red Nissan 4X4 Pathfinder was available. So, I climbed my way into my "Truark' armed with some Indian music tapes for the cassette player, and headed up into 'them thar hills!'

I was glad I had a 4-wheel drive as the road was slippery with ice and blown snow, on top of the pass the drifts were quite deep. Sometimes the fairytale landscape was disturbed by snowmobiles racing through the trees on tracks alongside the road. But it was a winter wonderland and safely inside the 'truark' with my heater on, I was enjoying it. The road wound down from the top of the pass, past Shell Canyon and pretty pine-strewn mountain scenery.

In Cody, the town made famous by Buffalo Bill, I stayed with some friends of Jim and Paige, an older couple called Lolli and Alan. They arranged a tour for me at the Buffalo Bill museum and pointed out other places of interest.

I came away from the museum with a new respect for Mr Bill Cody. Although he earnt his name 'Buffalo Bill' by killing thousands of the animals that the Indians needed for survival, he was acting under the orders of the army that he served in. As a white man in the America of his time, he was making a living the only way he knew. Because of his involvement with the Indian way of life, he grew up with a healthy respect for them and, while he couldn't go against the tide of American 'progress', he did his best to help the natives in his own manner. In a way, he was instrumental in preserving some of their customs by romanticising and displaying them in his 'Buffalo

Bill Wild West', a show that he took to the East where the Frontier was a novelty.

By taking many Indians on tour with him, Bill provided them with a living which, to some, was preferable to the confines of the reservation and temptation of the whisky bottle. He also paid fairly, not only Indians but also women. Equal pay for all which was a first in America. Annie Oakley, his gun-toting shooting star, made the same money as her male counterparts.

Bill was a showman, an entertainer and unknowing anthropologist. He made money with his shows but somehow managed to lose it backing other schemes. I strongly identified with his ideology and felt that I would have liked to have met him. Apparently he was a popular person and the town of Cody has definitely put his name on the map.

The town itself had a relaxed atmosphere and was attractively set amongst mountains with a scenic route leading out to Yellowstone Park. That was closed for the winter as the passes were snowbound. I was told that the buffalo, now a protected species, have increased in number and are making a nuisance of themselves in the park.

Lolli, my hostess, was a librarian at a local High School and, in an effort to keep abreast of the students, she was continuing studies herself, though now in her Sixties. On my last night in Cody she was due to attend a tutorial on Gay and Lesbian literature, and asked if I would care to join her. So, in contrast to the day's activity learning about the macho world of a buffalo hunter, I found myself in a classroom discussing a totally different view of life through the various readings presented. It was a very interesting and informative evening.

About 80 kms south of Cody lies the town of Thermopolis, named after its hot springs.

It is now becoming more well-known for its Dinosaur Centre. In 1992 a geologist and a fossil collector were vacationing in the area and saw some promising looking rocks. On investigation they found a remarkable collection of dinosaur bones. They took out a fossil lease, brought in more experts and, on unearthing still more species of dinosaur, decided to invest in building a centre which now serves for display and education. It includes a laboratory where the fossils are identified and preserved, and guided tours of the nearby excavation sites give the general public access.

On arrival at the Dinosaur Centre I was feeling quite ill. A head cold had set in and my sinuses were blocked. I drank coffee and took aspirin to try to clear my head before taking in the exhibition. Luckily, as I sat gathering myself together, a school tour entered and the head paleontologist guided them around. I tagged on the end of the group as a mature student and was treated to an expert explanation of the whole exhibition. Ed Cole was obviously very enthusiastic about his work and each dinosaur that he and his wife had excavated and restored was obviously a great source of excitement to him. It was certainly a pleasure to have someone so dedicated and knowledgeable to explain the wonders of different ages from Precambrian through Jurassic to Tertiary. The exhibits towered above me, most impressively, and must have been many schoolchildren's dream come true.

After my visit to the museum I braved the cold outside and found the thermal spring. The temperature of the water exiting the ground is 135 degrees F. There was so much steam it was hard to define the pool, but the water ran quickly out over a mass of flat, rocky ledge, mixing with the waters of a nearby river which rapidly cooled the flow. Dropping downhill, the watercourse was divided into sections with bowl-like rims, and on closer inspection I saw these rims were encrusted with multi-coloured calcium deposits. It was similar to the build-up in caves, but the colours were the result of algae in the water whose hues varied with the temperature. Overall the effect was stunning. A man-made viewing path wove around the water 'bowls' and the colours, reflections, steam and backdrop of snowy mountains left an indelible print on my mind as well as the camera film.

A public bath fed by the hot springs lay at the foot of this valley but, feeling the way I did, I thought it wiser to forgo this experience, so I jumped back in my 'truark' to take a different route over the mountains back to Sheridan. With the cold in my head, the high altitude as I climbed the pass, my ears felt as if they would explode and I kept swallowing to try and clear them, but to no avail. Despite having another half day on the car hire to explore further afield, I had to take the vehicle back early and retire to bed for the next 24 hours, fortunately being nursed by my hosts.

I revived the following night to be taken to the Christmas party of

Paige's bank colleagues. This was held in one of the women's homes and I was treated to a real taste of small town country life. The other girls spent the evening admiring the hostess, her house, children, husband, washing machine, jacuzzi and her huge collections of 'Precious Moments' – porcelain figures of a particularly twee nature. Being in a Panadol-induced stupor I sat quietly on the sofa and smiled and nodded when I thought I should. I could understand why Paige was so keen to get away on more travels. But then, we all have different practices and that's what makes the world go around. The women were kind, the food terrific—and I was no scintillating company either!

Another evening we all were to visit an art gallery which was opening an exhibition of work by T. Allen Lawson, a young man who had made several trips into the Big Horn mountains during different seasons to make working sketches for his paintings. These were varied in medium, texture and subject within the area. Not only did he have a collection of about 50 paintings, but also a display of his camping equipment, including snowshoes for his winter trips and an ordinance survey map with coloured pins to mark the locations of his sketches. It was most interesting, made more so by the music of the Mountain Winds Woodwind Quartet who played a selection of classical and medieval music. I felt more in my element on this occasion and couldn't help thinking that maybe the original Indian inhabitants would have approved more this style of 'progress'.

Before I left Sheridan, Jim and Paige showed me the tandem they had had specially built for their forthcoming trip around Australia and New Zealand. It was certainly a different mode of transport from the combi van. However, with weeks of training behind them during the summer months, they were hoping their leg muscles would soon be flexing again: they were due to uproot and travel in May '96. I gave them my Australian contacts and wished them well. Feeling much better, it was time to hit the road again. I needed to get up to the very northern part of Michigan to visit Beans and Kelli, more people I had met in Spain in '92. Beans, an energetic 'hornswaggler' in his late thirties, was another folk musician. He and I had written the show for the schools in Gibraltar and the Costa del Sol. The show was about the history of Gibraltar; we both had much fun in producing and performing it. His girlfriend, Kelli, had meanwhile worked on her paintings which she took back to sell in the States. She works in oils in a very stylised manner, much sought after by her clients both in Michigan and Florida.

I had also phoned Beans from Debby's place. When we eventually spoke, the conversation went something like this:

'Hi, Beans, it's Linda Bick from Spain speaking'. (Linda Bick is my stage name).

'Linda Bick—Holy Shit!!' (I'd like to think he was expressing pleased incredulity but with these Americans, who knows!!)

Beans was working in the bars in the Lake Michigan region. The idea was for me to stop over with his fiddler friend, Gary, at Grand Rapids and then, a couple of days later, take a connecting bus up to Levering. Good ol' Greyhound: their network was able to oblige. By tapping into their computer, the clerk at the bus station worked out a route for me via Billings, Montana, Chicago and Kalamazoo, another 1400 miles.

It was the Billings connection that nearly came unstuck.

Chapter Twenty-Nine

Going North

Jim and Paige saw me on to the Trailway bus at Sheridan depot, late evening, my tuckerbag crammed full of supplies for two days. We drove into the freezing night, arriving at Billings about 11.30. The Chicago connection was due in at midnight, but the snow had been flying out west and there was no sign of it—nor would be, the clerk informed me, until morning. I looked around at the bare, chilly waiting room and as I sat on a cold hard chair, thought of the warm bed I had left behind in Sheridan. However, it wasn't all bad as the bus station employers treated us waiting passengers to a bag of hot do-nuts. Then, about 1 a.m., they decided they may have a spare bus.

As the connecting passengers from the west hadn't arrived, there were only 3 of us from Billings for the next stage to Chicago. We climbed happily aboard, having the pick of seats, and the driver steered us out of the terminal and into the snowy night. But after about 5 blocks he turned around and announced:

'We aint goin' no damn place in this bus—the brakes are faulty.'

So, dejected, we turned back to base. 'That's it,' I thought resigning myself once more to a sleepless night on the chair. However, the angels were working overtime for another bus was found. We climbed aboard again somewhat more warily though the driver proclaimed the bus driveable. It was 12 years old, had a manual gear change and was very draughty. The central heating could not keep up with the streams of cold air coming in around the window seals and I had every stitch of clothing on I could find. Fortunately Connie had posted my thermal vest on to me.

The driver combatted the draught problem by soaking tissue paper in water, then plastering it around the outside of the window edges. It froze immediately in the -20 degrees conditions and did alleviate some of the discomfort. The driver complained about the bus, the bus company and life in general all through the night's drive.

When he left the bus at Minneapolis, his replacement did the same. However, they were both excellent drivers, battling against terrible road conditions and I felt they really earned their wages. It's wild country out there; had the bus broken down, I thought we would have all been in danger of freezing to death.

We made it to Chicago, a huge bus station full of interesting characters. Just as well I had something to watch as it was a 3 hour wait for the connecting bus and the terminal, although well-served with cafes and bookshops, was none too warm.

'Kalamazoo' is such a nice name and the bus/train station where we stopped for yet another connection, lived up to it. It was quaint, a wooden building in the style of English country stations, with its own supply of decorated Christmas trees outside. While I waited there for my final bus to Grand Rapids two young coloured girls, one with a babe in arms, asked me where I came from and then, what language was spoken in Australia.

When the bus arrived it was empty, once more only three of us had the choice of all the seats. I immediately sat at the front. The two girls dissented. The first said:

'Hey man, let's sit in the big seat at the back.'

Her friend replied indignantly, 'What! D'you know how much of a fight it took us darkies to get to sit in the front? We sit right here, man!' and indicated a forward position. I suppressed an amused chuckle.

At Grand Rapids Michigan, Marilyn, the fiddler's wife, picked me up in her little red Dodge sports car and we drove a further hour along country roads to what seemed like the heart of a pine forest. Their house was in an area called 'White Cloud'; under deep snow, it certainly earned the name. Marilyn was post-woman and drove every day, early in the morning, on these now snow-covered roads to her sorting office in Grand Rapids. During the year she faced all weather conditions as she delivered the mail on foot. Sometimes in the winter she called in to have a 'snow day' off. Then, the conditions were too bad for her to drive. I was surprised to hear it was only 2 or 3 days a year as the little red Dodge wasn't exactly 4x4, and the roads were treacherous.

However, it was cosy in the log cabin which Gary, a cabinet maker, had made very weatherproof. He had a huge workshop beside it and, across the road, a derelict barn that he hoped to renovate as a venue for musical shows and dances. Part of the large building could also be used as a music resource and craft centre. He had already begun on the roof, but I could envisage many months and dollars worth of work ahead. An interesting project. I spent a couple of days relaxing and watching videos before Gary drove me to Levering to meet my bus; it left at 5 p.m. on the Friday evening.

We left a little early, so sat in his van drinking beer at the look out point for the bus. Apparently in this part of America it is illegal to drink alcohol inside a vehicle, and any citizen can ring the police and report any culprit. Gary was paranoid that we would be seen and 'dobbed in'. So, whenever a car passed (which was often as we were parked next to a garage) we had to drop the cans below the window level. The procedure was so stressful that I didn't enjoy the drink. Fortunately, halfway through my can the bus arrived and I jumped out and ran to flag it down. It was the same driver that had piloted the bus from Kalamazoo and, as he grinned a welcome, I felt part of the family.

Michael Beans is a real showman. He was working with Kelli's brother, Kirby, entertaining in O'Leary's pub that night. The bus arrived at 10.30 and dropped me off right outside the door. Full of anticipation of our reunion, I walked toward the long, low building, bright lights on the exterior advertising its beers and entertainment. Parked outside, like a row of motorbikes outside a biker's pub, were skiddoos. I opened the door and walked past a row of one-armed bandits and cigarette machines to reach the bar. Pausing to adjust my eyes to the smokey pub atmosphere, I saw a smiling barman behind a counter lined with drinkers; they had all turned to watch the approach of this small, brightly clad figure with a big red rucksack. I heard a familiar tune and looked to the right to see Beans and Kirby playing enthusiastically playing on stage. Moving forward, I waved. Seeing me, Beans twirled his 'pirate' moustache, grinned from ear to ear and, on finishing his song, announced:

'Linda Bick from Spain has just arrived!'

Beans is never one to miss an opportunity for a special event and had been building up his audience's expectations all night, promising them a surprise guest. A cheer went up and suddenly I was receiving drinks from one and all. It was wonderful to watch my slim, attractive and 'fit for 40' friend performing his usual hand slapping, foot stomping style, thoroughly enjoying himself as always. His audience was appreciative of him and chatty to me.

When Beans finished his bracket he came rushing over and we embrace excitedly.

'Linda Bick, Holy Shit!' he reiterated. 'I just can't believe you are really here. It's wonderful. Of all the people we gave our address to in our travels, you are the only one who's actually come to visit us!'

In the next bracket I joined him on stage and played 'King of the Fairies' while my fingers were still in control. Beautiful Blonde Kelli arrived later and we continued the celebration back at their cabin by Carp Lake till early next morning.

Beans and Kelly

This northernmost tip of Michigan is a real tourist area which is just fine for Beans' job as a musician. He entertains in pubs and clubs there all summer and migrates to the Caribbean to run his shows from his boat, island hopping, in the winter. Here, by the Great Lakes, there are many beautiful spots which attract tourists summer and winter. During the hot summer months it is obviously ideal for all types of water sports and in the winter, when the snow lies deep, it's fun to hire a skidoo and ride out among the pine trees. Also ice fishing is a very popular weekend occupation for the city dwellers from Detroit. Carp Lake had numerous cabins dotted along its edge for those who wanted to use them in summer or winter. Beans and Kelli were hiring one of these and it was a cute picture postcard affair with the thick snow on the roof and long icicles hanging from the gutters. Just as well it was equipped with a good stove. Inside it was warm and cosy, serving the two of them just fine with a bathroom, bed-sitting room and kitchenette. I was allocated the sofa seat in the latter.

The next few days were a whirlwind of activity, which is how Beans lives his life. In order to cope with his hyperactivity, Kelli hides herself away in her studio with her oil paintings, joining in with his antics if and when she wants. The two artistic temperaments have managed to survive this way for some years and have great fun.

I met many interesting people and was able to play with good quality musicians who were familiar with several of my Celtic tunes. One of them, Dave Menefee from Ann Arbor, was a rotund, gnome-like figure with a big bushy beard. His slow drawl turned into a beautiful singing voice and he was a very apt instrumentalist on guitar and fiddle. Kirby, Beans' partner, also had a professional style and gentle voice. He was very popular with the locals and, like Beans, had made a lot of recordings. It was a real treat to play with these people.

The local recording studio was in Petosky, where Beans was in the process of making another tape. He wanted a whistle part laid down on one of the tracks and said he was lucky I was there to do it. So, in between Christmas parties and family visits, he briefly demonstrated what he wanted me to play.

The big day for the recording arrived and some other people came along to help with the narration: the new production was a folk story told with music. Beans drove us through the snow in his recently acquired Golden Cadillac. Although 20 years old, it was practically new as it had been garaged since his uncle had died almost as many years ago. What a treat to be driven to a recording studio in such style.

Petosky is another fairy tale village by Lake Michigan. In summer it is a holiday resort and has several trendy art and craft shops and fish restaurants. Bob Bollinger had a small but very well equipped recording studio there and we set up to start the action.

I was nervous when it came to my turn as the whistle part mainly called for improvisation and effect. So, each time Bob and Beans had a new idea I had to follow it with no practice. My stress level was rising and I was heating up with nervous energy. I kept taking off more layers of clothing.

'Give her another part and we'll have a strip show,' Bob joked. Eventually everyone was satisfied with the tale. Bob's Irish girlfriend,

Martina, arrived. We all went off to celebrate at the Park Garden Cafe, renowned as a previous haunt of Ernest Hemingway. My final night with my friend here was filled with laughter, and not a little relief that we'd got the music 'in the bag'.

Beans, Michigan

Chapter Thirty

The Reunion

My bus to London, Ontario was leaving from MacKinac City at 7.15 a.m. so Beans, Kelli and I were 'rigged and ready' to go well before. It was a cold, clear morning and it seemed that I wouldn't be snowed in after all, so it was time to bid yet another fond farewell and jump on the bus. For a change, the bus was crowded as now the Christmas migration was in full swing. I sat next to a lady who wasn't quite 'the full 9 yards' and who kept saying: 'Excuse me,' over and over again, under her breath.

The Bus to Meet Georgia

The route on Trailways joined the waters of Lake Huron at Bay City in Saginow Bay and came inland again through Flint to Detroit. Whenever I caught a glimpse of the Great Lake it was frozen, shining white in the winter sun. My connection was almost immediate and the drive through customs into Canada, efficient. The little that I could see before dark showed Canada's more conservative approach to life: people were less brightly dressed and the shops not so loudly decorated. It all looked quite English, or rather Australian, the in between stage—wide streets but traditional British housing.

I was two hours earlier than expected at the Bus Terminal and tried to phone Georgia but there was only the impersonal answer phone. So I had to wait, drinking cups of coffee and reading postcards, trying to contain my excitement until the appointed meeting time.

At last 9 p.m. arrived and Georgia was there. Her blue eyes sparkled with the joy of our meeting. She was rugged up in a beautiful full-length, deep pink woollen coat, a striking blue velvet hat over her now darker hair. She looked well, but what a different environment! The last time we'd seen each other was in the heat of Southern Morocco. She'd been in light cotton clothing with hair bleached blonde in the sun, her skin tanned. Now we were in a climate where gloves and ear muffs were a necessity against frost bite. We laughed, hugged and kissed in our pleasure at seeing one another, then hurried into the car she had luckily been able to borrow to meet me and take me back to her home.

In contrast to the arctic conditions outside, the Canadian buildings are centrally heated and most blocks of flats have a Jacuzzi in the basement area for the residents. Underground parking is available for some who pay extra, but a surprising amount of cars are left outside to suffer the ravages of the icy winter. It's necessary to have a good battery and several cans of de-icer.

Lesleigh, Georgia's best friend and flat mate, was another beauty: tall and slim, with a mane of black curly hair that set off her small impish face. Though a nurse by profession, her passion was acting and she was heavily involved with the local theatre group. Her natural grace and deportment gave her a larger than life presence, ideal for the theatrical world.

Georgia and I spent the first evening together talking non-stop to catch up on each other's news. Now home for three months, she had been delighted to reunite with her family and friends while enjoying hygienic and up to date medical attention. On regaining her health she easily found work, as a waitress, but was having difficulty in settling back in Canada after her adventures in warmer climes. She felt the cold and had often wondered why she was born a Canadian. She longed to return to the sun.

'Look, Georgia,' I said, 'I have this idea for an international folk music project back in Gibraltar and Spain. If you return, we can do it together.'

'If I know I can find work there, I'd be glad to,' she replied.

'Then we need to make a tape for me to show to the schools and Education Departments,' I said, glad that she was also keen. However, organising a demo tape and finding a studio proved to be more of a job than we expected. Georgia had to keep her scheduled shifts at the restaurant and she had no private transport. Between shifts we practised our music, and used the local bus service.

To catch a bus in Canada is a life or death experience. In sub-zero temperatures standing still for long is dangerous, so timing is very important. We would study the timetable in the warmth of the flat, judge how long it would take us to put on our outdoor clothes, take the lift down, walk tentatively across the icy car park to the road and slither to the bus stop. If for some reason the bus was delayed we would break into a walk or jog, carefully traversing the icy path toward the next bus stop. If the bus came in between stops it was permissible to flag it down as the driver was aware of the situation. It was also necessary to have the right change to save juggling money with gloved hands, causing a hold up getting into the warm bus.

One day we were confused as the buses were running on holiday time over the Christmas period. I jogged almost all the way into town before the bus arrived. Even with ear muffs, mitts and boots, my extremities were numb and I went through agonies as they thawed out in heated interiors.

Of course the restaurant where Georgia worked had been very busy leading up to Christmas, but she had the actual holy day off. When the 25th dawned Lesleigh, Georgia and I romped around in our pyjamas like a bunch of 10-year-olds. We squeaked with delight at each present opened from under the tree, pulled off the wrapping and ribbons, held it high to show one another. We eventually dressed to go out by car to Lesleigh's church, a few miles out of town. I was amazed that her car, parked outside, started as well as it did. After a few minutes of the car warming up while we shivered, the heater worked and we were away, driving past the snow-covered town houses into the frozen countryside. Many places were decorated with fairy lights, but none as ostentatious as the American displays had been.

The church was fairly modern and we were welcomed by a female priest who led a very warm, friendly service, ably backed by the choir (of which Lesleigh was a part) who sang gustily using folk instruments, including a South American rainstick, in some of their more up-beat numbers. It was an enjoyable, informal service and we chatted to the organ player and other people afterwards.

On the way back a country farm tea house was open, providing us with soup and mulled cider—a welcome Christmas treat. Later Lesleigh went off to join her family whilst Georgia and I had a full Christmas turkey evening meal with her cousin and his family. It certainly was a very white Christmas, the first I'd had for very many years. Unfortunately New Year was a bit of a fizzer. Georgia had to work and, as I could find no pubs to go to, we just shared a bottle of wine and some memories when she came home.

It was the start of a New Year which we both faced with hope in our hearts and the determination to get our tape made before I had to fly home. We had already listed and rehearsed enough material for a recording, but a suitable studio was proving elusive. We had not yet seen the whole selection in the area but those we had, didn't seem right or were too expensive, or both. How I wished Bob's Michigan studio was here and not 300 miles away.

While Georgia was still busy at her job in the restaurant, I set about exploring the urban part of Canada that I was in. In contrast to its English namesake, London Ontario was rather dull. Obviously much younger, the buildings were mainly modest and had little character. However, once inside they were warm. Downtown large shopping malls sold a vast variety of goods and I located plenty of interesting bookshops, both new and second-hand. I found a folk/classical specialist shop which kept me enthralled for hours—wishing for a limitless credit account. The library was enormous with an extensive ethnic music section; I could have spent weeks there. However, the part I enjoyed most was the central park with its communal skating rink. Scarved and muffed children of all ages skated to music played over the speakers while grey squirrels hopped among the trees. There was a festive feel over the winter holidays.

The most disappointing feature was the lack of pubs. Restaurants and trendy coffee houses, yes, but nothing that remotely resembles the public bar that we English (and Aussies) know and love. Maybe I was looking in the wrong places; after all, my experience was limited by bus routes and schedules or what I could discover on foot. By way of consolation there was a great do-nut shop about 20 minutes' walk along the river (the Thames, of course) from Lesleigh's flat.

One afternoon, dressed with many layers, Georgia and I took the walk, in bitter, misty weather—the temperature about minus 10 degrees. Despite the cold, young children wrapped up like polar bears were tobogganing, their laughter ringing out and their breath showing smokey around them. When we reached a bridge over the mainly frozen river, the do-nut place glowed like a beacon among a small group of shops.

We were glad to get inside and warm ourselves with hot chocolate and the pick of a selection of do-nuts in every form and flavour. People sat cupping their hands around their beverages, their gloves, hats and scarves momentarily discarded.

One thing I couldn't help but notice, being only 5' 2', was that the people were mainly in the 'giant category', towering over me. Georgia, only a few inches taller than me was also short by comparison. She put it down to the milk.

'It's all full of hormones,' she said. I must say that although I didn't grow any taller while I was there, my hair always seemed to need cutting. This, said Georgia, confirmed her theory.

The other thing I learnt was that a good many people in London were 'in therapy'. It was considered the norm to have a therapist and consult them at least weekly. Canadians, Georgia said, want to be correct about everything, politically and emotionally, and therefore seek guidance in this.

As far as political correctness goes, Canada is known internationally as being at the forefront in its anti-racism policies and until now, in its acceptance of many minority and persecuted people. At present it's a large country with a comparatively small population, not surprising: you have to be tough to survive the temperature extremes. The few indigenous Inuit people in the London area that I saw seemed fairly well-off and urbanised. Though I wasn't making a particular study of their conditions, on the surface they seemed more at ease in the western lifestyle than their aboriginal counterparts in Australia. While making such observations I was thinking of different places and people all around the world and one day, walking alone by the river, was inspired to write a song entitled 'Faraway Friends'.

Much as I enjoyed my time as a tourist, the most pressing subject was how to get our demo tape made, for we were running out of time. I had an idea that the end product would be enhanced if we had another person to help with the instrumentation while Georgia and I concentrated on the harmony singing. I thought of Dave Menefee, the guitarist and fiddler who I'd met at Beans' place. He lived not far across the border and was a self-employed stone mason, so might have been in a position and happy to make music with us. He had plenty of recording experience and our songs were easy to learn. I phoned him and he was interested, saying we should let him know when we had a studio arranged. But we simply couldn't find a studio we trusted—and there was only one more week before I had to leave.

I was racking my brains, Georgia was busy working at the restaurant and also fighting a sinus condition. It was beginning to look like we'd never get the tape done. In desperation I wondered if perhaps we went by bus to Ann Arbor, Menefee could take us to Petosky. I knew he wanted to do more recording there soon, and maybe it would benefit him too if we shared travel expenses. It sounded a bit too much to ask but I phoned him anyway. Incredibly, he said that it would be easier for him to come to London, pick us up and drive the more easterly route to North Michigan. We didn't know if we could trust the weather though. There was another problem: allowing two days for travel and two for recording, Georgia would be away from work for four consecutive days.

'Georgia, do you think you could get time off work?' It seemed another tall order.

'Well, I can only ask,' she said. It would entail swopping shifts with the other workers.

Yes, yes, yes, the power of positive thinking. By Tuesday evening it was all arranged. We were looking forward to seeing Dave early Friday morning and making the trip. I confirmed with Bob in Petosky that he had free studio time. However, our hopes were dashed again the following day: Dave rang to say he couldn't make it after all. We were back to square one. No studio in London; the one we really wanted, 300 miles away. Georgia went disconsolately to work the next morning while Lesleigh and I drove out to look at yet another studio in London. It was very expensive and snooty. I was feeling miserable.

There was one last hope of another place that Georgia and I were to investigate that night after she finished work. We braved the cold and the buses one last time; we came away still dissatisfied. It was stalemate but I refused to admit defeat.

'That's it, Georgia,' I said. 'We've got a studio waiting for us in Petosky. You've got the time off, we've both worked very hard practising. Really, all we are lacking is the transport and the luck for the weather to hold. What do you say if I hire a car and we drive up there first thing tomorrow?'

'Yes, let's do it,' she agreed. We phoned Bob and the hire company, arranged for a car at 9 a.m. then spent a night sleepless with excitement.

The conditions the next morning were grim. When the lady driver came to take us to meet our little red Chevrolet I was glad to let Georgia take the controls. The roads were slippery with heavily falling snow. On the open road, visibility was almost white-out. For a while I fought down a feeling of panic. What if we had an accident? I was due to fly out in four days time. We could easily get snowed in. Were we completely mad to try this journey?

However, being familiar with driving in these conditions, Georgia steered the car confidently and well, and we were soon at the American/Canadian border. As we crossed into Michigan the snow stopped and the sun broke through the clouds. Now that we could relax our concentration on the road, we burst into song.

The straight dual carriageway to the north that we were now on was easy to negotiate, the snow having been cleared to the sides where it glittered brightly in the winter sun. We felt elated to be travelling in this lovely little car – which had a great heater – on our way to achieve our goal. I'd worry about the expense later when the VISA bill came in. After a six hour drive we pulled up outside Bob's studio and he came out to meet us, grinning from ear to ear.

'I just couldn't believe you guys would do it,' he laughed, obviously flattered that we had turned down large Canadian Studios to drive 300 miles to his private outfit – and in the icy grip of midwinter too. Also, I had seriously stuck my neck out by coming north again when my plane left so soon from Detroit. There was still the possibility of more snow to stop our journey back to the city. If I missed the plane I'd be in big trouble. This was something I refused to worry about now as, having arrived at Bob's, we still had to run the gamut of more rehearsing and being able to feel confident amongst the jungle of microphones and headsets. Being used to tuning ourselves to each other acoustically, we were at first fazed by having to be wired into Bob's system. The first day saw us battling with phonics and not recording as much material as we'd hoped. Our doubts returned: would we complete the tape in time? It seemed a hopeless task after all – we only had one day left and things were not going well. We went to bed depressed, even though Martina had fed us magnificently and tried to restore our confidence. The next morning we went back to work early and finally solved our problems by turning down the volume on our monitor mikes. This had been throwing off our harmonies.

Now we could hear each other properly we raced on against the clock to put down the final tracks – and Bob reached for his tape-cutting machine.

On Sunday 7th January 1996, 17 months after our first meeting in Portugal, Georgia and I, with Bob and Martina, celebrated cutting our first tape together.

'What are you going to call it?' asked Bob, as he prepared to phone through the order for the tape covers. Georgia and I looked at each other and laughed. After all we'd been through individually and together in the last 17 months, it could only be 'Where Angels Fear to Tread.'

Georgia and Linda

POSTSCRIPT

I returned to Spain in mid-January (1996) to survive the wettest winter for many years: great for refilling the empty dam, but not too good for my house building project. My German 'Wanderschaft' friends arrived and together we battled the weather to complete a new roof for the visitors' house. A great start in the renovation process.

Soon after they left, Georgia flew in from Canada and we had many laughs rehearsing and producing the International Folk Music Show for schools in Gibraltar and the Costa del Sol. When this project finished, her many talents were in much demand so she accepted work offers further afield; I stayed in Castellar to continue the work on my guest house. With Georgia and other positive people's company, I combated the negative vibes from PC and his strange cronies next door. Now the house is finished. It has already welcomed visitors from many parts of the world.

I sit on my patio, a glass of wine in hand, gazing at the beauty around me, wondering what my next great adventure will be. I know wherever I go, I will meet old friends and make new ones. I would like to dedicate 'Faraway Friends' to them all.

PPS: More years have passed since the first edition of this book and my wandering wheels have taken me on other adventures in different parts of the world. Now living in Port Lincoln, South Australia I am writing more books about my travels. I have enough material to keep me busy for many years to come. I hope you enjoy them all.

To see the photographs from this book in colour format please go to Linda's website. www.lindab.id.au

Faraway Friends

Sometimes the road seems lonely and sad
And there's danger around every bend
But my troubles are halved when I hear in my heart
The voice of my faraway friends

Chorus: Those faraway friends give me hope when I'm down
I know I can reach journey's end
There'll be laughter and light when I ride into town
And we are together again

Wherever I go I take with me their smiles
Their songs and the words that they've penned
To share out the love, the music and dreams
Amongst other faraway friends

Chorus

There's times I'm not sure where I'm headed or why
And I don't seem to follow the trend
But I know more than once I've got back on the track
With the help of a faraway friend

Chorus

For all round the world I've scattered my life
Seen sights that would make the mind bend
But the trip's not complete unless I can meet
And make one more faraway friend

Chorus x 2

By: Linda Bick (Bootherstone)

Dedicated to all my friends everywhere.

The Author

Linda Bootherstone has spent most of her life exploring the world by motorcycle. She is now based in Port Lincoln, South Australia where she follows her other interests of art and music but also takes trips on her motorcycle whenever possible.

She has written two books previously and made several recordings of her own songs.

OTHER PUBLICATIONS
BY
LINDA BOOTHERSTONE

ALSO AVAILABLE ON AMAZON

DAISIES DON'T TELL
AN ILLUSTRATED ANTHOLOGY OF POEMS
LINDA BICK – 2010

THREE WANDERING POMS
LINDA BOOTHERSTONE – 2014

INTO AFRICA WITH A SMILE
LINDA BOOTHERSTONE – 2015

LOOKING AT LIFE
POEMS, SONGS AND STORIES
LINDA BOOTHERSTONE-BICK - 2020

www.ingramcontent.com/pod-product-compliance
Lightning Source LLC
Chambersburg PA
CBHW050308010526
44107CB00055B/2148